Water City

Water City offers practical solutions to some of the environmental challenges facing 21st-century cities as a result of climate change. The dense compact nature of the contemporary city makes it difficult to generate urban resilience to the effects of climate change, particularly coastal and pluvial flooding.

This book describes a design-led remediation methodology that draws on catchment planning and GIS mapping and analysis to redefine the city as a series of hydrological and ecological systems. Six case studies test the presented methodology, two greenfield and four brownfield sites based in the UK, USA, New Zealand and China. Each case study is illustrated with GIS maps and perspectives. Specific solutions to the environmental problems that will be intensified by climate change are presented.

Water City describes adaptation strategies to help practitioners in the urban landscape tackle these issues and make our cities better places to live. This practical guide is a key read for professionals and stakeholders in landscape architecture, urban design, planning and all those interested in how climate change will affect the future of our cities.

Matthew Bradbury is an associate professor at the School of Architecture, Te Whare Wānanga o Wairaka, Aotearoa/New Zealand and leader of the Masters of Landscape Architecture programme. Matthew's research explores the intersection of landscape practice and urban design in the development of a new urban model.

Water City

Practical Strategies for Climate Change

MATTHEW BRADBURY

Routledge
Taylor & Francis Group
LONDON AND NEW YORK

First published 2021
by Routledge
2 Park Square, Milton Park, Abingdon, Oxon OX14 4RN

and by Routledge
52 Vanderbilt Avenue, New York, NY 10017

Routledge is an imprint of the Taylor & Francis Group, an informa business

British Library Cataloguing-in-Publication Data
A catalogue record for this book is available from the British Library

Library of Congress Cataloging-in-Publication Data
Names: Bradbury, Matthew, author.
Title: Water city : practical strategies for climate change / Matthew Bradbury.
Description: New York : Routledge, 2021. | Includes bibliographical references and index.
Identifiers: LCCN 2020033995 (print) | LCCN 2020033996 (ebook) | ISBN 9780367425043 (hardback) | ISBN 9780367425067 (paperback) | ISBN 9780367853136 (ebook)
Subjects: LCSH: City planning—Environmental aspects. | City planning—Methodology. | Sustainable urban development. | Flood damage prevention.
Classification: LCC HT166 .B713 2021 (print) | LCC HT166 (ebook) | DDC 307.1/216—dc23
LC record available at https://lccn.loc.gov/2020033995
LC ebook record available at https://lccn.loc.gov/2020033996

ISBN: 978-0-367-42504-3 (hbk)
ISBN: 978-0-367-42506-7 (pbk)
ISBN: 978-0-367-85313-6 (ebk)

Typeset in Frutiger
by Apex CoVantage, LLC

To Alison, Sam and James

Contents

Figures

Whenuapai

Furong New Town

Wynyard Quarter

Jinan

Hazelwood Green

Osney Mead

Tables

Author biography

Dr Matthew Bradbury is an associate professor at the School of Architecture, Te Whare Wānanga o Wairaka, Aotearoa/New Zealand and leader of the Masters of Landscape Architecture programme. Matthew's recent research has been in the development of a new design model to help build a city resilient to the effects of climate change. By understanding the hydrological landscape that underlies the city, a new urban master plan can emerge, one that increases green space, encourages biodiversity, makes new public space for citizens and helps to reduce water contamination and flooding.

Matthew is also a director of BMLA (www.bmla.co.nz). The practice specialises in the integration of landscape, infrastructure and urban development for a wide range of projects, domestic, commercial and civic in New Zealand, PR China and the EU. Recent projects have included the restoration of urban streams, the daylighting of stormwater infrastructure, the planting of green corridors and the installation of stormwater treatment devices in the design of a number of public spaces in Aotearoa/New Zealand.

Foreword

This book is a must-have and a must-read for everyone who is interested in and concerned about one of the most challenging questions of the 21st century: how to deal with the effects of climate change in our urbanising world.

The 21st century is the century of the *city* as the dominant environment of the human species. In 2008, the population living in cities worldwide passed the 50 percent of the total world population. Somewhere in the second part of the 21st century, 75 percent of the world population will live in cities. The fastest growth of cities takes place in coastal areas and river deltas. In 2020, 21 of the 29 largest cities of the world can be found in deltas and coastal areas. The size as well the number of these cities will increase also in the near future.

The 21st century is also the century of *climate change*. The Intergovernmental Panel on Climate Change (IPCC) was founded by the United Nations in 1988 and delivered its first report in 1990. Since then, every three to four years a new assessment report into climate change has been published, with increasingly alarming conclusions concerning flood risk in densely populated areas.

Most urban areas, as well as agricultural and industrial zones, are a product of an idea which is a typical paradigm of the industrialised world of the 20th century. The idea is that we (humankind) have got everything under *control* – environmental processes as well as societal processes. The idea of being able to control is typical of the industrial process itself, elaborated by Frederick Taylor and Henry Ford. The idea was embraced by modern architects and urbanists like Le Corbusier, Giedion and many others, and it has infected whole generations of architects and urban designers. And not only architects and urban designers were infected by this idea, but also civil engineers, scientists and politicians. The idea of control resulted in a clear separation of different disciplines: every specialism focusing on its own thing, like in an industrial company.

However, the current process of unprecedented urbanisation and climate change shows that we haven't got urbanisation under control at all. These processes are far more complex, capricious and uncertain than was ever foreseen. Next to the need of mitigation, which includes strategies to avoid more extreme climate change, we are confronted with the need to make our cities more *adaptive*. This means that cities should be able to deal with the increase and uncertainty of changing conditions like sea-level rise and intensification of precipitation as well as with unforeseen societal and economic changes, like a coronavirus crisis. . . .

The rising awareness of complexity and uncertainty and the need to make our cities more adaptive has led to the insight that we need other approaches to the design and planning of urban landscapes. Cities shouldn't be regarded as industrial machines, but complex, evolutionary systems. Disciplines like landscape architecture, urban design, hydraulic engineering, environmental sciences and informatics are challenged to pay more attention to the mutual influences of landscape characteristics, built interventions, water systems, humanmade hydraulic systems and environmental processes. These disciplines are challenged to work *with* each other instead of next to each other.

This book by Matthew Bradbury shows how to develop such an interdisciplinary approach for making cities more adaptive, more prepared for an uncertain future. Landscape architect Bradbury delves into urban design, hydraulic engineering and GIS data analysis, and shows new solutions and perspectives for water-related cities in New Zealand, Asia, the UK and the USA. The development of the process is based on profound analysis of the local context, paying attention to many different aspects. The power of his case studies for different cities is deliberately simple. They are understandable for designers, engineers and scientists as well as for politicians and citizens. The case studies show that not only the water issue can be managed in a sustainable way, but also that the spatial quality of the cities will increase substantially by the proposed interventions. People will be safer but will also get a more attractive urban environment.

The lessons of this book are of great importance – not only for the cities described in the book, but for all cities and urbanising areas struggling with water problems in the world.

Han Meyer, Emeritus Professor of Urbanism, Delft University of Technology

Acknowledgements

This book would not have been possible without the support of Xinxin Wang, Kevin Zhu and Qianlin Luo. Xinxin has been responsible for not only helping with the production of the case studies but as a colleague at UNITEC has been an important collaborator in teaching and research. I am very grateful for her hard work and keen insights. Kevin Zhu, Rosie Luo and Anton Jones were invaluable in the preparation of the case studies.

Dr Marjorie van Roon's research into Low Impact Urban Design and Development first alerted me to the connection between urban form and environmental degradation within a definably ecological system. Dr van Roon's insights helped me to make the connection between urban development and how the consequences of climate change might be both measured and remediated through an understanding of the larger landscape.

Lastly, to all my friends, colleagues and students, who have all helped me with the long gestation of the book, many thanks, *Ehara taku toa, he takitahi, he toa takitini*.

Introduction

The environmental impact of climate change on the world's cities will be an enormous challenge to citizens, professions and urban agencies. Climate change will cause extreme weather events: flooding, severe storms, droughts and heat waves (Pachauri, 2014). The atmosphere is warming, increasing the capacity to hold more water and causing more rainfall. Widespread flooding will be the result. This will have catastrophic results for low-lying countries, especially around deltas like Bangladesh and a number of world cities that are built in low-lying areas.

The increase in air temperature is leading to the melting of the ice caps. This will have the effect of raising sea levels. According to the Intergovernmental Panel on Climate Change (IPCC), sea levels are expected to rise by 1.00 m by 2100, however, their figures have recently been reconfigured and now sea level is expected to rise by 2.00 m (Pachauri, 2014). The result will be increased coastal flooding and an increase in littoral damage from storm surges. The warming of the atmosphere will cause more heat waves, raising the temperature to levels that are intolerable to human life. The cumulative effect of these kinds of environmental changes on the biodiversity of the world's flora will also be profound; many native species are in danger of extinction due to adverse environmental effects (Mantyka-Pringle et al., 2015).

The city

Cities will be especially vulnerable to the effects of climate change. Existing cities are busy, crowded, densely populated places. The physical infrastructure of the city, the buildings, roads and public spaces, are usually hard impervious surfaces which are resistant to the absorption of rainwater. Typically, there is little green space in the traditional city, and hard urban surfaces accelerate the effect of heat waves. With little shading and heat absorbent surfaces cities exacerbate the effects of heat waves, warming up the urban environment to intolerable levels. Cities traditionally have low levels of biodiversity; but even the existing urban flora will be badly affected by the combination of all these environmental factors. Many cities are located on a littoral. Rising sea levels will damage these parts of the city which are often the location of vital infrastructure, such as ports, and expensive real estate, such as waterfront developments.

The design of new cities, while often better planned and with more efficient infrastructure, can also be characterised as being highly impervious with a low percentage of green permeable spaces. The current urban planning model (Steuteville & Langdon, 2009) emphasises an efficient grid structure. Public buildings, art galleries, theatres, museums, public spaces, squares, playgrounds, mini-parks and waterfront promenades leaven the mix of commercial, retail, and residential buildings that make up the majority of new urban development. The commercial reality of urban development is found in underlying development ratios: the Gross Floor Area (GFA) ensures a development return and the Floor Area Ratio (FAR) enables a developer to understand the maximum return from a development site (Ratcliffe & Stubbs, 2013). The result of a particular urban form and a readably understandable real estate formula has been an extremely profitable urban development model that has been replicated around the world.

However, the new city development has all the same environmental problems as the traditional city plan: highly impervious surfaces that will aggravate all the environmental consequences of climate change.

Climate change and the city

One of the environmental results of climate change will be that the increasing rainfall cannot be absorbed in the ground or readily directed to the nearest water body. This will have two immediate results. The first will be an increase in runoff from impervious urban surfaces. The runoff will pick up contaminants from roofs, roads and footpaths (Kelly, 2010). The discharge of this untreated water into urban streams and waterfronts will lead to an increase in the pollution of the receiving environment, such as lakes and harbours (Cromwell, 2009).

The other result will be widespread urban flooding (Boyd, Bufill, & Knee, 1993). The physical infrastructure of the city is obstructive to the quick and effective discharge of flooding. Blocked flooding pathways will cause increased damage to the city. In particular, waterfront development, usually at the downstream end of any urban flooding, will be the most affected (Houston et al., 2011).

The most obvious danger that the effects of climate change will present to cities is sea-level rise. Most cities in the world started life as port cities. Their existence was predicated on easy access to the sea.

Rising sea level means that their great advantage is now their downfall. Sea-level rise threatens port cities in a number of ways. According to how exposed they are to the open sea, more severe storms will cause storm surges that will cause catastrophic damage to the cities' edges. The areas closest to the sea are usually the most valuable in terms of real estate value. These areas are also where there is the most valuable public land. Parks, promenades and the cornice are usually located on the city/water edge and the likely inundation and destruction of this edge will remove some of the most valuable public space in many cities (Vitousek et al., 2017). For more inland cities that are protected by an archipelago, sea-level rise is more insidious, a gentler yet inexorable climb. Over time the inexorable rise of the sea will overtop the waterfront edge, causing littoral inundation (Hart, 2011).

There are a number of consequences of this condition. One is the increase of localised flooding in the waterfront area. This condition will combine with stormwater disposal. Surface stormwater is typically discharged in a localised, expedient manner directly into the adjacent receiving environment. The rising sea level will block these outfalls, causing surface stormwater to collect and create localised flooding.

Climate change will also cause an increase in temperature in cities. Urban heat is caused by solar radiation falling on hard, absorbent surfaces such as streets, pavements and buildings. These surfaces absorb the sun's energy and radiate that energy as heat after the sun sets. Depending on how densely the buildings are grouped and the amount or lack of vegetation, the ability of a city to release the heat build-up quickly can be compromised (Rizwan, Leung, & Liu, 2008).

The effects of the urban heat island effect (UHIE) are considerable. The obvious ones are on the health and well-being of the citizens. Excessive heat can cause injury and even the death of the city's more vulnerable inhabitants, particularly the old and young. An increase in demand for cooling, particularly from air conditioning, results in an increase in energy expenditure. The other effects are environmental problems, an increase in air pollution and a decrease in water quality, and even urban trees can experience physiological changes due to increased temperature with early budding and late leaf falls (Vogt et al., 2002).

While the environmental effects of climate change are just starting to appear, there are already a number of solutions to these problems. Many cities have made serious attempts at addressing these effects. Waterfront development agencies in particular are responsive to the environmental effects of climate change, especially in the problem of sea-level rise.

Remediation

Stormwater remediation

The new Toronto waterfront development by West 8 landscape architects (West 8, 2015) is an example of a stormwater remediation strategy. The waterfront master plan was a broad-ranging approach that acknowledged a wide range of urban, landscape and ecological and environmental issues on the Toronto waterfront. One of West 8's design strategies was to make a better connection between the city and the harbour. West 8 proposed to make Queens Quay, a busy eight-lane road, narrower by shuffling the existing traffic lanes northwards. The effect of this move was to create a combined pedestrian/tram/cyclist promenade along the length of the quay adjacent to the waterfront. This section of Queens Quay was repaved and replanted to create a new urban promenade. Where the new promenade meets the harbour, West 8 designed an extension of the quay with 8 m wide timber decks shaped as waves.

These new structures, known as Wave Decks, provide public meeting places with seats formed by the curving decking. The decks also have another purpose: they contain large storage tanks for the collection of contaminated stormwater from the urban catchment. The stormwater then moves through other systems located in the harbourside park before being cleaned and then discharged into the harbour.

The Toronto waterfront development demonstrates how a 'hard' engineered stormwater treatment solution can be used to treat stormwater contamination.

Waitangi Park (WAA, 2007), located on the Wellington, New Zealand waterfront, is another example of how stormwater can be cleaned before discharge. The park contains a structural stormwater device and a constructed wetland to clean contaminated stormwater from the surrounding urban catchment.

The park is located at the southern end of the Wellington waterfront between the National Art Museum, Te Papa and Oriental Bay. The park is 6.5 ha and has social functions that would normally be associated with an urban park: a playground, skateboard bowl, greenspace and café.

As part of the park development, the history of the Waitangi Stream was rediscovered. The Waitangi Stream used to run from the Basin Reserve to the harbour; it was then piped in the 19th century and used as a stormwater conduit for the highly impervious Te Aro valley. As part of the redevelopment of the park, Wraight and Associates daylighted the end of the stormwater pipe as an L-shaped canal and installed remediation ponds along the length to treat the contaminated water before it was discharged into the harbour.

Flooding remediation

Malmö and Copenhagen have both developed urban design strategies to address pluvial flooding (Haghighatafshar et al., 2014). For Malmö, this thinking has been an important consideration in planning the city's expansion for 20 years. The Copenhagen city authorities were more focused on the separation of stormwater and sewage rather than pluvial flooding.

However, an intense 1,000-year flood in 2011 caused a huge amount of property damage and focused the Copenhagen civic authorities on how pluvial flooding could be ameliorated in a dense urban environment like Copenhagen.

Malmö (Stahre, 2008) was an early adapter of SUD (sustainable urban drainage). In 2008 the city adopted the 'Storm-water Strategy for Malmö' (Malmö, 2008) strategy document. The document set out a typical aboveground structural stormwater system strategy. The strategy followed the established procedure: the creation of a stormwater treatment train starting in private property with a series of small-scale, localised interventions – grass roofs and detention tanks – before moving into the public realm. Measures such as permeable paving, rain gardens and swales are designed to slow down water flow. At the end of the pipe, large-scale end solutions such as wetlands and large ponds are also used.

The city of Malmö has been carrying out these measures since 2000. Stahre (2008) notes that installing structural stormwater devices within the existing city, which still has a combined sewer and stormwater infrastructure, has been difficult. However, in the new parts of the city, in suburban locations where a separate sewer/stormwater system has been installed, the building of an overground structural stormwater system has been possible.

One of the best-known recent examples of urban pluvial flooding is that of Copenhagen. The city was hit with a substantial storm event on 2 July 2011. It is estimated that 150 mm of rain fell within two hours. Rainfall intensity reached higher levels than predicted for a 100-year return event. The existing stormwater network soon failed. Many inner-city areas were flooded, with over 30 percent of building owners filing claims for storm flooding damage. Insurance claims for flood damage totalled over 800 million Euros (Divall & Strickland, 2016).

The City of Copenhagen had started to develop a strategy to address the way in which climate change would exacerbate pluvial flooding and sea-level rise in the Copenhagen Climate Adaptation Plan (The City of Copenhagen, 2011). This document suggested two strategies to combat pluvial flooding: separating stormwater and sewage systems, a long-term goal, and using the city's parks, sports fields and public spaces as water storage reservoirs.

However, the 2011 storm overwhelmed the city parks. Without modifications, the parks could only detain a small amount of water before flooding. The Cloudburst Management Plan built on the previous report and the practical experience of the 2011 flood. The management plan adapted the idea of using public space as a detention area and added the idea of conveyance, that is, using designated routes to convey stormwater flooding to the sea via roads and canals.

Landscape architects Ramboll Dreiseitl (Dreiseitl, 2012) produced a design study to illustrate how the Cloudburst Management Plan might be manifest for the worst-affected areas, west of the Copenhagen lakes. The designers started by making an inventory of all the available urban spaces and streets in the affected area (Hvilshøj, Lund, Goring, & Cathy, 2016).

The design study suggests that the parks and street should be modified to detain and convey stormwater as required by the overall Cloudburst Management Plan. The designers developed a hierarchy of types for modified public spaces and streets. Streets and boulevards could be used for flood conveyance or modified to detain the flood water as a green street or as retention boulevards. Public spaces such as parks and plazas could also be modified to form water detention zones to delay flooding.

The designers nominate specific sites in the city: Korsgade becomes a green street; Svend Trosts Veg, an urban canal; Vodrofsvei, an urban creek; and Gasvaerksvej, a retention boulevard. Hans Tavsens and Blagards Plads become a detention park and plaza respectively.

The Ramboll Dreiseitl master plan has been developed into a specific project, through the Norrebro competition. The competition was won by SLA (lead consultant), Rambøll, Atelier Dreiseitl, Arki_Lab, Social Action, Gadeidræt, Aydin Soei and Saunders Architecture (SLA, 2015). The winning design has adapted an existing park, the Hans Tavsens Park, and a street, the Korsgade, to form a flood detention zone and conveyance corridor.

The reconfigured Hans Tavsens Park is designed to detain up to 18,000 m^3 of water in a storm event. Floodwater will then be conveyed along the Korsgade to the Peblinge Sø (Lake), part of the Copenhagen lake system. In addition to conveying floodwater safely to Peblinge, the Korsgade will be refigured with an open water channel flowing through a series of indigenous biotopes. Stormwater will be cleaned in the newly configured street and by a small wetland constructed at the intersection of the lake and the discharge point.

The designers emphasise that the system will also work in summer with water from the lake being pumped back through the system. The designers have also allowed for a series of more conventional, engineered underground storage tanks. The Copenhagen lakes are also being looked at as part of the flood storage situation. As part of the Ramboll Dreiseitl master plan, Sankt Jørgens Sø, the lake to the south of Peblinge Sø, is being considered as a storage zone. Currently it has a depth of 4 to 5 m, and consideration is being given to lowering this depth to 2 m, enabling the lake to act as a major detention area for the city.

Sea-level rise remediation

One of the best-known examples of the impact on a major city of coastal flooding is the landfall of Hurricane Sandy on New York City in 2012 (O'Neill & Van Abs, 2016). Hurricane Sandy was a tropical hurricane that cut a path from the Caribbean through Cuba and the Bahamas as a category three storm travelling up the Atlantic coast before making landfall in New Jersey as a category two storm. Sandy was classified as the most destructive Atlantic hurricane, causing extensive material damage and loss of life along its path. However, the most profound effect was the realisation of the fragility of a large and important global city such as New York.

The impact of Hurricane Sandy on the New York region was considerable. The storm surge caused both coastal inundation and wastewater infrastructure failure. The influence of the storm surges on Manhattan was substantial. Much of Lower Manhattan, the financial centre of New York and, indeed, the United States, was flooded by the East River. The city's subway infrastructure was severely damaged with the flooding of seven subway tunnels. The New York Stock Exchange was forced to close, as were schools and universities. Coastal inundation also affected New York's outer boroughs and Long Island. The storm surges also caused damage to New York's wastewater infrastructure, and the surge overwhelmed sewage treatment stations, forcing the massive release of untreated sewage into the surrounding waterways (The City of New York, 2013).

The response by local government was to run an international national competition to develop innovative solutions to this address this problem (Rebuild by Design, 2014). The completion was won by the architecture superstars BIG with their proposal, the Big U (Rebuild by Design, 2014). In the winning entry, Bjarke Ingles proposed to combine a number of different flood protection techniques and soft and hard flood infrastructure to protect the Manhattan littoral. Soft techniques include the creation of a new coastal park system around the eastern tip of Manhattan. The parks will incorporate a series of topographical changes that will protect the housing and office infrastructure behind the parks from sea flooding (Schulz, 2018).

A new urban design

While all of these measures are laudable, the overall effect is piecemeal and disconnected. Localised contaminated stormwater might be able to be treated, but how is the volume of contaminated stormwater from the larger urban catchment able to be remediated? Urban flooding might be alleviated in one part of the city with flooding remediation measures but can the whole city be protected? In a similar way, one part of the city's waterfront might be protected from the effects of sea-level rise, but what about the other parts of the city that are adjacent to the new sea-level rise protection infrastructure (Cohen, 2016)?

When the inexorable effects of climate change become evident, all these environmental problems will develop an inescapable presence in the contemporary city.

To help address these environmental problems, a new urban form that accommodates the remediation of these difficulties in an inclusive and encompassing way will have to be found. The first step in building urban resilience is to understand that the environmental problems of climate change are not simply isolated incidents, such as occasional flooding events, but part of larger connected environmental systems. Once this is understood then a linked strategy that places the design of the urban master plan at the heart of the environmental remediation process, rather than a series of small haphazard interventions, becomes possible.

Building urban resilience to the effects of climate change means that an understanding of ecological systems in the city is necessary to address the problems. Engaging with the ecology of the urban development site, not as a fixed system but as a fluid set of environmental conditions, will help to both understand and address the dynamic effects of climate change.

The science of urban ecology (Marzluff, 2008) can help provide specific methods. Showing how specific urban/environmental issues are not limited by property boundaries but connected to larger environmental conditions is a key step in developing ways to address these issues in an inclusive manner. The dicta of urban ecology help to describe how specific environmental conditions, like hydrological systems, connect to each other at a series of scales. A city can be thought of in a hierarchical manner, from the room to the house to the street to the neighbourhood. Urban environmental conditions can likewise be thought about in a scalar fashion; for example, the scale of water flow can range from a kerb line to a major flood channel. This scale can be described as a series of conditions that are connected and intertwined with each other (Brown, 2017).

The concept of a hierarchy of nested conditions leads to specific techniques that address specific problems/issues. The hydrological catchment (Fryirs, 2012) is an example of how a collection of nested conditions can be defined through a topography at a certain scale. A catchment can be understood and mapped as a discrete scaled unit. A defined catchment system helps to appreciate the ways in which both the hydrological and ecological conditions of the catchment are intertwined and codependent. Catchment analysis offers specific techniques to place and order ecological conditions within a hydrological boundary (Hunter & Scrafton, 2012).

By placing a development site within a hydrological catchment, which can be part of an existing city or a greenfield site, the environmental impact of the climate change on the catchment and therefore the urban form of the development site can be understood. This way of integrating catchments analysis with urban design was pioneered by Ian McHarg in the publication of 'Design with Nature' (McHarg, 1969). In this publication, McHarg advances a method of mapping a development site within different environmental conditions of the catchment. Each map is drawn as a transparent layer with a specific environmental condition. The maps are overlaid and the result is that the most sensitive environmental conditions, especially hydrological and indigenous vegetation, are clearly outlined. The sites with the least number of sensitive environmental conditions are then allocated for the urban development programme.

This system of mapping overlays became digitised as the Geographical Information System (GIS) (Scally, 2006). GIS is a well-known software where different kinds of geographical and spatial data can be collected, scrutinised and analysed and the results presented in a map format.

For the purposes of this investigation, GIS will be used to map existing landscape and environmental conditions and to generate an analysis of the conditions, in particular, the hydrological condition of a site, such as overland flow paths. Catchment systems in all kinds of landscapes including the urban can then be located. This data can be presented graphically as both two-dimensional maps and three-dimensional images.

Once these adverse environmental conditions are understood, then the ways that the city can become resilient to these effects in a way that encompasses the whole of the catchment and not just as isolated incidents need to be consider. Low Impact Urban Design and Development (LIUDD) (van Roon & van Roon, 2009) offers a number of catchment-based design strategies that help to build resilience to the effect of climate change. The process starts with the development site being placed into the catchment and an environmental audit of the conditions is made. Identifying and protecting the existing hydrological structure of the catchment is important, and this can be done by using GIS to identify catchments, overland flow path and riparian margins. Mapping these corridors enables them to be protected from development pressures. The ability of a city to absorb rainfall by becoming more pervious is also critical. Making the city form more open and the building programme more compact by clustering building together are ways to achieve this goal. These two broad strategies, identifying and protecting existing riparian corridors and making the city more open and absorbent, can help the catchment to become more responsive to the impact of climate change.

Specific remediatory systems to help address three specific hydrological problems, stormwater, pluvial flooding and coastal flooding are well-known. Reducing water-borne contaminants is an important part of building environmental resilience. GIS mapping, the Rational Method (Thompson, 2007) and a number of software programmes can identify the sources and increase in stormwater occasioned by climate change. There are a number of well-known, tried and tested solutions, such as swales, rain gardens, green roofs and wetlands, that can help remediate these effects. In a similar way, the effect of pluvial flooding can be mapped and assessed via catchment mapping and assessments; once understood, there are a number of remediatory strategies such as ensuring that flood corridors are kept unimpeded and that flood detention zones are provided for (Maksimović et al., 2009). The remedies for coastal flooding are also very well understood and range from traditional hard solutions – walls, dykes and flood barriers – to so-called softer solutions that utilise the recreation of indigenous coastal ecosystem to help disparate the energy of storm surges (Morris, Konlechner, Ghisalberti, & Swearer, 2018).

Case studies

To illustrate how these ideas can form practical design strategies to help build resilience in our cities, six case studies are presented. These case studies are located in greenfield and brownfield development sites in New Zealand, the People's Republic of China (PRC), the UK and the USA. The case studies begin with two greenfield sites; they demonstrate how a planned development can be modified to make it more resilient to climate change.

The first project is a proposal for a new structure plan for Whenuapai, located in Auckland, New Zealand.

The second project is a design proposal for the Furong waterfront development in Guangdong, PRC. The two studies demonstrate a design process to deal with the environmental problems occasioned by waterfront and urban development and the ways in which these problems can be ameliorated

Both projects share a common analysis: the identification of what environmental problems are likely to be engendered with new waterfront/urban development. In these two studies, the main environmental problem was identified as being the production and entry of contaminated stormwater into the existing hydrological system and thence into the receiving environment.

The first goal was to increase the area of pervious surfaces. This goal will help decrease the amount of stormwater that will flow into the existing hydrological system. The Rational Method was used as a technique to understand the impact that the ratio of impervious to pervious surface within the catchment, before and after the development, would have on the production of stormwater. The second goal was protecting the existing hydrological network from the entry of contaminated stormwater. The technique was to buffer the existing stream systems. This operation was carried out using GIS mapping and analysis to identify the existing hydrological network, the streams and overland flow paths, then using the buffering function in ArcGIS to make protection zones around each OLFP and stream. The effect of this operation was to also increase the amount of pervious surface. The third operation was to cluster the urban form. By acknowledging and buffering the existing hydrological system, the loss of development GFA was inevitable. Clustering the development GFA into a new urban form was a way of ensuring that the projected real estate programme didn't result in a financial loss.

The suggested solution for the Whenuapai case study was to assemble the 'missing' GFA into apartment blocks at the intersection of the stream system with the littoral. In the case of the Furong waterfront, the waterfront building programme was clustered to form 'islands' within a new hydrological remediation landscape.

Four brownfield case study sites are then considered. The first is a brownfield site, the Wynyard Quarter, Freemans Bay, Auckland, New Zealand. This is an inner-city waterfront development on an existing reclaimed brownfield site. The proposed master plan follows the conventional urban development model, an intensely developed city grid with a strip of public space along the water's edge. An environmental inventory of the site within the urban's catchment area is undertaken. Three environmental problems are identified: contaminated stormwater from the catchment entering the harbour and pluvial flooding both on the waterfront site and from the catchment and sea-level rise. GIS mapping is used to identify the natural hydrological patterns of the site. The coastal edge and overland flow paths are identified and allocated for remediatory regimes. An exploration of the urban implication is made on site in the development, Wynyard Point. To achieve an increase in pervious surfaces for the site, the proposed development master plan is redefined to allow for an increase in pervious surfaces. The result is a new kind of urban development within a new urban park that connects to the natural world while ameliorating environmental problems.

The next case study is located in Jinan (PRC). The study starts with acknowledging a real problem, the flooding of the centre of Jinan. GIS mapping identifies the existing topography and the urban catchments that have contributed to the flooding. A hydrological analysis reveals the overland flow paths that confirm the location of the flooding routes. The study identifies existing green areas in the catchments that can be used to detain the flooding. Planners can use the case study as a document to guide the future urban development of the catchment, increasing the amount of green space for the citizens of the district and reducing the likelihood of flooding in the future.

The last two case studies are in the USA and the UK. The first case study site is a former steel works on the banks of the Monongahela River in Pittsburgh, Pennsylvania. GIS analysis reveals two catchments that discharge into the Monongahela River across the site with a number of overland flow paths. Environmental analysis also reveals a small amount of flooding from the river. With climate change, increased rainfall is likely to causes flooding across the site. In a similar way, flooding of the site from the Monongahela River is also expected. A planned urban development programme is modified to accommodate the remediation measures necessary to climate-proof the site. The proposed building programme is intensified on the remaining sites.

The last brownfield development case study is located on the periphery of Oxford, England. The 15 ha. site has an existing small-scale industrial park built in the 1970s. The site is bounded by the River Isis to the north and fields to the west, south and east. Hydrological analysis reveals that any development will be affected by flooding from the greater Thames catchment. A development programme has been proposed, a mixture of research centre, postgraduate student accommodation and incubator business for industry/academic research and development. To achieve the desired building programme within a flood landscape, a new landscape/urban configuration is tested. The site is divided into a series of eyots (small islands). Each island is raised above the flood plan and connected with bridges and boardwalks. An extensive replanting of water meadow and marginal indigenous plants is proposed. The building programme is divided amongst the islands.

Scope

The scope of the book is limited to investigating the hydrological problems of contemporary urban development that will be caused by the environmental effects of climate change. The book puts forward a number of strategic processes that will help build environmental resilience. The research is restricted to the investigation of the range and effect of three specific environmental issues: stormwater contamination, pluvial flooding and coastal flooding. The objective of the investigation is to demonstrate an awareness of these conditions, the ways in which they can be analysed and measured and the range of possible remediation measures. The aim of the book is to demonstrate how an understanding of these conditions can contribute to a design process that leads to a new urban development model. The urban implications of accommodating the necessary remediation measures are determined by a number of factors, including increased pervious surfaces areas, and making greener more open spaces to accommodate remediation systems.

The spatial implication of the new development strategies will be a fundamental change from the usual design solutions. In the conventional urban development model, social uses are often conditioned by specific urban formula around a residential zone, an entertainment precinct and a waterfront promenade, visitors and residents follow a programmed routine.

The new urban design strategies that have been developed in the book suggest a different model that results in an urban/landscape form, where residents and visitors experience a remediatory landscape; this could be a fragment of indigenous bush, wetlands or the recreation of a coastal ecotone. The social implications for the citizens that will experience this new model are thought-provoking.

An understanding of the implications of this new model of urban development in Aotearoa/New Zealand for the tangata whenua (the indigenous people of Aotearoa) is critically important. All New Zealanders have specific obligation under Te Tiriti o Waitangi (The Treaty of Waitangi) (Orange, 2015).

The articles of Te Tiriti are underpinned by the principles of partnership, participation and protection ensuring that Māori have equal rights and opportunities in any decision-making, and more specifically in issues that affect Māori and their taonga. How this might be manifest has led to the development of the Te Aranga Strategy, values and principles (tearanga.maori.nz). The principles are Mana, Whakapapa, Taiao, Mauri Tu, Mahi Toi, Tohu and Ahi Kā (http://www.aucklanddesignmanual.co.nz/design-subjects/maori-design/te_aranga_principles).

These principles have been formulated as a way in which stakeholders and designers who are working in the urban realm can acknowledge their obligations under the Te Tiriti o Waitangi. In developing this design methodology in Aotearoa, the principles cover a range of important aspects as they relate to Māori.

As an example, Mauri Tu is concerned with ensuring that the mauri (life force and vitality) of a site and the area around it are protected and enhanced thorough an understanding of the quality of wai, water, whenua, land, ngāhere, indigenous vegetation and air. It requires a holistic and regenerative approach. If these are damaged or impaired in any way, then solutions should be sought to repair this damage and therefore not to further impact the issue. Solutions can include cleaning stormwater through stormwater remediation systems, the remediation of contaminated soil, restoring waterways through daylighting and the planting of indigenous vegetation. It is important that a whole systems approach is adopted.

The second principle that is of particular relevance for case studies in Aotearoa is Taiao, relating to our natural environment. Here the emphasis is on enhancing and sustaining the natural environment through the return, use and care of local flora and fauna. Existing natural environments are to be protected and, if possible, enhanced and regenerated. Practical techniques seek to establish biodiversity through the use of ecological corridors and planting the appropriate indigenous flora in public spaces.

These two principles help to locate the exploration of the design methodology within an Aotearoa design case study.

Conclusion

This book will contribute to the goal of helping global urban development become more resilient to the effects of three specific environmental issues: stormwater contamination, pluvial flooding and coastal flooding that will be exacerbated by the effects of climate change. The proposed development process will enable major urban development stakeholders, such as local authorities, developers and citizens to clearly understand the ways in which larger-scale environmental problems, such as the discharge of contaminated stormwater and pluvial and maritime flooding, will impinge on the typical urban development site. Possible minimisation/remediation scenarios can be clearly measured and modelled, enabling a more transparent discussion over the environmental effects of any proposed development. The design process will give stakeholders the ability to manipulate an urban development master plan, leading to an open practice that can be modified through prioritising environmental remediation regimes. This process can give citizens a larger public realm in the urban development site.

A design process is outlined in which both the environmental problems that threaten urban development and the amelioration measures needed to make this development resilient to climate change.

Climate change has rapidly moved from being a fringe conversation to a central global concern. Yet this welcome attention has often led to an apocalyptic sense of doom and gloom where people feel that we can only wait for the end of the world. This book offers a way in which stakeholder, planners, engineers, designers and civic authorities can both understand the spatial consequences of climate change and the scope and shape of the necessary environmental remediation measures. The consequence of these measures for the future shapes of our cities will be profound; however, the consequences of not changing would be overwhelming.

References

Boyd, D., Bufill, M. C., & Knee, R. M. (1993). Pervious and impervious runoff in urban catchments. *Hydrological Sciences Journal*, *38*(6), 463–478.

Brown, I. T. (2017). Managing cities as urban ecosystems: Fundamentals and a framework for Los Angeles, California. *Cities and the Environment (CATE)*, *10*(2).

The City of Copenhagen. (2011). *Copenhagen Climate Adaption Plan*, Copenhagen. Retrieved from https://stateofgreen.com/files/download/1038

The City of New York. (2013). *A Stronger, More Resilient New York; Sandy and Its Impacts*. Retrieved from http://s-media.nyc.gov/agencies/sirr/SIRR_singles_Lo_res.pdf

Cohen, M. (2016). *NYC May Get a Big Ugly Wall Instead of Bjarke Ingels' Storm Protection System*. Retrieved from www.6sqft.com/nyc-may-get-a-big-ugly-wall-instead-of-bjarke-ingels-proposed-big-u-storm-protection-system/

Cromwell, J. (2009). *Implications of Climate Change for Adaptation by Wastewater and Stormwater Agencies*. Alexandria, VA: Water Environment Research Foundation.

Divall, S., & Strickland, L. (2016). *We Can't Keep Building Higher Walls: So How Can Cities Deal with Flood Risk?* Retrieved from www.citymetric.com/horizons/we-can-t-keep-building-higher-walls-so-how-can-cities-deal-flood-risk-1969

Dreiseitl. (2012). *Copenhagen Strategic Flood Master plan*. Retrieved from www.dreiseitl.com/en/portfolio?region=europe#copenhagen-strategic-flood-master plan

Fryirs, K. A. a. B., G. J. (2012). Catchment Hydrology. In K. A. F. a. G. J. Brierley (Ed.), *Geomorphic Analysis of River Systems*. Hoboken, NJ: Wiley-Blackwell.

Haghighatafshar, S., Jansen, J., Aspegren, H., Lidström, V., Mattsson, A., & Jonsson, K. (2014). Storm-water management in Malmö and Copenhagen with regard to climate change scenarios. *VATTEN: Journal of Water Management and Research*, 70, 159–168.

Hart, G. (2011). *Vulnerability and Adaptation to Sea-Level Rise in Auckland, New Zealand*, Wellington. Retrieved from www.wgtn.ac.nz/sgees/research-centres/documents/vulnerability-and-adaptation-to-sea-level-rise-in-auckland-new-zealand.pdf

Houston, D., Werritty, A., Bassett, D., Geddes, A., Hoolachan, A., & Millan, M. (2011). *Pluvial (Rain-Related) Flooding in Urban Areas: The Invisible Hazard*. York: Joseph Rowntree Foundation.

Hunter, P., & Scrafton, C. (2012). *Integrated Catchment Management Plans and Catchment Management Plans: How Well Are They Working with Land Use Planning?* Paper presented at the Water New Zealand Conference. Retrieved from www.planning.org.nz/Attachment?Action=Download&Attachment_id=3115

Hvilshøj, S., Lund, A. A., Goring, N. H. M., & Cathy, L. V. (2016). Copenhagen cloudburst concretization plan, Denmark. *Landscape Architecture Frontiers, 4*(5), 54–67.

Kelly, S. (2010). *Effects of Stormwater on Aquatic Ecology in the Auckland Region*. Retrieved from www.aucklandcouncil.govt.nz/SiteCollectionDocuments/about council/planspoliciespublications/technicalpublications/tr2010021ecological impactsfromstormwaterintheaucklandregion.pdf

Maksimović, Č., Prodanović, D., Boonya-Aroonnet, S., Leitão, J. P., Djordjević, S., & Allitt, R. (2009). Overland flow and pathway analysis for modelling of urban pluvial flooding. *Journal of Hydraulic Research*, *47*(4), 512–523.

Malmö, S. (2008). *Dagvattenstrategi för Malmö*, Malmö. Retrieved from www.google.co.nz/search?client=safari&rls=en&q=Dagvattenstrategi+fo%CC%88r+Malmö%CC%88+(2008)+Malmö%CC%88+Stad.&ie=UTF-8&oe=UTF-8&gfe_rd=cr&dcr=0&ei=YvMUWq3aCczN8geopIOYCg

Mantyka-Pringle, C. S., Visconti, P., Moreno, Di M., Martin, T. G., Rondinini, C., & Rhodes, J. R. (2015). Climate change modifies risk of global biodiversity loss due to land-cover change. *Biological Conservation*, *187*, 103–111.

Marzluff, J. M. (2008). *Urban Ecology: An International Perspective on the Interaction between Humans and Nature*. New York: Springer.

McHarg, I. L. (1969). *Design with Nature*. Garden City, NY: American Museum of Natural History.

Morris, R. L., Konlechner, T., Ghisalberti, M., & Swearer, S. E. (2018). From grey to green: Efficacy of eco-engineering solutions for nature-based coastal defence. *Glob Chang Biol.*, *24*(5), 1827–1842. doi:10.1111/gcb.14063

O'Neill, K. M., & Van Abs, D. J. (2016). *Taking Chances: The Coast after Hurricane Sandy*. New Brunswick: Rutgers University Press.

Orange, C. (2015). *The Treaty of Waitangi*. Auckland: Bridget Williams Books.

Pachauri, R. K. (2014). *IPCC, 2014: Climate Change 2014: Synthesis Report: Contribution of Working Groups I, II and III to the Fifth Assessment Report of the Intergovernmental Panel on Climate Change*. Retrieved from www.ipcc.ch/report/ar5/syr/

Ratcliffe, J., & Stubbs, M. (2013). *Urban Planning and Real Estate Development*. Abingdon, UK: Routledge.

Rebuild by Design. (2014). *The Big U*. Retrieved from www.rebuildbydesign.org/our-work/all-proposals/winning-projects/big-u

Rizwan, A. L., Leung, D. Y. C., & Liu, C. (2008). A review on the generation, determination and mitigation of Urban heat Island. *Journal of Environmental Sciences*, *20*(1), 120–128.

Scally, R. (2006). *GIS for Environmental Management* (1st ed.). Redlands, CA, USA: ESRI Press, Independent Publishers Group.

Schulz, D. (2018). *First Phase of Bjarke Ingels' BIG U Storm Protection System Begins Planning Process*. Retrieved from www.6sqft.com/first-phase-of-bjarke-ingels-big-u-storm-protection-system-begins-planning-process/

SLA. (2015). *Climate Adaptation Copenhagen: The Soul of Nørrebro*. Retrieved from http://sla.dk/files/7014/7887/6332/SLA_Nordic_Built_Challeng_Hans_Tavsen_Park.pdf

Stahre, P. (2008). *Blue-Green Fingerprints in the City of Malmö, Sweden: Malmö's Way to Sustainable Drainage*. Malmö, Sweden.: VA Syd.

Steuteville, R., & Langdon, P. (2009). *New Urbanism: Best Practices Guide*. Ithaca, NY: New Urban News Publications.

Thompson, D. B. (2007). *The Rational Method*. Retrieved from https://pdfs.semanticscholar.org/a4e9/37c1b58958f3add38f934df85810d41b63b3.pdf

van Roon, M., & van Roon, H. (2009). *Low Impact Urban Design and Development: The Big Picture: An Introduction to LIUDD Principles and Methods Framework* (Vol. 37). Lincoln, NZ: Manaaki Whenua Press.

Vitousek, S., Barnard, P. L., Fletcher, C. H., Frazer, N., Erikson, L., & Storlazzi, C. D. (2017). Doubling of coastal flooding frequency within decades due to sea-level rise. *Scientific Reports*, *7*. doi:10.1038/s41598-017-01362-7

Vogt, K. A., Grove, J. M., Asbjornsen, H., Maxwell, K., Vogt, D. J., Sigurdardottir, R., & Dove, M. (2002). *Linking Ecological and Social Scales for Natural Resource Management*. Cambridge, MA: Cambridge University Press.

WAA. (2007). *Waitangi Park*. Retrieved from www.waal.co.nz/our-projects/urban/waitangi-park/

West 8. (2015). *Toronto Central Waterfront*. Retrieved from www.west8.nl/projects/all/toronto_central_waterfront/

Chapter one

Introduction

This chapter discusses the effects of climate change on the way our contemporary cities are planned. The discussion begins with a description of the genesis of the current urban planning model. This model emphasises constructing urban density through a grid infrastructure network and an intensive building programme. The antecedents of this model are found in the ideas of New Urbanism (CNU, 1993). The model has developed into a highly successfully urban morphology that has been replicated globally. The success of this formula is due to the way that the formula has been adapted to the exergies of real estate planning (Ratcliffe & Stubbs, 2013). A discussion of the structure of real estate planning is outlined with the important metrics described. While this model has proved to be enormously successful both socially and economically, the consequences are that the city becomes highly impervious. The contemporary city model emphasises hard surfaces, building roads, infrastructure, footpaths, bike lanes and hard public spaces, such as squares and plazas. The hydrological consequences are profound: with the paucity of green space, there simply isn't the ability to absorb rainfall. This means that pluvial flooding and stormwater contamination will increase. A hard-impervious coastal edge also exacerbates the effects of coastal flooding. With climate change these three hydrological conditions will become much more insistent. A closer discussion of how three environmental issues that will be exacerbated by climate change – pluvial flooding, sea-level rise and stormwater contamination – is then considered.

Contemporary urban design

The contemporary urban planning model has its roots in a reaction to modernist urbanism that occurred in the 1980s and 90s. Architects and urbanists started to develop a new model of urban development, taking their inspiration from traditional European urban forms, in particular the use of the grid as a structuring device, and the city block.

Many of these ideas became codified in the Congress for New Urbanism (NU), which was founded in America in 1993 (CNU, 1993). Peter Calthorpe, Michael Corbett, Andrés Duany, Elizabeth Moule, Elizabeth Plater-Zyberk, Stefanos Polyzoides and Daniel Solomon issued a manifesto, the Charter of New Urbanism, which codified the debate of the 1980s into a prescriptive and easy-to-follow formula (Talen, 2013).

The charter begins by defining the problem of contemporary American urbanism: sprawl, environmental degradation and a lack of investment in the central city (though this concern has definitely been reversed with the extraordinary real estate bubble of the 2010s).

The principles of the charter are enunciated at three scales, from the regional to the individual building. The first chapter/section is concerned with the urban configuration within the region, the metropolis, the city and the town. Urban structures within a region should be more clearly defined, that is, there is a well-defined difference between the city/town and nature/agriculture. Social goals such as equable development opportunities throughout a region, the provision of affordable housing and improvement of transport connections with an emphasis on public transport are noted.

The next scale is the neighbourhood, the district and the corridor. This section refers to the action that an individual can take to improve an existing city. The emphasis is on community-driven action that helps people to lead better urban lives. The first building block is the neighbourhood, and these are linked together with corridors (roads, rail and trams). The streets in the neighbourhood are designed for walking and community interaction. The community should have a wide diversity of people through the provision of housing types, including low cost. A mix of civic, business and commercial ventures within a district is advocated; the single use of zone is deliberately avoided.

The last scale addresses more architectural issues: the block, the street, the building. Here the concerns are how the design of new buildings can address urban issues. All urban spaces, the street, the square and the park, are defined by buildings. Important buildings and public spaces should be distinguished from other buildings and spaces by location, prominence and form.

The principles of the NU Charter have filtered down and become a more prescriptive, buildable formula (Steuteville & Langdon, 2009) able to be used by urbanists and architects to build new towns, cities and waterfronts. For the design of a residential quarter, the formula starts with the neighbourhood block. Each neighbourhood should have a centre, a public space, a square or park. The centre is also the location of a public transport stop. All buildings should be within a five-minute walking distance of the centre, giving a distance of roughly half a kilometre. The neighbourhood is to be made up of a variety of different kinds of buildings. A street grid of different widths is advised, with a hierarchy of main streets and smaller mews (or service lanes). The buildings on the main streets are placed close to the street with minimal front yards while garages with dwelling space above occupy the mews.

Since the 1990s the New Urbanist ideas have become extremely influential on urban planning throughout the world (Grant, 2005). This has occurred in two ways: the first is the adoption of the new urbanist principles in toto. This has occurred mostly in the USA in the building of residential subdivisions, often on greenfield sites. The adoption of the new urbanist protocols has often been accompanied by a building programme in traditional architectural styles.

One of the most famous examples is the resort town of Seaside in Florida (Seaside Institute, 2008). This development was begun in 1991 on a 23 ha site on the Florida Panhandle coast. The town has a small civic centre and is made up of mostly small, freestanding residential buildings built in a traditional timber construction with bright colours. This has proved an extremely lucrative real estate development. The other famous (or perhaps infamous) development is the design and construction of the town Celebration by the Disney Corporation in Orlando, Florida (Knack, 1996). The site is 20 km^2, and the downtown area was completed in 1996. The town is organised around a central axis lined with shops and terminates at an urban promenade on a central lake.

A second development of new urbanist protocols has been a hybrid of NU planning with modernist architecture. Here, the adoption of the new urbanist street grid, the provision of civic buildings in important locations and the creation of public spaces has been combined with modernist high-rise buildings and modernist planning, especially functional zoning. This particular urban model has been most prevalent in the design and construction of new Chinese cities (Wu, 2006).

Property development

This new urban model was accompanied with a move, in the western world, away from government-based property development to private development driven by the free market reform of the 1980s (Hofman & Manuel, 2019; Peiser & Frej, 2003). The uncertainty and complexity around private urban development, especially given the nature of the property cycle, has led to the importance of a knowable development formula. The NU urban model has helped to develop this winning blueprint.

The first part of the NU/developer formula for a successful urban development is a public space, an entertainment zone for the new citizens. This is marketed as a drawcard to attract visitors and citizens to visit the new location and enjoy the new public realm. This space is often built by public money either directly or through tax credits, as an incentive for the development. Once the public infrastructure is in place, private real estate investment is built around the public space. The buildings are often consciously designed as mixed use, with retail activities on the ground floor, and residential and/or commercial above. However, the use, retail, commercial or residential, can be modelled and analysed to find the best fit according to the real estate cycle. The buildings occupy a grid-like master plan (either existing or new) that brings new customers and residents to the urban development. This formula has been successful, especially in waterfront developments. The first recognised waterfront project, the Baltimore Inner Harbor, USA, initiated in the early 1970s, is an example of this model (Fitzgerald, 1998). The project was driven by the proximity of the old Baltimore river port to downtown Baltimore. The harbour had gradually silted up, resulting in port operators moving away and abandoning the old port infrastructure. A new waterfront master plan was developed in the 1970s to reinvent the port as a commercial real estate opportunity (Breen & Rigby, 1996). The new waterfront design encompassed a mixture of public and privately financed projects along a public promenade at the edge of the old dock. The first building constructed was the publicly financed Baltimore Convention Centre, finished in 1979; followed by the Harbor Place Mall, developed by the Rouse Company, opened in 1980; then the National Aquarium in 1981; Pier 6, an outdoor entertainment facility, in 1991; the Power Plant, a multiuse building with bookshops, restaurants and a gym, in 1997–1998; and Port Discovery, a children's museum, in 1998. Along with this development programme was the construction of 11 hotels and two sports stadia. The buildings along the harbour edge are all linked with new public space, including a waterfront promenade, squares and parks. The success of the Inner Harbor development has been aggressively promoted with claims that the project receives more visitors a year than Disneyland, produces $786 million a year in revenue and has generated 16,000 jobs (Hambleton, 2016).

The resilience of this particular urban model is shown in a contemporary urban development, the proposed Aarhus Waterfront (Rosenfield, 2014). The master plan, designed by BIG (Ingels, 2010), proposes seven freestanding residential buildings in an L-shaped configuration around a former dock/basin. The buildings, while formally distinct, all share a similar building footprint. They also follow the traditional form of the European perimeter block with a large internal courtyard for the private use of the building's occupants. While the seven residential blocks define the basin, the public space, a waterfront promenade, mediates between the blocks and the water's edge. The architects have 'bent' the promenade to extend over the water, producing greater 'free' public space. The architects then strung a series of public activities along this new promenade that are more usually associated with summer beach events, such as a lido and an artificial beach. Against the building line are a series of pavilions of different sizes and typologies, including a line of beach huts.

Comparing the Baltimore Inner Harbor to the Aarhus Waterfront, there are obvious stylistic differences; however, there are recognisable similarities, especially the littoral promenade/public space with the programmed public activities backed with the commercial development.

While the architectural style has changed, the essential urban morphology conforms to the NU-derived development model.

While the first part of any urban development relies on an accepted urban morphology, the second part of any private development is understanding the financial return on the project.

Real estate planning

The viability of any property development is determined by specific financial analysis and investment models. The first stage of a property development is driven by a comprehensive development study. This has two parts, a market analysis and financial planning (Peiser & Frej, 2003). The latter stage is made up of a development feasibility study and an understanding of the mechanics of the development contribution.

Market analysis

The market analysis is usually divided into two parts, the first being an analysis of the existing market. This looks at a region's demographics, work opportunities and economic future. The second part of the analysis looks at the market's existing real estate history, in particular residential and commercial sales. For this analysis, past records are used to determine which real estate products are liable to do well in a certain area, for example, single-storey houses versus apartments. Similarly, commercial real estate products can be usefully divided into groups: offices, power centre, retail and mixed use. Deborah L. Brett and Adrienne Schmitz (2009) define a mixed-use real estate development in North America as having three or more revenue-producing functions. These usually include retail, office, residential and hotel components, each of which should be larger than 10,000 m^2. The shape of the development can take a number of forms. One follows a megastructure model where the functions are grouped around a single atrium/public space. Another model can link the different buildings with aboveground walkways and lobbies; the best-known example of this is the Houston model (Mostafavi, 2012).

More contemporary examples of mixed-use development take a new urbanist model with building uses being broken into a number of ostensibly different buildings, often different façades facing a common building floor plate that surrounds a public space designed to look like a civic square. Shops, bars and restaurants are located on the ground floor with office and retail above, and underground parking is often provided (Talen, 2013).

Master-planning the car infrastructure, parking and circulation, ensuring a mix of on- and off-street parking, discussing the possibility of shared parking and ensuring car and truck access to all buildings are critical parts of a successful development in the North American market.

Before planning the mixed-use development, an analysis of the market potential for a mixed-use development needs to be undertaken. Each development element should be able to be an economically stand-alone unit, but also the potential synergy between the different buildings' uses must be considered. The synergy creates a 'captive use' plus gives economies of scale from shared infrastructure. By understanding these possible synergies, such as residential with retail, the types of residential developments can affect what types of retail activities are offered. While people may live in a mixed-use development, they will not be the sole customers. Other uses in a mixed-use development are office, retail and entertainment spaces like restaurants and bars, hotels, movies theatres and museums. Retail in most mixed-use development will be the high-end boutique type. Facilities such as health clubs and spas can also be part of the retail mix. There are a number of problems with mixed-use development. Firstly, there is the often high building cost of multiple-use developments. Mixing services like garbage collection, loading docks and shared parking can be problematic in mixed-use buildings. Office, retail and residential buildings all have different floor plate designs. Retail floor plates are typically 27 m deep, with a post and beam grid, with columns at 7 to 9 m centres, whereas residential construction is generally 18 m deep with load-bearing walls and a 4 m column grid. Each building use must be able to generate support from outside of the development rather than relying just on the internal synergies of the development. Another problem, especially over a long build-out, is that each component will have different market appeal at different times in the real estate cycle. And lastly, the development can often be a victim of its own success: if a mixed-use project is successful, then other developments will locate nearby and copy it, which will ultimately mean a lower return.

Financial planning

The second part of a development study is understanding how a development will make an adequate financial return (Kahr & Thomsett, 2005). Property developers use a financial feasibly study to understand the costs involved in a property development. They are used for three reasons; firstly, to understand the value of a piece of land. By understanding the cost involved and the limitations imposed by local government and civic authorities, the developer can start to understand how much to pay for a site. Secondly, the study will be used to determine the return on the project: a developer can model different returns under different scenarios. And thirdly, banks and other lending institutions can use this information to determine the lending risk of advancing financing. Are the assumptions made in the study realistic? Will the development be able to realise the selling programme? Are the construction costs realistic? These are important questions that can be addressed in the feasibility study. There are three stages in which a financial feasibly study can be used. At the beginning of the project a low-cost appraisal can be made to see whether the developer should go further with the project. If this study is favourable, then the developer can move to a more detailed study. This will involve more costs, such as preparing a detailed development scheme with consultants and buying or getting an option on the site. The last use of a feasibility study is as a monitoring tool during the construction process; the real costs of the development can be compared to the study costs, helping to ensure the project is kept to time and within costs.

Development feasibility study

The development feasibility study is, in its simplest form, the value of the completed building – the developments costs (the cost of construction, the cost of the finance and all the fees – the land costs = the profit of the development) (Miles, 2007).

The value (profit) on the completion of the project is made up of three components: the rental value, or how much money will be accruing in the different income streams on the development; the capitalisation rate, that is, the net income divided by the cost of the development; and the capital valuation, which is found by multiplying the total income by the yield.

Property developers use a number of ratios to understand the financial costs and returns on a development site. The first is Gross Floor Area (GFA). This term refers to the total floor area within the building walls. This term includes all the structure and spaces but excludes the roof. The term Net Floor Area (NFA) refers to the GFA minus the structural area, while the Usable Floor Area or Leasable Floor Area (LFA) is the NFA minus the functional areas and circulation areas (corridors, atrium and lobby) (BOMA, 2017). The amount of allowable GFA on the site is usually regulated by local governments. They often use a ratio known as the Floor Area Ratio (FAR). This is the relationship of the building GFA to the area of the building plot. This ratio can be refigured in different ways: the typical example is a FAR of 1. This can be a one-storey building occupying 100 percent of the site, or a four-storey building occupying 25 percent of the site. If planning authorities wish the building footprint to be totally occupied but want to indicate a building height, then the ratio could be 1.5 or 2.0 (Bertaud & Brueckner, 2005).

The building costs can be divided into different components according to the type of building, i.e., office buildings and retail have different costs against them; external works, roads and landscaping infrastructure are separate costs, as are the professional fees; architect, lawyer and quantity surveyor are initially lumped together in one sum. A contingency sum on the building cost should be allowed for. If the development is to be leased, then letting fees are calculated as a percentage of the rentable value. Selling the development will incur sales, advertising and marketing fees. Finally, the developer's profit margin is normally calculated at an average of 20 percent.

There are a number of approaches to understanding the surplus of the development project. Dr. Tim Havard, author of a number of property development text books (Havard, 2014), characterised these as the traditional residual approach, the accumulative cash flow (ACF) approach and the discounted cash flow (DCF) approach. These models look at the income and costs of a project projected into monthly segments over the time period of the development. ACF takes the estimated monthly interest plus the total expenditure at the end of the project, i.e., when the project is sold, to determine whether profit has been made; DCF does the same thing but discounts the amount by projecting the cost in present-day terms via a discount at an agreed rate.

The viability of the contemporary urban development has a number of critical factors. For the property developer, understanding how to make a profit on an urban development through the manipulation of the size and space of saleable spaces and the way that this space is marketed is a key part of any development. For a government agency the building of public space to make a city or town meaningful to its citizens is a central concern. The NU model promotes the importance of the neighbourhood, a mixed-use area with retail, commercial and residential uses, both within the same building and within an area. Residents can gain access to all the new urban amenities by walking or taking public transport.

The financial attraction of a successful property development and the more intangible factors that are generated by the attraction of public space join in many contemporary urban projects.

Environmental problems

Contemporary urban design relies on a street grid to organise the building programme. Buildings occupy the whole block; public space is defined as an urban promenade or urban square; any green space is confined to a traditional park. The financial and social success of this model is attested to by the way this form has been replicated around the world.

However, one clear downside to this model is that the resulting city form is highly impervious, that is, the building infrastructure and public spaces are incapable of absorbing water. In simplistic terms, there is not enough green space in the contemporary city model to be able to absorb rainfall. This gives rise to three specific problems.

Buildings, streets, squares and footpaths all produce rainfall runoff that is polluted from urban street detritus. The water is collected in a piped infrastructure and discharged into a local receiving environment, often the local harbour. The discharge of these toxins into a receiving environment has a deleterious effect on marine biota (Schiffa, Baya, & Stransky, 2002; Kelly, 2010).

Because of the highly impervious nature of the typical urban development, the existing stormwater infrastructure can often be overwhelmed by sudden storm events. This causes surface flooding to varying levels of intensity (Houston et al., 2011). In many urban developments these effects have been concealed; however, with the effects of climate change these two hydrological conditions will worsen, causing more frequent and greater intensity of pollution and flooding. There will be obvious consequences for the infrastructure of the city and the lives of the citizens.

The third problem is coastal flooding. The water's edge of the typical urban development is the most critical part of a waterfront project. This is also the location of the main public space, the promenade, and the location of the most valuable real estate. This is also a place directly affected by coastal flooding. This condition will be exacerbated by the effect of sea-level rise and storm surges.

Stormwater Contamination

The construction of an urban development – the typical residential, commercial and industrial building and infrastructure – results in the removal of vegetation and the amendment of the natural topography and soil structure, which leads to a disruption of the natural hydrological system of the development zone.

Rainfall is no longer absorbed into the vegetation or the open ground; instead it is deterred by the new impervious surfaces of the city. Roads, pavements and buildings all contribute to increasing water runoff into adjacent water bodies, the receiving environment (Liu, Goonetilleke, & Egodawatta, 2015).

The increase in impervious surfaces has two effects on the native hydrological system. The first is an increase in the volume of rain not absorbed by the ground, and the second is the transformation of streams and rivers into artificially enclosed drainage systems of pipes and channels that are designed to smooth the progress of water through the network (Boyd, Bufill, & Knee, 1993). These two conditions, the volume and the speed of runoff, have the effect of increasing the discharge of water within a shorter amount of time. These two factors also have an effect on increasing the speed and the height at which the runoff volume will peak. The quickness or 'flashy' nature of peak flow runoff has a deleterious effect on the receiving environment, with flooding and damage to the littoral at the discharge point of the runoff. The last effect of increased urbanisation on the native hydrology is the shortness of time it takes to reach peak flow (Shuster, Bonta, Thurston, Warnemuende, & Smith, 2005).

The other effect of an increase in impervious surfaces is the increase in contaminated stormwater. There are a number of urban activities that generate the pollution of urban stormwater. These include contamination from paved and road surfaces; construction processes in the building industry such as the removal of topsoil as preparation for the construction; and the debris and particles from different kinds of building materials. This leads to the contamination of stormwater with suspended solids. The effect of the contamination on the receiving environment is a smothering of the flora and fauna in the littoral zone with the suspended particles, and a reduction in water transparency (Chester & Gibbons, 1996).

Different industrial processes contribute to the different pollutants from direct sources and from processes. Methods of storing and finished and unfinished industrial products can cause contaminated runoff to enter the stormwater system, as well as the more obvious sources like waste generated from industrial processes and emissions.

Roof and gutter corrosion lead to runoff becoming contaminated by corroded materials. This causes both toxicants and suspended solids to enter the water system. Incorrect waste disposal practices, leaks from existing sewer systems and chemical spills on impervious surfaces all contribute to runoff contamination. Vegetative waste can also cause stormwater contamination; leaf litter and bark can contribute to a heightened organic carbon load. The effect of this condition is to decrease the presence of oxygen in the water. This can lead to smells in the receiving water. Organic carbon can also combine with other particulates and toxicants (Balloa, Liua, Houb, & Changa, 2009).

The sources of contamination effects not only the quality of the runoff but also the way in which contamination occurs. This phenomenon is referred to as build-up and brush-off pollution. The build-up of pollutants on urban surfaces is related to specific urban conditions: the amount and form of the impervious surface and the weather, especially the duration of dry periods. The brush-off phase refers to movement of pollutants from the surface to the receiving environment via the stormwater process.

All these pollutants contribute to the contamination of the receiving environment, leading to a loss of native flora and fauna in the adjacent water bodies – the sea, lakes and rivers – resulting in a loss of marine biodiversity (Schiffa, Baya, & Stransky, 2002). All these effects will be exacerbated by climate change.

Pluvial flooding

Pluvial flooding (terrestrial flooding) is usually caused by high-intensity, short-duration rainfall. Soils become saturated with excess water and the existing stormwater system is unable to cope with the downpour because it exceeds the design limitation of the drainage network. The excess water becomes a flood before it reaches the receiving environment, the sea, lake or river (Houston et al., 2011). This phenomenon is called exceedance.

The conditions that contribute to the process of pluvial flooding are the topography of the city and location of infrastructure. These conditions influence the way in which the runoff will flow over the ground and pond or flood. The steepness of the ground condition and what barriers there are to the flooding, infrastructure and buildings will also affect the shape and extent of urban flooding.

Two further conditions affecting the process of pluvial flooding, then, are the threshold of when rainfall starts to become runoff, and at what rate runoff will start to flow. The soil condition in the flood zone also has an effect on the rate of flood build-up according to how saturated the ground is.

The capacity of the existing drainage system is also critical. There are usually four stages in the failure of a drainage system. The first phase is where stormwater enters a fully functioning, underground drainage system via a gully or manhole. The designed system has plenty of capacity to cope with the runoff. The next phase is surface flooding where the piped system still has capacity. The third phase is where the inflow and the pipe system are full. And the last phase is when the pressure within the stormwater -system is higher than outside, giving rise to overflow from the stormwater system, the so-called manhole popping (Maksimović et al., 2009). Pluvial flooding can often occur in sync with fluvial flooding, flooding from rivers and streams; and coastal flooding, flooding from the sea. These two conditions can exacerbate the effect of pluvial flooding.

Coastal flooding

Inundation is defined as the level of water on dry ground that is above the normal high tide mark (Mean High Water Springs [MHWS] in New Zealand). Inundation is caused by storm tides and storm surges. A storm surge is defined as the level of water that has been produced by a storm event above a normal tide. A storm tide is the level of water that is produced by the storm surge plus the normal tide, measured from a base datum (MfE, 2014).

Coastal flooding occurs when seawater inundates coastal land, usually as the result of a storm event (NOAA, 2013). These storm events are caused by a number of factors. Storm surge is one, when onshore wind and low atmospheric pressure cause higher than normal waves. This results in direct flooding of coasts, the overtopping of coastal flood barriers and the breaking down of coastal barriers, breaching sea defences. Tsunamis, though not as frequent as storm events, can also cause widespread coastal flooding (Vitousek et al., 2017).

While storm surges and tsunamis are examples of force majeure, sea-level rise is a wholly human-made phenomenon. The IPCC has assessed the average sea-level rise in the world to be around 2 m for the 21st century as a result of climate change. The panel also points out that an extra 100 to 200 mm of sea-level rise could occur by 2100 if the Antarctic sheet ice melts at a more rapid rate.

These three conditions have often been disguised or concealed in many urban developments. However, with the advent of climate change (Pachauri, 2014), these hitherto acquiescent conditions will become serious and enduring problems.

The increase in storm events will produce more rainfall which will cause the production and discharge of contaminated stormwater into the urban littoral. Increasing numbers of storm events will overwhelm existing stormwater infrastructure, causing urban flooding. The increase in sea warming is a well-known consequence of climate change and will produce sea-level rise and storm surges that will directly affect the viability of any urban development that is adjacent to the sea.

Remediatory measures certainly exist for these problems, however, they demand space for the remediation functions to work. For example, structural stormwater remediation systems require space at the discharge point of a stormwater system for a wetland or raingarden treatment system. Pluvial flooding remediation requires space for overland flooding conveyance channels and detention ponds. Coastal flooding prevention measures similarly require a large amount of space for both hard and soft remediation devices such as a littoral buffer zone.

If remediating the serious hydrological problems that will soon threaten the viability of the contemporary urban development is important, then a new urban development model in which the remediation of these problems will be given precedence is critical.

Conclusion

This chapter has outlined current urban design practice, its genesis in the ideas of NU and its alliance with contemporary real estate planning. The result is an urban design prescription intermeshed with a real estate formula. The success of this model is proven by its enviable global success; however, this success comes at the expense of the silencing of important environmental problems, in particular, pluvial and coastal flooding and stormwater contamination. With the effects of climate change becoming more insistent, the option of simply continuing the accepted urban model will become increasing redundant.

References

Balloa, S., Liua, M., Houb, L., & Changa, J. (2009). Pollutants in stormwater runoff in Shanghai (China): Implications for management of urban runoff pollution. *Progress in Natural Science*, *19*(7), 873–880.

Bertaud, A., & Brueckner, J. (2005). Analyzing building-height restriction: Predicted impacts and welfare costs. *Regional Science and Urban Economics*, *35*, 109–125.

BOMA. (2017). BOMA 2017 for Office Buildings: Standard Methods of Measurement: ANSI/BOMA ZZ.1-2017.

Boyd, D., Bufill, M. C., & Knee, R. M. (1993). Pervious and impervious runoff in urban catchments. *Hydrological Sciences Journal*, *38*(6), 463–478.

Breen A., & Rigby, D. (1996). *The New Waterfront: A Worldwide Urban Success Story*. London: Thames and Hudson.

Brett, D. L. & Schmitz, A. (2009). *Real Estate Market Analysis: Methods And Case Studies* (2nd ed.). Washington, DC: Urban Land Institute.

Chester, L. A., & Gibbons, J. (1996). Impervious surface coverage: The emergence of a key environmental indicator. *Journal of the American Planning Association*, *62*(2), 243–258.

CNU. (1993). *The Charter of New Urbanism*. Retrieved from www.cnu.org/who-we-are/charter-new-urbanism

Fitzgerald, P. (1998). Balitimore inner harbour. In *Wikimedia: OpenStreetMap* [CC BY-SA 2.0]HTML.

Grant, J. (2005). *Planning the Good Community: New Urbanism in Theory and Practice* (Vol. 9). London: Routledge.

Hambleton, R. (2016). Place-based leadership: A new perspective on urban regeneration. *Journal of Urban Regeneration & Renewal*, *9*(1), 10–24.

Havard, T. (2014). *Financial Feasibility Studies for Property Development: Theory and Practice*. Oxford: Routledge.

Hofman, A. A., & Manuel, B. (2019). A finance- and real estate-driven regime in the United Kingdom. *Geoforum, 100*(2019), 89–100.

Houston, D., Werritty, A., Bassett, D., Geddes, A., Hoolachan, A., & Millan, M. (2011). *Pluvial (Rain-Related) Flooding in Urban Areas: The Invisible Hazard*. York: Joseph Rowntree Foundation.

Ingels, B. (2010). *Big: Bjarke Ingels Group*. Seoul, Korea: Archilife.

Kahr, J., & Thomsett, M. C. (2005). *Real Estate Market Valuation and Analysis*. Hoboken, NJ: Wiley.

Kelly, S. (2010). *Effects of Stormwater on Aquatic Ecology in the Auckland Region*. Retrieved from http://www.aucklandcouncil.govt.nz/SiteCollectionDocuments/aboutcouncil/planspoliciespublications/technicalpublications/tr2010021ecologicalimpactsfromstormwaterintheaucklandregion.pdf

Knack, R. E. 1996. "Once upon a Town. Walt Disney Co. building the town of Celebration near Orlando, Florida." *Planning* 62 (3):10.

Liu, A., Goonetilleke, A., & Egodawatta, P. (2015). *Role of Rainfall and Catchment Characteristics on Urban Stormwater Quality*. Singapore: Springer.

Maksimović, Č., Prodanović, D., Boonya-Aroonnet, S., Leitão, J. P., Djordjević, S., Allitt, R. (2009). Overland flow and pathway analysis for modelling of urban pluvial flooding. *Journal of Hydraulic Research*, *47*(4), 512–523.

MfE. (2014). *3 Implications for New Zealand's Coastal Margins*. Retrieved from www.mfe.govt.nz/publications/climate-change/coastal-hazards-and-climate-change-guidance-manual-local-government-n-21

Miles, M. E. (2007). *Real Estate Development: Principles and Process*. Washington, DC: Urban Land Institute.

Mostafavi, M. (2012). *In the Life of Cities*. Baden: Lars Müller.

NOAA. (2013). *Defining Storm Surge, Storm Tide and Inundation*. Retrieved from www.nhc.noaa.gov/news/20130806_pa_defineSurge.pdf

Pachauri, R. K. (2014). *IPCC, 2014: Climate Change 2014: Synthesis Report: Contribution of Working Groups I, II and III to the Fifth Assessment Report of the Intergovernmental Panel on Climate Change*. Retrieved from www.ipcc.ch/report/ar5/syr/

Peiser, R. B., & Frej, A. B. (2003). *Professional Real Estate Development: The ULI Guide to the Business*. Washington, DC: Urban Land Institute.

Ratcliffe, J., & Stubbs, M. (2013). *Urban Planning and Real Estate Development*. Abingdon, UK: Routledge.

Rosenfield, K. (2014). *New BIG-Designed Neighborhood to Activate Aarhus' Waterfront*. Retrieved from http://www.archdaily.com/551290/big-designs-7-building-waterfront-development-in-aarhus/

Schiffa, K., Baya, S., & Stransky, C. (2002). Characterization of stormwater toxicants from an urban watershed to freshwater and marine organisms. *Urban Water Journal*, *4*(3), 215–227.

Seaside Institute. (2008). *Views of Seaside: Commentaries and Observations on a City of Ideas*. Santa Rosa Beach, FL: Rizzoli.

Shuster, W. D., Bonta, J., Thurston, H., Warnemuende, E., & Smith, D. R. (2005). Impacts of impervious surface on watershed hydrology: A Review. *Urban Water Journal*, *2*(4), 263–275.

Steuteville, R., & Langdon, P. (2009). *New Urbanism: Best Practices Guide*. Ithaca, NY: New Urban News Publications.

Talen, E. (2013). *Charter of the New Urbanism* (2nd ed.). New York, NY: McGraw-Hill Education.

Vitousek, S., Barnard, P. L., Fletcher, C. H., Frazer, N., Erikson, L., & Storlazzi, C. D. (2017). Doubling of coastal flooding frequency within decades due to sea-level rise. *Scientific Reports*, *7*. doi:10.1038/s41598-017-01362-7

Wu, F. (2006). *Globalization and the Chinese City*. London, New York, NY: Routledge.

Chapter two

Introduction

This chapter discusses the development of specific strategies that will help build resilience to the consequences of climate change for the contemporary city.

Firstly, the concept of resilience is explored, especially a contemporary definition that describes a fluid and hybrid response to external disturbance. Then the science of landscape and urban ecology is put forward as a framework to understand how urban development works within a larger realm. Developing an understanding of the urban development site within knowable and measurable environmental conditions is discussed, in particular using the framework of the hydrological catchment to help understand and address environmental problems.

Ways in which this framework can become engaged with the pragmatics of site development are explored in a discussion of the work of Ian McHarg (1969). The use of GIS digital mapping software to both uncover environmental problems and model possible remediatory regimes is considered (Skidmore, 2002). Specific strategies drawn from the ideas of Low Impact Urban Design and Development are explored for their relevance (van Roon & van Roon, 2009). These particular strategies are protecting riparian margins, reducing impervious surfaces through building clustering and reducing contaminates.

From this background, a specific design process is sketched out that gives practical design strategies to remediate the effect of climate change.

Resilience

Making our cities resilient to the environmental effects of climate change is the first step in developing an alternative urban model. Definitions of resilience have passed through three phases, according to the ecologist Carl Folke (2006). Folke finds the beginning of the idea of resilience within ecology studies in the 1960s and 70s. From observations of interacting natural phenomena, ecologists found connections between random events and ecological processes. Resilience was described as 'the capacity to persist within such a domain in the face of change' (Folke, 2006, pg. 254). Folke describes how these ideas came up against the steady state theory, the dominant paradigm in ecology at the time. The steady state theory held that nature was in a state of equilibrium with small movement that would always return to the same state. As the concept of resilience became more accepted, the concept of engineered resilience emerged. This view attempted to address the presence of disturbance in a system by concentrating on the return to the steady state after disturbance. This view of resilience concentrates on conserving and husbanding resources to ensure a constant functioning regime. Difficulties with measuring the recovery of a system after disturbance became pronounced. Another definition of resilience emerged: the adaptive system. The emphasis was on describing a fluid, unstable, dynamic world. Rather than a return to equilibrium, the condition/state will undergo new processes after disturbance. Folke describes how new ideas about systems moved from beliefs that systems are stable and predictable to ideas that systems can be described as complex and adaptive. Some common terms include nonequilibrium dynamics (a process of continual adaption), lack of hierarchy organisation and nonlinearity.

Disturbance to these systems takes many forms but with the advent of climate change the role of human-made disturbance has become increasing obvious, leading to a lowering of resilience in many systems. The concept of the adaptive system led to the development of a second stage of thinking about resilience that Folke (2006) describes as ecological/ecosystem resilience. Folke sees this category as being an advance on engineered resilience, with the focus now on maintaining a stable system though a robust organisation. The characteristics of a resilient system are its ability to withstand disturbance in a robust manner and to maintain functionality.

A third category, social-ecological resilience, has recently emerged. This is a departure from the other two definitions, untethering the concept of resilience from any idea of fixity or stability. Instead Folke (2006) argues for a reconceptualisation of nature from a state of equilibrium to a more open, dynamic field of flows into openness. Folke sees the way in which disturbance can create the possibility of a renewal of systems through the recombination of different regimes and structures. This leads to the ability of regimes to self-organise into new configurations. The characteristics of this definition are the capacity of the system to absorb disturbance and yet retain an internal coherence, to be self-organising and able to learn and transform from disturbance.

The concept of resilience offers a way to conceptually rethink the current urban development model. The classic definition of resilience is the ability of an environmental/social system to return to its natural state after a disruptive event. The implication for building a resilient urban development is that it should be able to resist disruptive environmental events such as sea-level rise and flooding so that the development can continue to function as a financially and socially viable urban proposition.

However, expecting our existing urban structures to simply bounce back in the same shape after a catastrophic environmental event is not going to be possible after the repetition of disruptive events.

The concept of adaptive systems in thinking about the effect of climate change on urban waterfronts is explored by Klein, Nicholls and Thomalla (2003). The authors identify five ways in which adaptive processes can be used to increase the resilience of the urban project. These are: helping to increase the ability of physical infrastructure located on the development site to withstand flooding; changing specific management practices that are vulnerable to the effects of climate change; helping vulnerable ecosystems to adapt to the changes brought about by climate change;

identifying vulnerable systems and processes and strengthening them (for example, using natural ecosystems like wetlands and marshes to protect against storm surges); and raising public consciousness about how vulnerable the development site is to the effects of climate change, thus helping stakeholders prepare for adaptive measures.

The third, more contemporary definition sees resilience (Folke, 2006) as the capacity of a system to transform to another state, yet to keep certain integral qualities, structures, identity and functions. The implications for the contemporary urban design model are that the accepted master plan must be transformed into a new configuration that accepts the disruption of environmental events such as flooding and provides the appropriate remediation regime. In the provisioning of this solution, the existing conventional urban development master plan has to transform; the plan cannot return to the existing pattern after the disruptive event. However, while the architectural, formal and spatial qualities of the urban master plan may be transformed, the internal qualities of the urban development, the provisioning of public space, the connection to natural processes and, most importantly, the economic return can remain intact.

The potential of this definition of resilience is that it can be manifest as a hybrid city form that can absorb the effects of climate change yet can still retain the development dogma of the 21st century city. To help understand how the shape of this new city might develop, the science of landscape and urban ecology can provide ways of conceptualising the position of the city within an ecological system and ways of defining and naming the location of natural features within the system.

Urban and landscape ecology

The science of urban ecology uses the ecology model, the study of the way living organisms relate to each other and the environment, and places this study within an urban milieu (Niemela, 1998). Techniques and methods used in ecological studies are transferred to the study of the ecology of the city. Jari Neimela defines urban ecology as being 'ecological research in the urban setting' (Rebele, 1994). Neimela discusses how to incorporate ecological knowledge within urban planning regimes, what kind of nature exists in the city and how can it be quantified. Neimela also discusses the knowledge of specific processes of human-induced disturbance and the effects of this disturbance on ecological succession.

Urban ecology is a science that gives a knowable and assessable framework in which to connect the urban development site to critical environmental issues. Rather than see the development site as an island that is assailed by unknowable external conditions such as flooding, sea-level rise and polluted runoff, the study of urban ecology gives a framework in which to place the development site within a series of nested scales that vary according to specific environmental conditions. For example, the effect of pluvial flooding and stormwater contamination on an urban development site is caused by water movements that are generated within the surrounding zone.

Landscape ecology is a science that spatialises ecological systems within a particular location, a landscape. Ecological processes are studied within a specific locale. The scale of a specific landscape setting will have an effect on a specific ecology or, more particularly, a specific ecotone (Forman & Godron, 1986). A landscape can be conceptualised as a series of cascading scales in relationship to each other (or nested within each other). Decisions made within a certain landscape at a certain scale cannot be seen in isolation but will inevitably have an effect on another system at another scale. A good example of this landscape is the catchment.

The sciences of urban ecology and landscape ecology give a specific landscape form, the catchment, to help place an urban development within a known and knowable structure.

The hydrological catchment is a defined landscape unit can be used to spatially locate the urban development site. In this way the effects of climate change on the catchment and thus the urban development site can be apprehended.

The catchment

A catchment is a geographical unit in which the hydrological cycle and its components can be analysed (Cretu, Nagy, & Boncia, 2010). To understand how water will behave in the city or the countryside, the catchment (known as a watershed in the USA) is defined as a specific geographical unit. The catchment is a hydrological system within a geographically specific terrain. The extent of the watershed/catchment can be measured by taking a cross-section at 90 degrees to a watercourse including the rising ground on both sides until the terrain drops into the neighbouring catchment. This point is known as a divide and defines the edge of the catchment.

A catchment/watershed works in three ways. Once the rain has fallen into the catchment/watershed, the water percolates into the ground. The infiltration process is influenced by a number of factors: the topography, the climate, the sort of vegetative cover present and the soil type. Secondly, the catchment stores rainwater within the ground as an aquifer or spring. The type of surface cover of the catchment will often determine how deep the percolation goes. And, thirdly, once the soils are saturated, the rainfall begins to run off and form creeks, streams and rivers. They will lead to a point where the runoff discharges into a receiving environment, a larger river, a lake or the sea (Calow & Petts, 1992).

The catchment/watershed contains and is defined by a hydrological network. The network is made up of all the watercourses that discharge into a receiving environment. The operation of the network is influenced by four factors: the geology of the catchment, the slope, the climate and the environment (Robinson, Sivapalan, & Snell, 1996). The watercourses themselves are classified, from upstream to downstream, into a hierarchy of orders, from their origin to confluence to termination. The entire network can be described as a river continuum. The model is based on an understanding of how a hydrological system within a catchment acts as an ecosystem. The watercourse is dynamic; it interacts with the adjacent riparian zone, soil, vegetation and topography. Changes to the surrounding or buffer conditions affect the condition of the watercourse. The river continuum can be divided into three sections: the headwaters, the middle reaches and the lower reaches. Each section can be described by the order of streams it contains and their typical gradient. Thus, the headwaters contain first- to third-order streams, usually with a steep gradient. The middle reaches contain fourth- to seventh-order streams, which are usually wider and with a lower gradient. This zone is usually industrialised/urbanised, so this water is usually the receiving environment for pollution. The last section, the lower reaches, is of larger-order rivers (Thorp, Thoms, & Delong, 2008).

By rethinking the urban development site as part of a catchment, critical environmental issues, especially hydrological, can be located within a greater landscape/ topography.

To start an investigation into an urban catchment, the elected development site can be reframed beyond its immediate property boundaries to be located within the larger urban catchment. The urban catchment locates the urban site within a scaled relationship to the greater landscape.

Design with nature

A design process to understanding the importance of the site within the catchment in terms of the environmental impact of an urban development, and to ensure the protection of important ecological features such as streams and native bush fragments, was originally developed by Ian McHarg in his seminal text, *Design with Nature* (McHarg, 1969).

The book is a strange blend of autobiography, apocalyptic warnings, design case studies and geographical mapping techniques. The central dialectic of the McHargian universe is city and nature. That Manichean choice – city bad, nature good – is repeated throughout the text, from reminiscing about his childhood growing up in Glasgow to confronting the environmental damage to the New Jersey shore after the storm of 1962 (eerily prefiguring the damage of Hurricane Sandy).

McHarg introduces what he describes as the ecological view. A landscape inventory is taken of the development site: slopes, drainage, erosion; then wider environmental criteria: flooding zones, recreational areas, habitats, forests; then social values such as land values, scenic values and historical values are mapped. These are all represented as grey tones on individual transparent maps. The transparencies are laid on top of each other; the darker areas with the most accumulated values are the most ecological and socially valuable. The lighter areas are therefore of less value; these are the areas that can be developed.

McHarg demonstrates the methodology of the ecological view by carrying out an ecological inventory of the Philadelphia region, starting with a hydrological inventory: surface water, flooding zones, marshes and aquifers, followed by a valuable land review with a mapping of forests and agricultural land. Using the inventory, McHarg suggests which areas should be zoned for open space conservation and which areas could be zoned for development. The Baltimore Valleys study demonstrates the growing sophistication of McHarg's methodology. Approached by a community group apprehensive about the threats of growing suburban sprawl from Baltimore, McHarg uses what he calls 'physiographic determinism' to reveal where development could be allowed to happen without spoiling the natural beauty of the valleys. Concurrent with this process he also carries out a study demonstrating what would happen to the valleys if standard strip sprawl was allowed to happen. After carrying out an ecological inventory using a wide range of environmental data, McHarg uses a combination of agricultural values and the protection of the rivers and streams to prohibit the use of the valley floors for any development. Instead, the surrounding valley tops, the plateaus, are deemed as the best sites for development. McHarg suggests that the most intense development should occur on the forested ridge. This case study demonstrates two of McHarg's methods coming together to form a three-dimensional understanding of the site: the mapping sets up the basic nature of the plan while the section or transect helps to make the overall disposition.

McHarg's mapping strategy, the gathering of data about the location of most ecologically important parts of a site, and then the logic of combining this data to demonstrate a hierarchy from the most ecologically important/valuable to the least, is easily digestible.

The graphic representation of this data in the form of transparent maps is a magic wand that enables everyone, from experts to the general public, to understand both the process and the inevitability of the results. One of the critical assumptions that McHarg adopts is that human activity, especially urban activity, is inherently deleterious to the environment. These activities are to be relegated to the areas not occupied by environmentally sensitive uses. Since McHarg's analogue layering of maps, the process has been transformed digitally into what is now GIS mapping.

GIS

Geographic Information System (GIS) is software that helps in the analysis and design of data, especially environmental data (Schuurman, 2004). GIS can be used efficaciously to map a catchment and to analyse the hydrological pattern. GIS catchment analysis starts with the construction of a digital three-dimensional model of a given landscape. A digital elevation model can take two different forms according to the base data. The first is a digital surface model – that is, a model that represents the surface of the earth plus all objects on the surface such as trees and buildings. The base data for this model might come from drone mapping. The second model is a digital terrain model that represents just the earth's surface (Moore, Grayson, & Ladson, 1991). Base data for this model often comes from a surveying method such as Lidar.

A digital elevation model is represented in GIS in both raster and vector files. The raster forms a grid with elevation points, and is known as a digital terrain model. In the vector form the model is known as a triangular irregular network (TIN). This is a series of points with three-dimensional coordinates that are joined in a triangular network. Using one of these base models, a number of environmental conditions of a site can be modelled, such as the aspect of the site, its relationship to the cardinal points of the compass, the slope of the site and the gradient of the topography.

Using a digital model of the site, the hydrological behaviour and pattern of a landscape catchment can also be modelled (Shamsi, 2005). Using ArcGIS (ESRI) software, the original digital elevation model (DEM) data can be integrated with hydrological information to determine the boundaries of a catchment network on any given terrain. ArcGIS is also able to map the area of rainfall within the catchment from point data. Using ArcHydro and, more recently, ArcPro, a range of tools in the ArcGIS toolkit can define the hydrological pattern and behaviour of the catchment area. The software can help define the catchment boundaries of the site and the stream order pattern of the site catchment from the edges to the discharge point. The modelling can also show the effects of an increase in rainfall and the effects of a lessening or increase in perviousness of the different surfaces in the catchment (Skidmore, 2002).

While this software is typically used to determine the hydrological behaviour of unmodified catchments, it can also be used to determine the hydrological behaviour of urban catchments. However, when carrying out GIS analysis of an urban catchment, a number of specific urban/landscape conditions need to be considered to ensure an accurate measurement of catchment runoff. These conditions are artificial changes to the terrain through contour modification, an increase in impervious surfaces through building and infrastructure construction and the installation of reticulated stormwater systems (Maksimović et al., 2009). These are all conditions that are not found in natural catchments but will affect the accurate measurement of the effect of runoff within the urban catchment.

The percentage of pervious and impervious surfaces within a catchment is a critical measure in understanding the hydrological behaviour within a catchment, how much of the catchment is capable of absorbing rainfall. If this information is not available as a shape file then there are a number of ways of deriving this information. The simplest way to understand this ratio is through an aerial photo survey to measure the percentage of buildings and roads versus unbuilt surfaces such as parks and reserves. This method doesn't allow for any complex analysis to include factors such as the soil condition and the types of absorbent vegetation. To give more certainty, ground truthing (a site inspection) of the selected landscape can yield a more accurate analysis of the specificity of the ground conditions. Finally, a specialist investigation of soil and subsoil conditions will yield hard data on the ability of soils to absorb runoff.

The McHargian design process helps in the selection and preservation of ecologically important zones within a site and in planning possible locations for urban development. The process helps in gaining an understanding of the hydrological behaviour of a catchment, both in the generation of stormwater and pluvial flooding. GIS mapping helps to outline the shape of the urban catchment to graphically represent the environmental features and provide an inventory of the existing conditions of the catchment. A simple mapping of the landscape, the topography, aspect, slope and ratio of permeable to impermeable can be configured. A more complex understanding of the hydrological conditions of the site can also be made, such as the overland flow paths, the areas of flooding and the amount of stormwater produced. Important data about the vulnerability of a development site can also be gathered from a study of the larger catchment. GIS software can carry out the mapping and analysis required to understand the three critical environmental problems that have been identified: where and when urban flooding will occur, an understanding of the production of urban stormwater and the effects of sea-level rise. GIS mapping can also be used to model the remediation measures for these issues.

Stormwater modelling

There are also a number of simple mathematical formulae that can determine the amount of runoff within a catchment. The Rational Method is a commonly used mathematical equation to calculate the maximum value of flood runoff from a small catchment. This is a formula that relates the intensity of rainfall, the area of the catchment and the consequent runoff (Thompson, 2007).

Rainfall intensity is the relationship between four conditions: the geographic location of the catchment, storm duration, storm intensity and storm return interval. This figure has already been calculated for a number of geographical locations and has been developed into readily classifiable formulae on the internet. For example, in New Zealand, the National Institute of Water and Atmospheric Research (NIWA) has developed an online calculator for any New Zealand location. There are also a number of online tools to help with this calculation (LMNO Engineering Research and Software, 2015).

> The Rational Method Equation Q = C**u**CiA
>
> where:
> Q = design discharge (L**3**/T),
> Cu = units' conversion coefficient,
> C = runoff coefficient (dimensionless),
> i = design rainfall intensity (L/T) and
> A = watershed drainage area (L**2**).
> The units' conversion coefficient, **3** C**u**, is necessary because the iA product, while it has units of L/T, is not a standard unit in the traditional units' system.
> C = runoff coefficient
> The runoff coefficient is the fraction of the rainfall that is converted to runoff, that is, the rainfall that is not absorbed into the ground. The runoff coefficients of different ground conditions can be found in a number of commonly available tables. This figure can be manipulated by increasing the permeable surface through the provision of new public spaces like parks, and by decreasing building footprints.
> i = design rainfall intensity (L/T)

The amount of runoff from the catchment and the size of the remediation or detention devices required to remediate or alleviate the effect of excessive runoff due to impervious surfaces can be modelled using a number of software programmes. Some programmes are more suitable as conceptual design tools for the study of how an urban stormwater management regime could be integrated into the urban landscape, rather than for more specific hydrological analysis.

Certain software can be used to model water and pollutant runoff, transport and routing. This data is important in assessing future land-use policies. Large-scale catchment modelling can be used for assessing regional water quality and pollutant loads and for assessing broad-scale management actions. More specific programmes can be used to model the performance of conventional and innovative water supply, stormwater and wastewater provisions. These programmes are useful for measuring the impact that innovative water service regimes can have on various urban development options. Programmes can be specifically designed to determine water quality and to demonstrate how a range of stormwater treatment measures will operate. Remediatory regimes for stormwater cleaning and flood prevention can then be modelled. Other programmes can be used to size stormwater infiltration systems, and to help in the design of rainwater tanks, grass swales and bio-retention systems.

McAlister et al. (2006) describe and evaluate six rainfall-runoff models. XP-SWMM (Phillips, Yu, Thompson, & de Silva, 2005) is a model for assessing the performance of conventional and innovative water supply, stormwater and wastewater provisions. The authors suggest that the model is useful for measuring the impact that innovative water service regimes can have on various urban development options. MUSIC (Dotto et al., 2010; Wong, Fletcher, Duncan, Coleman, & Jenkins, 2002) is a model specifically designed to determine water quality and to determine how a range of stormwater treatment measures will operate. The authors suggest that this programme should be used as a conceptual design tool rather than a more specific hydrological analysis, or any study of how an urban stormwater management regime could be integrated into the urban landscape. XP-AQUALM (Dotto et al., 2010) is a model that will generate both water and pollutant runoff, transport and routing. The authors (Dotto et al., 2010) suggest an important use for this model is for assessing future land-use policies. E2 is software useful for large-scale catchment modelling; the authors suggest that the model is best used for assessing regional water quality, pollutant loads and broad-scale management actions.

Remediatory regimes for stormwater cleaning and flood prevention can be modelled after analysis. SWITCH is a model to size stormwater infiltration systems, which has been expanded to help in the design of rainwater tanks, grass swales and bio-retention systems. Elliot and Trowsdale (2007) discuss the ability of ten programmes to model stormwater remediation devices. They found that WBM was able to model the effect of green roofs; MOUSE, MUSIC P8 SLAMM StormTac, SWM and WBM were able to model the effect of swales; MUSIC and WBM, the effect of bio-retention devices. MOUSE, MUSIC P8 RUNEQUAL SLAMM StormTac, SWM UVQ and WBM can model the effect of ponds and wetlands.

Conclusion

This chapter describes the lineaments of a process that can help address the challenges that climate change present to the future development of the city. The complexity of the environmental problems described suggests that a number of different disciplines will have to be utilised. The discussion starts with thinking about the connection between resilience and urban ecology. Moving the discussion into the world of urban design suggests a consideration of more disparate sources, including 1970s landscape architecture, mapping software and stormwater calculation. This multi-disciplinary approach is developed in the next chapter where the discussion is manifest as practical design methods. These techniques address directly the problems that urban designers, developers and agencies will engage with on greenfield and brownfield sites.

References

Calow, P., & Petts, G. E. (1992). *The Rivers Handbook: Volume One: Hydrological and Ecological Principles*. Oxford: Blackwell Scientific.

Cretu, G., Nagy, C., & Boncia, F. (2010). Watersheds. *VICAIRE (VIrtual Campus In Hydrology and Water Resource Management)*. Retrieved from http://echo2.epfl.ch/VICAIRE/mod_1a/chapt_2/main.htm

Dotto, C. B. S., Kleidorfer, M., Deletic, A., Fletcher, T. D., McCarthy, D. T., & Rauch, W. (2010). Stormwater quality models: Performance and sensitivity analysis. *Water Science and Technology*, *62*(4), 837.

Elliott, A. H., & Trowsdale, S. A. (2007). A review of models for low impact urban stormwater drainage. *Environmental Modelling & Software*, *22*(3), 394–405.

Folke, C. (2006). Resilience: The emergence of a perspective for social-ecological systems analyses. *Global Environmental Change*, *16*, 253–267.

Forman, R. T. T., & Godron, M. (1986). *Landscape Ecology*. New York: John Wiley.

Klein, R., R. Nicholls, and F. Thomalla. 2003. "Resilience to natural hazards: How useful is this concept?,." *Global Environmental Change Part B: Environmental Hazards* 5 (1):35–45.

LMNO Engineering Research and Software. (2015). *Rational Equation Calculator Compute Peak Discharge from a Drainage Basin Using the Rational Equation Method*. Retrieved from www.lmnoeng.com/Hydrology/rational.php

Maksimović, Č., Prodanović, D., Boonya-Aroonnet, S., Leitão, J. P., Djordjević, S., Allitt, R. (2009). Overland flow and pathway analysis for modelling of urban pluvial flooding. *Journal of Hydraulic Research*, *47*(4), 512–523.

McAlister, T., Mitchell, G., Fletcher, T., & Phillips, B. (2006). Modelling Urban Stormwater Management Systems. In T. H. F. Wong & Engineers Australia, National Committee on Water Engineering (Eds.), *Australian Runoff Quality: A Guide to Water Sensitive Urban Design* (Vol. 1). Crows Nest, NSW: Engineers Media.

McHarg, I. L. (1969). *Design with Nature*. Garden City, NY: American Museum of Natural History.

Moore, I. D., Grayson, R. B., & Ladson, A. R. (1991). Digital Terrain Modelling: A Review of Hydrological, Geomorphological, and Biological Applications. *Hydrological Processes*, *5*. doi:10.1002/hyp.3360050103

Niemela, J. (1998). Ecology and Urban Planning. *Biodiversity and Conservation*, *8*, 119–131.

Phillips, B. C., Yu, S., Thompson, G. R., & de Silva, N. (2005). *1D and 2D Modelling of Urban Drainage Systems Using XP-SWMM and TUFLOW*. Paper presented at the 10th International Conference on Urban Drainage, Copenhagen, Denmark.

Rebele, F. (1994). Urban ecology and special features of urban ecosystems. *Global Ecology and Biogeography Letters [0960-7447]*, *4*(6), 173–187.

Robinson, J. S., Sivapalan, M., & Snell, J. D. (1996). On the relative roles of hillslope processes, channel routing, and network geomorphology in the hydrologic response of natural catchments. *Water Resources Research*, *31*(12). doi:10.1029/95WR01948

Schuurman, N. (2004). *GIS: A Short Introduction*. Malden, MA: Blackwell.

Shamsi, U. M. (2005). *GIS Applications for Water, Wastewater, and Stormwater Systems*. Boca Raton, FL: Taylor & Francis.

Skidmore, A. P. H. (2002). *Environmental Modelling with GIS and Remote Sensing*. London and New York: Taylor & Francis.

Thompson, D. B. (2007). *The Rational Method*. Retrieved from https://pdfs.semanticscholar.org/a4e9/37c1b58958f3add38f934df85810d41b63b3.pdf

Thorp, H. J., Thoms, M. C., & Delong, M. D. (2008). *The Riverine Ecosystem Synthesis: Toward Conceptual Cohesiveness in River Science* (1st ed.). Amsterdam and Boston: Academic Press and Elsevier.

van Roon, M., & van Roon, H. (2009). *Low Impact Urban Design and Development: The Big Picture: An Introduction to LIUDD Principles and Methods Framework* (Vol. 37). Lincoln, NZ: Manaaki Whenua Press.

Wong, T., Fletcher, T. D., Duncan, H. P., Coleman, J. R., & Jenkins, G. A. (2002). *A Model for Urban Stormwater Improvement Conceptualisation*. Paper presented at the Global Solutions for Urban Drainage, Portland, Oregon.

Chapter three

Introduction

The previous chapter sketched out a possible structure in which to frame the environmental impact of climate change on an urban development site. Using key concepts from urban and landscape ecology, the hydrological catchment was advanced as a locus in which the effects of climate change could be both measured and mitigated.

This chapter will elucidate some of the concrete strategies and techniques to help build environmental resilience to climate change. From the previous section, we see that placing the urban development site within the catchment and carrying out an environmental inventory is the first step. Once these consequences are understood, a number of broad catchment-based strategies and specific remediation techniques can be put in place to help build resilience to climate change and in particular to the three hydrological problems outlined in chapter 1; the increasing contamination of the receiving environment from stormwater, terrestrial flooding and coastal flooding.

Understanding the type of development site determines what the most appropriate mitigation strategies and tools are. Urban development sites can be divided into two types, greenfield and brownfield. A greenfield site is generally defined as a rural site, mostly grass, possibly with some native vegetation, but generally 100 percent pervious. The site is capable of absorbing rainfall and has a functioning hydrological system of overland flow paths, streams and rivers. A brownfield site is an existing urban site, typically highly impervious, where the natural hydrological pattern has been subsumed by development. Mitigation strategies can be shared between both types; however, specific remediation techniques are generally tailored to a specific site.

Greenfield site

In examining the impact and potential for the mitigation of climate change for a greenfield development, the theory and practice of LIUDD (van Roon & van Roon, 2009) is explored. LIUDD demonstrates how an urban development can be built with the least impact on the natural environment, in particular, the original hydrological cycle. The thesis of LIUDD is that by understanding and privileging environmental criteria, the urban development site is shaped to achieve a low-impact urban development. As the environmental effects of climate change worsen, the ways in which the urban design of a new settlement can lessen the impact of these effects will become increasingly important.

The theory of LIUDD begins by shaping the urban development site within the larger catchment through a series of ecologically derived goals. Making the best use of the existing infrastructure, minimising the effects of the development through site selection, matching the development to the carrying capacity of the ecosystem and minimising the energy inputs and outputs within the catchment are the goals of LIUDD.

These goals are developed through the use of specific strategies: protecting terrestrial and marine biodiversity through protecting existing sensitive areas on the development site; trying to maintain the natural hydrology of the catchment; reducing or containing contaminants on the development site through the restoration and protection of the natural landscape; and developing new kinds of urban form to help retain or create pervious space by clustering the building programme.

Hydrological neutrality

Once an inventory of the catchment is understood, an important aim of LIUDD is to retain/enhance the biodiversity and health of the existing aquatic ecosystem within a catchment during and after the urban development process. The objective of LIUDD is to ensure that even after an urban development there is no change to the health of the water ecosystem. A primary driver for this condition is the concept of hydrological neutrality. Van Roon (van Roon & Moore, 2004) defines the state of hydrological neutrality as being actions that cause little or no change to the hydrologic system within a catchment.

Van Roon credits the invention of the idea of carrying out urban development with no effect on the hydrologic/ecosystem health to American researchers in Washington State. They christened the concept Zero Impact Design (ZID) (Holz, 2002), in which any urban development must 'retain or recreate' the indigenous hydrological conditions. As much of Washington State is covered in forest, the ZID regime is specifically oriented toward the protection of indigenous forest within a catchment. The duplication of forest-like functions such as evapotranspiration and ground infiltration on runoff is promoted in an urban development.

Techniques that are available to designers to ensure hydrological neutrality for urban developments are protection of riparian margins, increasing evapotranspiration, using clustering to reduce the building footprint and limiting the effective impervious area of the development to 15 percent of the catchment.

The effect of these strategies is to lessen the amount of runoff in the catchment, thus decreasing the possibility of pluvial flooding and runoff becoming contaminated from dirty urban surfaces.

Reducing contaminants

Reducing or containing contaminants on the development site through the restoration and protection of the natural landscape is another critical strategy to minimise any environmental damage from an urban development. It is especially important to prevent contaminants from entering the water cycle. Many contaminants can attach to and travel with fine sediment particles. To prevent this occurrence, an urban development can employ structural stormwater devices to prevent any contaminants from getting into a natural waterway (see the next section).

Protection of riparian margins

Protection of riparian margins is critical to the protection of a stream network. This goal can be accomplished with the indigenous planting of high biomass species in a buffer zone around the stream. This method helps to increase aquatic and terrestrial biodiversity within the riparian corridors. In addition to riparian corridors, wetland and flood detention areas should also be protected by planning a buffer area around these zones. By protecting the areas around urban streams through the replanting of indigenous species, erosion can be reduced, sediment trapped and phosphorus, nitrogen and other contaminants present in urban runoff can be filtered before reaching the stream, protecting and enhancing both aquatic and terrestrial wildlife habitats (Wenger & Fowler, 2000). To ensure buffer zones function, the planting should be a 15 to 30 m margin. While grass will help absorb pollution in overland flows, the planting of indigenous vegetation, preferably from the appropriate ecotones, is a best-practice solution. The buffered hydrological network can also act as a flood corridor during extreme rainfalls (Viavattene & Ellis, 2013), as well as being used as a connector of urban ecopatches (Farr, 2008). Social activities such as parks, reserves and sport facilities can be located along stream margins, as they help to increase the amount of pervious surface within the urban development (Murphy, 2010). A specific GIS function, buffering, can be used to delineate a buffer around existing stream and overland flow paths (ArcGIS, 2015).

However, research has found that protecting existing stream networks by themselves is not enough to replicate the predevelopment hydrology (Walsh, 2016). Even the smallest streams and overland flow paths contribute to the hydrological health of the catchment, so their protection is also critical.

Increased evapotranspiration

Increased evapotranspiration rates are important in building resilience in the greenfield catchment. Van Roon suggests that the catchment should be planted with species that have a high biomass to help increase evapotranspiration. Research shows that water loss to deep seepage is small but water loss to evapotranspiration in an undeveloped catchment can vary from 30 to 60 percent, while from impervious surfaces the rate rapidly decreases to 10 to 25 percent (Walsh, 2016). The change in vegetation cover also affects the rate of transpiration; grass has a much lower transpiration rate than trees; native forest cover has the best rate. Researchers have found that a combination of topography and vegetation cover, specifically hill slopes and native forests, proved the best and most effective measure for both the soil absorption of runoff and increasing evapotranspiration (Walsh, 2012). The rate of evapotranspiration is also dependent on the climate and the particularities of the location.

Reducing the percentage of impervious surfaces

Reducing the percentage of impervious surfaces within the catchment helps to reduce the amount of stormwater runoff (van Roon & Moore, 2004). Van Roon qualifies this technique further by defining an 'effective impervious' surface as being an impervious area that drains directly into a waterway. This can mean an impervious surface directly adjacent to a waterway, or an impervious surface that is linked to a waterway via a piped system. If the runoff from the impervious area can be intercepted with a pervious surface, or a structural stormwater device such as a swale, a green roof or a rain garden, then the impervious surface is no longer considered part of the effective impervious area.

Restoring natural spaces

By protecting and, where necessary, restoring natural spaces within the catchment, the ability to deal with environmental problems such as littoral and pluvial flooding is increased.

Restoring, enabling and protecting indigenous terrestrial and aquatic biodiversity is critical to ensuring the continuing ecological health of a catchment. This can be helped by protecting any existing indigenous ecotones and indigenous habitats. If damaged ecotones and/or indigenous habitats can be identified within the catchment, then prioritising the restoration by replanting on sensitive slopes, riparian corridors and ridges is important.

The New Zealand Biodiversity Strategy (Department of Conservation, 2016) emphasises the importance of ensuring the effective functioning of natural ecosystems within the catchment. This can be accomplished through maintaining and enhancing indigenous ecosystems. Indigenous vegetation can also be used to manage stormwater within the catchment through the preservation of hydrological corridors.

Clustering

Conventional urban development models usually assume that the building and associated infrastructure will cover most of the site irrespective of any areas of environmental vulnerability, such as overland flow paths or native bush fragments. LIUDD uses techniques originally developed by McHarg (1969) and Arendt (Arendt, Brabec, Dodson, Reid, & Yaro, 1994) to understand the location of critical existing environmental systems within a catchment. Using this data, these areas are protected while the less environmentally sensitive zones can be developed. The question of accommodating the required building programme within the area allocated as being the least environmentally sensitive is critical. How is the amount of building required to fulfil the real estate criteria to make a profitable development able to be accommodated on a site that will almost inevitably be smaller than the normal development model requires? Van Roon points to the use of clustering as a planning technique that can accomplish this task (Whyte, 1964). Clustering the building programme will maintain and help to restore the existing hydrological network within the catchment.

All these catchment-based strategies help to shape an urban development within a catchment so as to lessen its effect on the natural hydrological cycle. With the effects of climate change, in particular the increase in rainfall, strategies that increase the absorption of rain into the ground and help direct rainfall into an existing hydrological system are welcome. Strategies that reduce impervious surfaces from which rain can pick up contaminates are useful. The restoration of littoral zones is a strategy that can be directly used to help buffer the effect of sea-level rise.

Brownfield site

Techniques to help mitigate the effects of climate change for a brownfield site are more structural in nature.

Stormwater

From 1988 to 2020 there have been a number of environmental initiatives to develop methods to increase the ability for cities to treat stormwater pollution (Ferguson, 1998). These techniques are known by different acronyms: Low Impact Design (LID) in Australasia and Sustainable Urban Design (SUD) in the UK (Fletcher et al., 2015). What characterises this research is the emphasis on small-scale, local techniques. The measures are conceptualised as interventions in the typical journey of stormwater from its genesis as it first falls on an urban surface: roof, pavement or road, to its eventual discharge into an adjacent water body: river, harbour or lake. The task of a structural stormwater design is to retard, retain and clean this water through a series of small-scale measures which form a 'treatment train' (National Research Council, 2009).

Stormwater remediation practice

There are a number of devices and structural interventions to both improve stormwater quality and attenuate stormwater flow. Roofs are an important starting point in the treatment train. A green roof is a layer of vegetation in a growing medium on top of a waterproof roof structure. It is used to minimise runoff from conventional roof surfaces such as metal or rubber. A green roof can help to delay and reduce the runoff from a storm event by absorbing the first part of the rainfall. This helps to detain part of the volume of water that would have been treated by a conventional stormwater system. The green roof can also help to remove contaminants in rain water. Metal roofs, especially zinc and copper, contribute polluting metals into the stormwater train. By using a green roof this pollution is avoided (Carter & Rasmussen, 2006).

Water quality can also be improved by using buffer strips, which work by using vegetation to filter out pollutants and the soil mix then binds contaminants (Cantor, 2008). Buffer strips are usually grassed areas adjacent to impervious surfaces, typically roads and car parks over which runoff will travel. Buffer strips are effective at removing sediment and some pollutants. Another technique to help detain and filter stormwater is the use of swales. They work like a conventional kerb and channel system, conveying water away from a road or parking area but using an open, vegetated channel. The vegetation acts in two ways: one, to attenuate the flow of stormwater; two, to remove a variety of pollutants and trap sediments (Davis, Stagge, Jamil, & Kim, 2012). Bioretention systems or rain gardens are also used to treat contaminated runoff from roads and car parks. They actively treat stormwater in situ by filtering the runoff through vegetation and fine media layers within one location. The effect is to slow down runoff flow and to improve stormwater quality (Roy-Poirier, Pascale, & Filion, 2010). The vegetation layer acts to remove larger sediment while the below-ground layers trap certain pollutants.

Larger-scaled ponds or wetlands are usually placed at the end of the treatment train. These act as the last resort before the stormwater hits the receiving environment. Constructed ponds are dammed water bodies with a low range of water-level movement and marginal vegetation. Ponds help trap sediments and pollutants in silt layers (Moore & Hunt, 2012). Ponds are also able to uptake some pollutants through phytoplankton. Constructed wetlands are contained shallow-water systems that regularly fill and empty with aquatic vegetation (Malaviya & Singh, 2012). Wetlands trap sediments and pollutants and the vegetation helps to uptake dissolved pollutants (Wong, 2006).

Recent research on the efficacies of constructed wetlands has investigated some of the ways in which wetlands can treat road runoff and sewage, as well as their performance under the new conditions of climate change.

Constructed wetlands are a common way to remediate petrochemical pollutant from roads. The wash-off of heavy metals from car-produced pollutions is particularly damaging to surrounding ecosystems (Gill, Ring, Higgins, Neil, & Johnston, 2017). The use of constructed wetlands to prevent road wash-off and the associated petrochemical pollutants from entering streams is a widespread technique to prevent damage to water biodiversity.

As the pollutants move through the water body of the wetland, the pollutants are extracted through a number of means such as sedimentation, heavy pollutant participants sinking to the bottom of the wetland and evaporation. Pollutants are also filtered and absorbed through biological processes that are encouraged by plants in the wetland and the associated microorganisms. These specific processes are phytoextraction, which is the way pollutants can build up within plant tissues, and phytostabilisation, which is the way pollutants can be stabilised within the soil structure.

However, the efficacy of the ways which wetlands actually remove harmful heavy metals from the environment has been questioned. Gill et al. (2017) looked at a number of studies and found that sedimentation seems to be the most efficient process to help in the negation of heavy metal pollution. The ability of plants to efficiently uptake heavy metals seems, at best, limited. However, the authors suggested that over time heavy metal accumulation within the pond can be linked with the production of natural organic matter (NOM) from the plants in the wetland.

Urban stormwater often contains nitrogen from sewage. Many inner-city piped drainage systems still carry stormwater and waste water. Even if stormwater and sewage have been separated into different piped systems, there can still be sewage overflows into stormwater systems. The results of excess nitrogen getting into the recovering environment, whether seawater or freshwater, can affect the biodiversity of the receiving ecosystem through hypoxia, acidification and eutrophication. Constructed wetlands can be used to treat nitrogen within stormwater runoff (Vymazal, 2007). However, the conventional wetland pond is unable to remove all forms of nitrogen. Only a wetland process that provides aerobic and anaerobic conditions will be able to accomplish this goal. Jan Vymazal (2007) puts forward four constructed wetland models to address this specific issue. These are the constructed wetland with floating plants (CWFFP), the constructed wetland with free-flowing water and planted macrophytes (CWFWS), the constructed wetland with horizontal surface flow (CWHSSF) (a swale) and the constructed wetland with vertical surface flow (CWVSSF) (or what we might call a rain garden). The author notes that each of these process modes can remove certain types of nitrogen. For example, rain gardens can remove ammonia but cannot denitrify, whereas swales are good at denitrification. Vymazal (2007) argues that to comprehensibly remove or rehabilitate nitrogen in stormwater, a hybrid wetland system should be constructed that incorporates different treatment systems.

Climate change will not only cause an increase in the number of storm events leading to an increase in stormwater and flooding, it will also cause an increase in the pollutants in stormwater. In a recent study of urban road runoff in Queensland. Mahbub et al. (2011) found that increasing rainfall, longer rainfall and more intense rainfall will cause an increase in runoff of car-related pollutants into estuaries and the marine receiving environment. The authors identify a number of pollutants from cars, heavy metals, total petroleum, hydrocarbons and polycyclic aromatic hydrocarbons. The authors are particularly interested in volatile organics such as benzene, toluene, ethylbenzene and xylene. These pollutants are specific products of exhaust, brakes and oils. The study simulated the heightened rainfall that will occur under climate change on a selection of Gold Coast urban streets. The study found that there would be an increase in the wash-off of some of the volatile organics. The carrier of these compounds was Total Organic Carbon (TOC). The majority of TOC is found in NOM, the detritus of plants and animals and their waste products. To remediate this condition, targeting the carriers of the TOC particles would be most effective (Mahbub, Goonetilleke, Ayoko, & Egodawatta, 2011).

Pluvial flooding

Reducing pluvial flooding on a brownfield site also required specialist techniques.

Pluvial flooding is the result of an extreme storm event in a city. When pervious ground fails to absorb the rainfall naturally and the runoff overwhelms the existing piped stormwater infrastructure, the result is an overground flood (Falconer, 2009). The increase in the pluvial flooding of European cities in the last decade and the acknowledgement of more extreme weather patterns due to climate change have led to a number of research and policy initiatives (Fratini, Geldof, Kluck, & Mikkelsen, 2012).

European flood control in urban areas has traditionally concentrated on underground piped engineered networks. In Australasia, where storm events are more intense than in Europe, 'dual drainage' systems are designed (Fratini, Geldof, Kluck, & Mikkelsen, 2012); that is, an underground system for normal, everyday rainfall and an overground system of overland flow paths using streets and landscape contouring for major storm events.

Fratini et al. (2012) suggest that by taking this multilayered approach, the implications for urban design and in particular the design of public space must be reconsidered. The technical demands of pluvial flooding and benefits of using urban design to accommodate excess flooding require water professionals to change to a multifunctional and transdisciplinary practice. The term multifunctional is used by the authors to refer to an urban space that can cope with a number of different functions, public and social, as well as being able to ameliorate the effects of urban flooding.

The three-point approach (3PA) for urban flood risk management (Fratini, Geldof, Kluck, & Mikkelsen, 2012) is an example of this new kind of practice. Fratini et al. draw a conceptual framework for water professionals to understand the technical/design/social response to urban flooding. The first point of the approach is the traditional urban stormwater drainage system where expected storm events are met with technical solutions within the limitations of a traditional drainage system. The second point of the approach is for extreme rain events outside of the expected technical design for storm occurrences such as with climate change. The objective is effectively to use aboveground urban space to provide for the storage and conveyance of stormwater within urban areas.

Point three is about the everyday life of the city. Here, the approach is more about the social and cultural sphere where education about the need for resilience for extreme stormwater events is inculcated. This part of the approach is as necessary as the other two as it is within the social world that the important (and expensive) decisions will need to be made to ensure that the necessary urban infrastructure is put in place to accomplish point two.

The result of the 3PA is a graph where the x-axis is the flood return period and the y-axis is the infrastructure and human life cost of flooding to the city. The three points are arranged along an ascending line on the graph, beginning at point three. This is the everyday world of little or no rain, with the emphasis on education and cultural change in the way a community will approach and understand how a city has to become more resilient to storm events and the consequences of urban flooding. The line of increased cost and increased storm events ascends, and point one is the typical engineered response to a storm event by a conventionally engineered underground rainwater infrastructure. At the end of the line is point two, with the extreme storm events that cause damage to both the city's structure and citizens' lives. This is where the connection between pluvial flooding, remediation and urban design should be made. The design of public spaces in the city should offer multifunctional solutions as a public space and space for flooding detention and conveyance.

Pluvial flooding remediation practice

There are two specific overground techniques to ameliorate the effects of pluvial flooding: conveyance and detention.

The SusDrain handbook (SusDrain, 2012) sets out the critical factors to assuage the worst aspects of pluvial flooding. The most important step is to allow for an unimpeded aboveground flow path to ensure that pluvial flooding can be conveyed away from the flooding zone.

These paths can be mapped using a Digital Terrain Model (DTM). All the flow paths must connect and avoid any depression. It is these areas that will experience flooding. Because the flood path will only become active on rare occasions, the land should be designed as a multifunctional space, though it is important that nothing is built or planted in the space which will impede any flooding. Citizens should also be aware of having to evacuate the space in the event of a flood. Cleaning up the consequences of a flood, the subsequent debris in the public space, is also an important consideration.

If it is not possible to convey the flooding away from a site, then flood storage areas will have to be found until after the storm event. Flood detention areas can also be treated as multifunctional spaces. When designing a surface storage area, a number of critical factors have to be resolved. These are: what are the environmental conditions downstream of the detention area? For example, will the release of flood water into a stream environment adversely affect the biota of the watercourse?

If the flooding is being discharged into a coastal environment, then certain water conditions, such as a high tide or storm event on the coastal edge, can cause the discharge of flooding from the hinterland to be slowed or even reversed. Conditions such as these may affect the locations of detention zones. For example, low-value land could be used to store exceedance water: a 'sacrificial' zone.

When designing a detention area, the use of the proposed site and the amount of water to be stored is important. Calculating the volume of water, the depth of storage and the time it will take to drain is critical. Understanding the technical requirements of the flood detention zone will affect the other uses of the site like a park or public space. Where the design of an urban master plan and the construction of the building programme lie in a greenfield/brownfield development, avoiding building on overland flow paths or in flood plains or depressions is common sense.

Pluvial flooding planning

There are many different methods for understanding how pluvial flooding will affect an existing city. A simple approach is outlined by Falconer (2009). He characterised two methods: dry and wet. The dry method uses GIS mapping to make a DEM, giving a high-level map of where topographical depressions occur on a site.

Falconer describes the dry method in more detail (Falconer, Smyth, & Maani, 2008). LIDAR data is used as a base for the DEM, then by using a screening technique, Contour Polygon Screening (CPS), to identify not only the location of topographical depressions but the depth of the depression. A shallow depression presents a low flooding hazard while a deeper depression may be more of a threat.

This mapping analysis is accompanied with a GIS analysis of overland flow paths on a bare earth DTM without the buildings. The combination of the flow paths and the topographic depressions (sinks) can give a general idea of where pluvial flooding will occur. The author notes that this analysis ignores the presence of an existing underground drainage network but assumes that in the case of a storm event these systems will be overwhelmed and be unable to function, i.e., drain excess water.

This is a simple, high-level process that can help civic authorities identify areas where pluvial flooding will occur. To address the amount of water that will occupy the depression, Falconer recommends a specific software, the Rapid Flood Spreading Model (RFSM). This model calculates the rainfall depth based on the probability and duration of a specific storm event on a 1 km grid. The final depth calculation can be made by looking at the impact of zone cells and calculating the filling and spilling process from each cell until an equilibrium is reached.

Understanding the maximum velocity of the discharge from each impact zone can also be modelled. Using depth and velocity maps can help establish a danger hazard hierarchy, for example, shallow depth and low-velocity zones can be discounted as not being critical to life or property in the event of pluvial flooding. This model is explored in more depth in a paper looking at mapping the pluvial flood mapping for all of Ireland by Kellagher et al. (2010).

Coastal flooding

While coastal flooding has always been an important consideration in the development of any port city, the effects of climate change and especially sea-level rise make the provision of flooding remediation extremely important. There are three broadly accepted strategies for the amelioration of coastal flooding in the urban environment. The first is a coastal barrier, which can be a traditional hard-engineered bulwark or a green-engineered solution. Secondly, changes can be made to the design of infrastructure and housing stock to allow for coastal flooding. And lastly there is abandoning the coastal edge and retreating from the effects of coastal flooding (National Research Council, 2014).

Coastal flooding remediation practice

The first strategy is the traditional approach of protecting the existing coastal littoral/property by establishing a protective barrier at the coastal edge with an engineered structure. Traditionally these are hard structures such as:

- Sea walls, a solid wall parallel to the sea. While an obvious answer to flooding, they can produce a wave backwash action, undercutting the base of the wall and undermining the effectiveness of the wall to resist flooding.
- Groynes, hard structures that extend into the sea at right angles to the coastal edge. These structures work with coastal longshore action (sand is moved across the face of a beach). The groyne retards this action and causes sand to be retained on the beach, helping to protect the coast edge from flooding.
- Gabions, metal cages filled with rocks that are placed at the bottom of cliffs to present erosion.
- Revetments, a version of a sea wall that is built against the base of a cliff to prevent erosion.
- Rip-rap, large rocks that are placed at the base of a sea cliff or on a coast edge, with the purpose of absorbing wave energy and preventing beach erosion.

- Breakwaters, large structures like a wall or a line of piles that are placed at sea parallel to the coast. The structures break up wave energy before the waves reach the coastline.
- Tidal barriers, retractable walls that can close an estuary or river mouth to prevent flooding. The best-known example is the Thames Barrier (Environment Agency, 2014).
- Soft-engineered structures can also be used (New York State Department of Environmental Conservation, 2014). These structures utilise natural coastal processes to protect the coastal edge according to the particular ecology, for example, the planting of mangroves on subtropical/tropical coastal edges.
- Beach nourishment, whereby wave energy can be dissipated by adding to the depth of coastline, and sand can be added to the beach, making the coast wider and pushing storm action out to sea.
- Existing sand dunes, which can also be used to protect against coastal flooding. However, the dune system must be protected from human use by using clearly marked entry points and prohibiting access to the rest of the dune system. Coastal wetlands, preservation of existing coastal wetlands or their re-creation can help in breaking up wave energy and helping to prevent flooding.

Some of these operations can be described as Adaptive Topography (Heikkila & Huang, 2013), that is, prevention of flooding is carried out by modifying the topography of the affected landscape. Apart from dykes and levees, filling the land behind the coastal edge can also avoid a flooding disaster.

The second strategy is to accommodate flooding through the design of coastal settlements. The strategy connects to policy advice, such as the regulation of building in hazard zones, and providing information about flooding dangers for coastal residents. An important strategy here is the concept of Location Avoidance (MfE, 2008). This suggests an active planning policy where flood-prone areas are mapped and located, and building construction in these zones is discouraged through policy instruments.

If a building already occupies a flood zone, then retrofitting the building by making the basement and ground flood resistant is important. New buildings can be built on a raised platform. This strategy has been used in the Hafen City development (Samant & Brears, 2017). Because of concerns with flooding, building heights have been set at 7 to 8 m above the Mean High Springs datum. This has been achieved by using compacted fill. Service areas such as car parking have been concealed within the fill zones.

In the Netherlands, new buildings have to be designed with the ground floor designated as a sacrificial level (Pelsmakers, 2013). There are a number of floating building designs that are able to rise and fall on a normal tidal rhythm. These strategies could be termed as being an adaptive architecture.

The last option is retreating from the areas on the coast that will be prone to flooding caused by sea-level rise. This option is the most radical when owners of threatened coastal properties have to abandon their land (Turbott & Stewart, 2006).

Summary

The new urbanist design model, as outlined in chapter 1, relies on a street grid to organise the urban building programme. When buildings occupy the whole block, public space is defined as a park or square and there is often very little green space, the result is a highly impervious urban plan. The real estate formula for the typical urban development is predicated on this knowable urban formula.

However, the effects of climate change and the remediatory regimes for the three environmental problems, as described in the brownfield section, demand space for the structural remediation functions to work. Structural stormwater remediation systems require space at the discharge point of a stormwater system for a wetland or raingarden treatment system. Pluvial flooding remediation requires space for overland flooding conveyance channels and detention ponds. Coastal-flooding prevention measures similarly require a large amount of space for both hard and soft remediation devices such as a littoral buffer zone.

If remediating the serious environmental problems that will become more insistent through climate change is critical to the success of an urban development in an existing city, then the previous survey of remediation measures for a brownfield site points to the necessity of a new urban development model in which space for the remediation of environmental problems will be critical.

In the greenfield development section, the form of an urban development was shaped by environmental criteria, especially hydrological.

Greenfield remediation strategies for brownfield sites

This section discusses how LIUDD strategies used in greenfield development such as maintaining hydrological neutrality, reducing impervious surfaces, protecting and enhancing natural spaces, restoring/enabling/protecting biodiversity and finding new urban forms through clustering might be adapted to the development of a brownfield site.

Maintaining hydrological neutrality

An important method of reducing any detrimental effect of urban development on the environment, especially the hydrological network, is to maintain or restore the natural hydrology of the catchment. As described in the previous section, LIUDD has a number of techniques that help accomplish this goal. These are protecting the riparian margins of streams and overland flow paths, planting trees to increase evapotranspiration and reducing impervious surfaces, buildings, roads and footpaths.

While these techniques are developed for use in a greenfield site, some specific environmental problems in the urban brownfield site could be addressed by the insights and techniques that this aim presents, in particular for the problem of pluvial flooding.

The pattern of urban flooding within the urban catchment often mimics the hydrological network of overland flow paths. To remediate this problem, some of the recommended techniques, such as the protection of the hydrological network, could be modified to include the protection or enlargement of the urban overland flow paths network to form conveyance channels and detention zones for pluvial flooding. The direction of the excess runoff can be mapped using GIS software.

Reducing impervious surfaces

An important LIUDD aim is the striving for an effective impervious surface of 15 percent within a catchment (the effective impervious surface of 15 percent means a continuous and unbroken impervious surface from the source to the discharge point into an adjacent water body, *not* a total of all the impervious surfaces in the catchment).

The aim of having more pervious surfaces in an urban development is desirable. This measure will allow a number of outcomes that will help to build resilience to the effects of climate change, such as more rainwater absorption, space for stormwater treatment, encouraging biodiversity though increased planting, reducing solar gain through tree planting and increasing social interaction though the provision of public space.

The practical difficulties in achieving an effective impervious surface of 15 percent within an existing brownfield catchment are complex. Urban catchments are an accretion of many impervious surfaces: buildings, streets and footpaths, built up over many years. To 'disconnect' the continuity of these surfaces, to create greater areas of impervious surfaces, within often highly contested sites with multiple ownership patterns, is difficult to conceive.

However, with some large-scale urban development projects, such as an urban waterfront, the possibility of attaining an effective impervious surface of 15 percent seems to have the most chance of success. A typical waterfront development site is generally organised under a single government structure with authority over the whole of the development site. In this situation, the possibility of reducing impervious urban surfaces becomes viable. The LIUDD techniques and associated tools in real estate planning can become creditable. Impervious surfaces can be reduced by reducing the building footprint by clustering building forms and urban layouts, making them malleable and responsive to the location of environmental remediation zones. The mechanics of real estate development could help provide the motive power to undertake the clustering. The manipulation of the required GFA with a new FAR (see chapter 1) could reveal new development configurations. Ironically, the almost totally impervious industrial waterfront may be the one urban development site capable of increasing the absorption and amelioration of stormwater and flooding.

Protecting and enhancing natural spaces

While the typical urban brownfield development is hardly a natural space, indigenous ecotones can be constructed to help address specific environmental problems such as coastal flooding. To accomplish this goal the development site should be mapped using GIS software to understand where coastal flooding is going to occur, and then ensuring these areas are protected and not built on. To readjust the necessary urban development building programme, the practice of clustering buildings and moving the building programme away from environmentally sensitive areas such as coastal zones is necessary. Coastal flooding can be measured by modelling sea-level rise using GIS. The effects can be ameliorated with techniques ranging from traditional hard storm barriers to soft-engineered solutions using natural systems like barrier planting and the restoration of littoral vegetation.

Restoring/enabling/protecting biodiversity

Increasing the environmental resilience of urban sites is a critical part of response to the challenges of climate change. The construction of terrestrial and aquatic biodiversity will help to build up the ecological health of the site. Increasing pervious surfaces and planting trees, especially indigenous species, will all help to build up biodiversity. Amelioration devices such as linking the waterfront development site to viable ecotopes within the urban region via corridors will help create a larger ecological network (Meurk & Hall, 2006). One important consequence of the increase in the site's biodiversity is the potential for reducing heat build-up causing the urban heat island effect (Gunawardena, Wells, & Kershawa, 2017).

New urban form through clustering

A critical element in ensuring the environmental resilience of the urban development site is the reduction of impervious surfaces, in particular, the reduction of the building footprint. This can be achieved through the clustering the building programme technique. The application of the idea of clustering to the urban development site may prove to be, initially, conceptually difficult. The new urbanist model, an infrastructure city grid, has proved to be very successful both socially and financially. However, the indubitable effects of the environmental problems of climate change as outlined in the first chapter suggest that a radical alternative urban form is necessary.

Clustering is an idea that uses the amalgamation of buildings in an urban development to free up land for other purposes such as amenity, recreation, utility or, in the LIUDD world, protecting environmentally sensitive zones. The traditional way in which building clustering occurs is the village, an urban form where houses are grouped together. This basic housing morphology can be amended in a different way to produce a number of different housing types that can still meet the definition of clustering, such as row housing.

William Whyte (1964) offers an early definition of cluster housing. Whyte, like many American urbanists in the 1960s, was concerned with the results of the great suburban boom of post-war America and the concomitant phenomenon of urban sprawl. Whyte put forward the idea of cluster housing as a panacea to this problem. Whyte suggests that housing should be built at a greater density than conventional suburban housing by grouping conventional suburban houses onto smaller sections. Whyte justifies this action by outlining the economic and social benefits of clustering including the ways in which closer neighbours mean more cooperation and less maintenance of the private section.

Whyte gives examples of cluster housing at different scales, starting with the more palatable examples that have a deliberate stylistic association with picturesque

New England villages. The examples change to different house typologies, firstly the double-storey house (which Whyte comments on favourably in comparison to the transparency of the single-storey, modernist range house). Whyte includes examples of housing developments not just on greenfield sites but ones that are close to the centre of established cities such as Washington, DC, and Pittsburgh. In the River Park project in Washington, the development is to the south of the Capitol. Designed by Charles M. Goodman, the development is a mix of what we might call terraced houses and an apartment block (Whyte, 1964). The terrace houses are two storeys high with an extra storey provided by a barrel vault. These are grouped in short 'bars' of up to eight townhouses facing each other across a private courtyard. The parallel bars are arranged across the site in a tictac formation, and public spaces and car parking are located outside of the bar formations. To the rear of the town houses is a long eight-storey housing slab block.

Whyte (1964) moved the definition of clustering beyond a physical gathering of single-storey buildings into the idea of the clustering of people, or intensification. Along with the change in housing type comes a commitment to the importance of open space. Whyte points out that cluster housing cannot simply be an excuse for cramming more housing onto a site but can also preserve the natural features of the site such as topography or existing vegetation. This is an important connection in thinking about urban development that links Whyte and McHarg (McHarg, 1969).

Christopher Alexander (Grabow, 1983) discusses the idea of cluster housing in his famous book, *A Pattern Language* (Alexander, 1977), under the title 'Number 37 House Cluster'. Alexander draws on his observations of suburbia where he sees that even within a suburban street, people will form an informal association of houses through social connections. Alexander suggests how these social connections can be given formal and spatial coherence through the physical grouping or clustering of individual houses around a common space or green. Alexander suggests that each cluster should comprise a maximum of 12 houses, which equals a maximum social equation of one representative from each house gathering around a kitchen table for discussion on the community direction (no couples allowed!). Alexander discusses the formal expression of this social organisation: the housing will be denser and closer together around the green while tapering off towards the boundary of the property.

In a similar way to Whyte's writing, Alexander then moves beyond the simple, physical clustering of single houses to an examination of a denser form of housing including row housing and what Alexander calls a Housing Hill (Alexander, 1977). With this housing model Alexander suggests retaining the family house as a basic building unit, and literally stacking individual houses on top of one another in an ascending four-storey form. The houses are located on terraces and, as the terraces ascend, the house numbers contract thus giving each house a small terrace/garden plot. Alexander suggests that the house hill be oriented towards the sun and has a central access stair. With this model, Alexander is suggesting that when greater density is required, an aggregation of the family house is better than turning to the apartment building or tower block.

Klaus-Dieter Weiss (2004) writes about the history of an apartment conceptualised as a cluster of houses. All the benefits and individuality of the single-family dwelling are retained with the concurrent benefit of the house/apartment being located in the centre of the city. Weiss maps out an inventory of the 'house apartment' homes, starting with a number of unrealised paper projects from Le Corbusier in the 1920s (Le Corbusier, 1929) where evocative drawings are used to create the charm of the individual family home, especially outdoor living on the terrace, within the cellular structure of an apartment block.

More contemporaneous examples are the famous Habitat for the 1967 Montreal Expo (Merin, 2013) designed by Moshe Sadie. Here two contemporary concerns of the time meet: an interest in prefabricated modular construction, and the desire for the individual form of the dwelling unit to be expressed. A similar approach was taken in the design and construction of the Lillington Garden project in Pimlico designed in the late 1960s by Drabourne and Drake (Amery & Wright, 1977). The low-rise building used a complex sculptural elevation of terraces and roof garden planters, built in brick.

Another example of clustering in housing practice is Kelling House in Clarkdale Street, Bethnal Green, London, designed by Denis Lasdun (Curtis, 1994) in 1957. The building is a collection of four 15-storey blocks around a central circulation lift core. Lasdun consciously rejected the modernist housing solution of the tower and slab in favour of a broken organic form which he referred to as 'clusters'. Curtis comments that Lasdun's use of the cluster was trying to accomplish two things: keeping the old working-class social patterns while at the same time affirming the importance of building density in the city centre and avoiding the suburban.

The result of these housing experiments is a new housing form that gives a similar density as the traditional housing form but with a much smaller footprint. In this way the landscape natural or designed assumes a much greater importance.

The implication of this history for the conventional urban development model is twofold. Firstly, the economic rationale of the urban master plan based on a certain amount of saleable space can be reconfigured into a different urban form, thus ensuring the same economic return. Secondly, the fluidity of site planning demonstrated in this history could be drawn upon in response to the necessity of ameliorating critical environmental issues.

Conclusion

This chapter seeks to offer practical strategies for a stakeholder in an urban development site, whether a greenfield or brownfield site, who wants practical ways in which to build resilience against the coming depredation of climate change.

This section outlines strategies that are specific to a greenfield site, drawn from the ideas and techniques of LIUDD. By understanding the ways in which a proposed urban development will disrupt the natural hydrology of the urban catchment, the developer has a range of practical strategies and tools to help privilege the existing hydrological system. By protecting the existing hydrological conditions, the development can be buffered against future flooding and stormwater contamination. This ensures that the proposed urban development is disrupted as little as possible.

Brownfield sites can also be protected against the environmental effects of climate change, such as flooding both pluvial and coastal, with a range of well-known and accepted remediation measures. However, the size and location of these measures is problematic in an existing city.

The third section of this chapter discusses techniques drawn from the LIUUD canon that could help determine the placement of such remediation measures in a brownfield site and explore the consequences for the existing urban form.

The next chapter outline a design method, drawn from chapters 2 and 3, for urban stakeholders (citizens to developers) to use when approaching an urban development site. By placing the site within its larger landscape context, the potential damaging effects of climate change on the site can be apprehended and range of practical methods and techniques that will both build resilience to climate change and to ensure commercial return can be developed. Six design case studies demonstrate how these techniques can be utilised for a range of urban development, both greenfield and brownfield, in the PRC, New Zealand, the USA and the UK.

References

Alexander, C. (1977). *A Pattern Language*. Oxford: Oxford University Press.

Amery, C., & Wright, L. (1977). *The Architecture of Darbourne and Darke* (J. Lever, Ed.). London: RIBA Publishing.

ArcGIS. (2015). *Riparian Buffer Land Cover by Watershed*. Retrieved from www.arcgis.com/home/item.html?id=ad099d6faaf94984a51c70d054e94e37

Arendt, R., Brabec, E. A., Dodson, H. L., Reid, C., & Yaro, R. D. (1994). *Rural by Design: Maintaining Small Town Character*. Chicago: American Planning Association.

Cantor, S. L. (2008). *Green Roofs in Sustainable Landscape Design* (1st ed.). New York: W.W. Norton & Co.

Carter, T. L., & Rasmussen, T. C. (2006). Hydrologic behavior of vegetated roofs. *Journal of the American Water Resources Association*, *42*(5), 1261–1274.

Curtis, W. J. R. (1994). *Denys Lasdun*. London: Phaidon.

Davis, A. P., Stagge, J. H., Jamil, E., & Kim, H. (2012). Hydraulic performance of grass swales for managing highway runoff. *Water Research*, *46*(20), 6775–6786. doi:10.1016/j.watres.2011.10.017

Department of Conservation. (2016). *New Zealand Biodiversity Action Plan*, Wellington 6143 New Zealand. Retrieved from www.doc.govt.nz/Documents/conservation/new-zealand-biodiversity-action-plan-2016-2020.pdf

Environment Agency. (2014). *The Thames Barrier*. Retrieved from www.gov.uk/guidance/the-thames-barrier

Falconer, R. (2009). *Pluvial Flooding and Surface Water Management*. Paper presented at the 5th EWA Conference, Brussels. Retrieved from www.dwa.de/portale/ewa/ewa.nsf/C125723B0047EC38/CC41A2CC77C52058C125768E0030232E/$FILE/Pluvial%20Flooding%20and%20Surface%20Management.pdf

Falconer, R., Smyth, P., & Maani, L. (2008). *Pluvial Extreme Event Risk Appraisal Techniques with Recent Applications in Ireland and the UK*. Paper presented at the Irish National Hydrology Conference, Dublin. Retrieved from https://web.actuaries.ie/sites/default/files/erm-resources/05_pluvial_extreme_event_risk_appraisal_techniques.pdf

Farr, D. (2008). *Sustainable Urbanism: Urban Design with Nature*. Hoboken, NJ: Wiley.

Ferguson, B. K. (1998). *Introduction to Stormwater: Concept, Purpose, Design*. New York: John Wiley.

Fletcher, T. D., Shuster, W., Hunt, W. F., Ashley, R., Butler, D., Arthur, S., . . . Viklander, M. (2015). SUDS, LID, BMPs, WSUD and more – The evolution and application of terminology surrounding urban drainage. *Urban Water Journal, 12*(7), 525–542. doi:10.1080/1573062X.2014.916314

Fratini, C. F., Geldof, G. D., Kluck, J., & Mikkelsen, P. S. (2012). Three Points Approach (3PA) for urban flood risk management: A tool to support climate change adaptation through transdisciplinarity and multifunctionality. *Urban Water Journal*, *9*(5), 317–331. doi:10.1080/1573062X.2012.668913

Gill, L. W., Ring, P. C., Higgins, B., Neil, M. P., & Johnston, P. M. (2017). Long term heavy metal removal by a constructed wetland treating rainfall runoff from a motorway. *Science of the Total Environment*, *601–602*, 32–44.

Grabow, S. (1983). *Christopher Alexander: The Search for a New Paradigm in Architecture*. London, UK: Routledge Kegan & Paul.

Gunawardena, K. R., Wells, M. J., & Kershawa, T. (2017). Utilising green and bluespace to mitigate urban heat island intensity. *Science of the Total Environment*, *584–585*, 1040–1055.

Heikkila, E. J., & Huang, M. (2013). Adaptation to flooding in urban areas: An economic primer. *Public Works Management & Policy*, *19*(1), 11–36. doi:10.1177/1087724X13506559

Holz, T. W. (2002). *Zero Impact Development: Source Control for Stream Protection*. Paper presented at the Washington Hydrological Society Seminar Series, Mercer View Community Centre, Seattle, Washington.

Kellagher, R., Panzeri, M., L'Homme, J., Cesses, Y., Gouldby, B., Martin, J., Nicholson, O., & Adamson, M. (2010). *National Pluvial Flood Mapping for All Ireland: The Modelling Approach*. Paper presented at the National Hydrology Conference. Retrieved from www.opw.ie/hydrology/wp-content/uploads/2016/11/06-National-pluvial-flood-mapping-for-all-ireland-the-modelling-approach.pdf

Le Corbusier. (1929). *The City of Tomorrow and Its Planning*. London: John Rodher.

Mahbub, P., Goonetilleke, A., Ayoko, G. A., & Egodawatta, P. (2011). Effects of climate change on the wash-off of volatile organic compounds from urban roads. *Science of the Total Environment*, *409*, 3934–3942.

Malaviya, P., & Singh, A. (2012). Constructed wetlands for management of urban stormwater runoff. *Critical Reviews in Environmental Science & Technology*, *42*(20), 2153–2214. doi:10.1080/10643389.2011.574107

McHarg, I. L. (1969). *Design with Nature*. Garden City, NY: American Museum of Natural History.

Merin, G. (2013.). *AD Classics: Habitat 67/Safdie Architects*. Retrieved from <www.archdaily.com/404803/ad-classics-habitat-67-moshe-safdie/>

Meurk, C. D., & Hall, G. M. (2006). Options for enhancing forest biodiversity across New Zealand's managed landscapes based on ecosystem modelling and spatial design. *New Zealand Journal of Ecology*, *30*(1), 131–146.

MfE. (2008). *Meeting the Challenges of Future Flooding in New Zealand*, Wellington, New Zealand. Retrieved from www.mfe.govt.nz/sites/default/files/meeting-challenges-of-future-flooding-in-nz.pdf

Moore, T. L. C., & Hunt, W. F. (2012). Ecosystem service provision by stormwater wetlands and ponds: A means for evaluation? *Water Research*, *46*(20), 6811–6823. doi:10.1016/j.watres.2011.11.026

Murphy, Y. (2010). *Urban Water Modeling and Impervious Surface Analysis with GIS (Annotated Bibliography)*. Retrieved October 2011, from http://dusk.geo.orst.edu/gis/student_bibs/murphy.html

National Research Council. (2009). *Urban Stormwater Management in the United States*. Washington, DC: National Academies Press.

National Research Council. (2014). *Reducing Coastal Risk on the East and Gulf Coasts*. Washington, DC: National Academies Press.

New York State Department of Environmental Conservation. (2014). *Shoreline Stabilization*. Retrieved from www.dec.ny.gov/docs/permits_ej_operations_pdf/shorelinestable.pdf

Pelsmakers, S. (2013). Future-proofing London. In *Imagining the Future City*. London: Ubiquity Press.

Roy-Poirier, A., Pascale, C., & Filion, Y. (2010). Review of bioretention system research and design: Past, present, and future. *Journal of Environmental Engineering*, *136*(9), 878–889. doi:10.1061/(ASCE)EE.1943-7870.0000227

Samant, S., & Brears, R. (2017). Urban waterfront revivals of the future. In P. Y. Tan & C. Y. Jim (Eds.), *Greening Cities: Forms and Functions*. New York: Springer.

SusDrain. (2012). SusDrain. *The Community for Sustainable Drainage*. Retrieved from www.susdrain.org

Turbott, C., & Stewart, A. (2006). *Managed Retreat from Coastal Hazards: Options for Implementation*. Retrieved from www.waikatoregion.govt.nz/assets/PageFiles/5405/tr06-48.pdf

Van Roon, M., & Moore, S. (2004). *Evaluating the Ecological Efficacy of Low Impact Urban Design and Development*. Paper presented at the Sustainable Engineering and Science Conference, Auckland, NZ.

Van Roon, M., & van Roon, H. (2009). *Low Impact Urban Design and Development: The Big Picture: An Introduction to LIUDD Principles and Methods Framework* (Vol. 37). Lincoln, NZ: Manaaki Whenua Press.

Viavattene, C., & Ellis, J. B. (2013). The management of urban surface water flood risks: SUDS performance in flood reduction from extreme events. *Water Sci Technol*, *67*(1), 99–108. doi:10.2166

Vymazal, J. (2007). Removal of nutrients in various types of constructed wetlands. *Science of the Total Environment*, *380*, 48–65.

Walsh, C. (2012). Urban stormwater runoff: A new class of environmental flow problem. *PLoS One*, *7*(9), e45814.

Walsh, C. (2016). Principles for urban stormwater management to protect stream ecosystems. *Freshwater Science*, *35*(1), 398–411.

Weiss, K.-D. (2004). *High-Density Housing: Concepts, Planning, Construction*. München: Birkhäuser.

Wenger, S. J., & Fowler, L. (2000). *Protecting Stream and River Corridors*, the University of Georgia. Retrieved from www.lerf.eco.br/img/publicacoes/2000_12%20Protecting%20Stream%20and%20River%20Corridors.pdf

Whyte, W. H. (1964). *Cluster Development*. New York: American Conservation Association.

Wong, T. H. F. (2006). *Australian Runoff Quality: A Guide to Water Sensitive Urban Design*. Crows Nest, NSW: Engineers Media.

Chapter four

Introduction

This chapter draws on the finding of the previous chapters to help outline concrete strategies to make both brownfield and greenfield urban development projects resilient to the effects of climate change. In chapter 1 the dimensions of the contemporary urban planning model both in terms of planning and economic use was discussed. The financial structure of this model was outlined, in particular the uses of real estate formula, FAR and GFA to understand the financial return on a particular building form. The vulnerability of this model to the depredation of climate change, the three hydrological conditions, stormwater contamination and pluvial and coastal flooding, was then canvassed. In chapter 2 the lineaments of a methodology to approach the problems were laid out. The idea of resilience and its many implications formed the first part of the discussion. Urban and landscape ecology offered specific strategies to help locate the urban development site within a larger milieu. The hydrological catchment was advanced as a form in which an understanding of how both climate change will affect urban sites and how the effect of different remediatory regimes will be measured. The way in which the catchment can be used in both design thinking, via the work of Ian McHarg, and in analytical thinking, with the use of GIS mapping and simple hydrological formula such as the Rational Method, was also explored. Chapter 3 provided specific techniques that could be used for the urban design of greenfield and brownfield sites to build resilience to climate change. Techniques from LIUDD were canvassed for their use in greenfield site development while more conventional techniques were discussed to combat specific issues of stormwater pollution and pluvial and coastal flooding for brownfield sites. The use of LIUDD techniques for brownfield sites was explored, and while acknowledging that this discussion seems to be counterintuitive, connections were suggested.

This chapter has two sections. The first is a description of the design process; the second contains six case studies showing how the design process is used for both greenfield and brownfield sites in a number of countries.

Design process

This section details how a design process, drawn from the previous chapters, is constructed.

The section is divided into three parts. The first part of the design process is building an inventory and analysis of the development site within the hydrological catchment. The inventory consists of the definition of the catchment, the location and boundaries of the development site and the location and boundaries of the catchment. The placement of the development site within the catchments is further defined through aerial photos, the topography of the catchment, the vegetation and the hydrology, in particular the overland flow paths. The inventory also encompasses a study of any existing environmental problems with the site, in particular the ratio of pervious to impervious surfaces and the possibility of flooding.

The second section is concerned with the urban development potential of the site within the catchment. This can be measured in a number of ways. The financial return of the site can be understood with simple development ratios, the GFA and the FAR. The development potential of a site can also be understood through the development of structure plans and master plans; these show how the site might be developed to different degrees of detail, from simple zoning layouts to detailed infrastructure layouts with building distribution.

The implication for building environmental resilience to the environmental problems that the development plan will engender can be analysed in a number of ways. The environmental implications of a development ratio, the potential GFA and FAR of a site, can be translated into a simple ratio of permeable and impervious surface for a development site. This can demonstrate how the hydrological balance of a site will be affected by a development.

The impact of a more sophisticated master plan on the environmental character of a site can be tested by superimposing the plan over the existing site analysis. Some of the environmental implication of the master plan that can be understood in the way the urban development might, for instance, block an overland flow path, thus preventing the conveyance of future flooding or the way a development might be flooded by sea-level rise. The implication of an increase of impervious surfaces can also be understood through the use of the Rational Method.

The third part of the design process can be divided into two parts, landscape and architectural. Into these categories fall the actual techniques used to make the development site resilient to the effects of climate change. Some of the techniques that can be used are derived from LIUDD techniques and GIS operations such as protecting the hydrological pattern of the site by buffering the overland flow paths that run through the development site from the greater catchment and protecting the littoral through buffering the harbour/river edge. The design consequences of these operations are varied; for example, the buffered overland flow path (OLFP) could be used for pluvial flooding conveyance and detention. The OLFP could also be planted with indigenous vegetation to help encourage evapotranspiration and lower the urban heat island effect. The buffered OLFP network could also be used to locate stormwater treatments devices such as wetlands to treat stormwater from the larger catchment. The buffered harbour water edges could help to form and locate soft barriers to coastal flooding.

The net effect of these remediation techniques on the catchment can be measured through a recalculation of the permeable/impermeable surface ratio. This has two consequences. The first is the development of a new urban master plan that is more open and greener with a number of remediatory regimes to help build urban resilience to the effects of climate change. The implication of this new master plan on the conventional real estate programme requires a change in thinking about how the required amount of GFA to make the project financially viable might be allocated. This can be accomplished through the LIUDD strategies of clustering the building programme. By recalculating the GFA into a new FAR, a reconfigured building footprint driven by the dictates of the environmental remediation programme, the financial returns of the original real estate investment can be accomplished. The urban and architectural consequences of the reconfigured urban programs can be modelled in ArcGIS, graphically represented through the extrusion of the proposed building footprint.

The inventory

The first stage of a design process is to build an environmental inventory of the development site and an analysis of the hydrological qualities.

Catchment – location and boundaries of site

Locate the urban development site within hydrological catchment using GIS mapping. This gives a physical boundary to both carry out an inventory of the environmental qualities of the site and a landscape analysis. Understanding the relationship of the development site to the catchment through the use of aerial photographs and study of ownership patterns through a study of cadastral mapping is also critical in establishing the political dimension of the development project.

Topography/slope/aspect

Mapping the contours of both the development site and the catchment are critical for understanding the hydrological behaviour of the project. Understanding the quality of the topography, in particular the different slopes within the catchment and their degree of steepness and the relationship of the topography to the solar orientation or aspect, are also important. (Two specific GIS operations, slope and aspect, can help build this data.)

Vegetation

Understanding the extent and type of vegetation within a catchment is important for both brownfield and greenfield development sites. For a brownfield site, the presence of vegetation is an indication of an open or pervious surface. This can have a number of potential uses: the absorption of stormwater or as a potential flood detention area. Patches of remnant indigenous vegetation are important to be identified as they as can act as the nucleus of the ecological centre that helps to promote urban biodiversity.

In a greenfield site, the location of any existing vegetation, especially indigenous vegetation, is important to help preserve and build biodiversity. They can be used to link to other area of indigenous vegetation in the catchment forming networks of green space. Preserving these areas in any future urban development is critical as they can be used in the planning process as to form parks/public spaces.

Hydrology

The next operation is gaining an understanding of the hydrological conditions of the site within the catchment; both where rainwater will fall in catchment and the amount of rainwater that will fall are important data. In a brownfield site, the existing urban infrastructure of streets and building will determine the amount of stormwater that will accumulate and the direction in which water will flow.

A greenfield site will be mostly pervious surfaces which will absorb much of the rainfall and the existing topography that will direct the runoff as overland flow paths.

GIS software will be able to determine the location of OLFP and the Rational Method can be used to understand how much rainfall is being accumulated in the catchment for both greenfield and brownfield sites.

Many development sites have existing environmental problems, in particular flooding, both coastal and territorial, and the contamination of receiving environment through polluted stormwater.

Brownfield sites

Understanding the extent of site flooding can be done through a number of sources. Data on existing littoral flooding can often be found from governmental agencies. With the importance of climate change for urban development policies, governmental agencies are becoming more proactive in modelling the hydrological effects of sea-level rise.

In a similar way, pluvial flooding and stormwater contamination are well-known events in many cities, and governmental agencies often have existing data about the number of occurrences and the amount of water in pluvial flooding events. Data of the effect of climate change for increased pluvial flooding and stormwater contamination have also been extensively canvassed for many cities by respective agencies.

Greenfield

Greenfield sites typically have fewer existing data about the effects of flooding or stormwater contamination, as the consequences for property, often farms on the city's periphery, are not so critical as for an existing urban area. Analysis of the effects of flooding and stormwater contamination is affected by the ratio of pervious to impervious services in the catchment can be affected by the degree of slope of the catchment.

Development assessment

A new urban development whether in a brownfield or greenfield site will have an effect on the existing environment, especially on the hydrological pattern. An urban development is typically highly impervious; thus, the development will alter a number of landscape conditions, vegetation topography and hydrology that will have an impact in the catchment.

Greenfield site

The environmental effects of a traditional urban development will have more of an impact in a greenfield site. The ratio of pervious to impervious surfaces is altered; more impervious surfaces will have the effect of producing more runoff. There are a number of hydrological consequences: more runoff will result in more contaminants picked up from streets and roofs entering the receiving environment, such as rivers, lakes and harbours. There will also be an increase in pluvial flooding. Another consequence of urban development in a greenfield site is the destruction of existing vegetation, often native bush. The damage can lead to a loss of biodiversity (Aronson et al., 2017), and the lack of tree cover can lead to an increase in the heat island effect (Gunawardena, Wells, & Kershawa, 2017).

Brownfield site

The effects of the typical urban development on a brownfield site would seem to have a less deleterious effect on the environment than that on a greenfield site. The development site will likely already be highly impervious and there is little chance of the presence of any existing vegetation let alone indigenous flora.

However, the environmental effects of climate change, with increased storm events leading to increased flooding and sea-level rise, have important implications for the conventional urban development. Increased pluvial flooding from a dense impervious catchment can cross or bisect a development site, leading to loss of property and possible loss of life. A conventional urban development does not have the capacity to be able to respond to this problem. In a similar way, a conventional waterfront development project with the typical urban promenade offers little protection against the predation of sea-level rise and the effect of storm surges.

Assessment

A development plan can range from a structure plan, a simple map that shows a rudimentary infrastructure grid with the location of urban functions (housing, commercial, industrial), indicated in broad zonal patterns, to a developed urban master plan. Here the infrastructure network, public and private spaces, building layouts, the overall GFA and individual site FAR are shown in detail.

There are a number of ways in which to assess the environmental impact of a proposed urban development on a greenfield or brownfield site.

Superimposing the proposed development plan over a map of the existing site that shows the environmental conditions as detailed in the inventory section is a useful technique to immediately highlight clashes and disparities. The most important conditions are the existing hydrological conditions, especially pluvial and coastal flooding, both under current circumstances such as storm events and the speculative conditions that will arise from the effects of the climate change.

By superimposing the proposed development plan over the pluvial flooding map, the potential of the development to obstruct the flow of water from an overland flow path is revealed; in a similar way the juxtaposition of the development plan over a pluvial flooding map will reveal which parts of the development are vulnerable. If the development site is located on a river, lake or coastal edge, superimposing the GIS map of edge flooding over the proposed development plan will clearly indicate the potential of damage to the edge condition of the development.

By overlaying the development plan on the existing stormwater infrastructure, the increase in the direction of contaminated stormwater can be seen. If the development site is located at the end of a catchment that is near a river, lake or the sea, then there will often be an increased discharge of contaminated stormwater, an unsightly, smelly and dangerous result.

The other way that a proposed development master plan can be used to highlight its environmental impact on the catchment is by understanding how much more impervious surface the development plan will add to the catchments impervious/pervious surface ratio. As described in chapter 2, the Rational Method (Thompson, 2007) can help in understanding how much more runoff will be generated. The result will be a measurable increase in stormwater and possibly an increase in flooding.

Measurable data that shows the environmental problems that the development plan will exacerbate leads to the development of specific remediatory techniques. To make the urban development resilient to these effects, the project will have to be able to spatially accommodate the environmental problems and remediatory regimes. To address the environmental issues that will be caused by future urban development, a series of specific strategic urban design interventions that address specific environmental problems such as flooding, sea-level rise and the heat island effect can be modelled using GIS software.

The design process

So far the process as outlined is able to elucidate some of the environmental complexities of the development site, reveal key environmental issues (particularly around flooding and stormwater contamination) and demonstrate how these problems will escalate through the imposition of an urban development plan.

This section draws on a number of specific design techniques, explicated in chapter 3. These range from accepted remediatory methodologies such as Water Sustainable Urban Design (WSUD) (Fletcher et al., 2015) to more strategic methodologies such as LIUDD (van Roon & van Roon, 2009) to techniques that are specific to problems, such as soft-engineered flooding barriers to combat sea-level rise.

GIS mapping software was discussed in chapter 2 as helping to visualise both existing environmental conditions, the results of proposed urban development and what the possible remediation technique might look like.

The next stage is testing how best these remediation techniques will address the environmental issues of the development site. Confronted with the exergies of the site and the development plan, the range of ameliorative techniques cannot be used singularly but instead connect to each other.

Pluvial flooding

Mapping of a development plan over a site plan can help make simple planning decisions such as avoiding building on an overland flow path. This has a number of immediate advantages. This action avoids buildings being damaged by flooding. Using the location of these paths can also lead to a number of other remediatory operations. By enlarging the space of the OLFP and making topographic modifications, the paths can be used to accommodate possible pluvial flooding in two ways. Firstly, as a conveyance path through an urban development, and secondly, as a possible site for detention zones (Falconer, 2009).

Stormwater

The size and shape of these OLFP zones can also be used for other purposes. The discharge of contaminated stormwater into the sea, while a common technique in most waterfront developments, is becoming increasingly problematic. There are a number of techniques for the treatment of stormwater before discharge, such as wetlands (Malaviya & Singh, 2012). The areas around the OLFP can be used to accommodate treatment areas for contaminated stormwater next to the receiving environment. Urban biodiversity can be improved by widening the OLFP to establish wildlife corridors that are planted with indigenous vegetation (Aronson et al., 2017). These corridors can also treat overland stormwater flow, filtering out pollutants before they enter the OLFP system.

Coastal flooding

The mapping of a waterfront development plan over a site map that shows the effects of rising sea level and storm surges will soon demonstrate the need for remediatory action. Many waterfronts have a waters-edge public space, a promenade, a corniche. This is a space in which citizens are invited to traverse a zone between the spectacle of the water and the commercial/public building programme. The spatial implication of the space is a smooth, uninterrupted transition from the spectacle of the water to the commercial opportunity of the buildings on the edge of the promenade. If the urban development is to be protected from sea-level rise, then the edge needs to be used as a flood barrier.

There are many different techniques to prevent coastal flooding. Broadly speaking, we can divide these into hard and soft measures: hard, such as the traditional armoured flood wall, and soft, a reconstructed indigenous coastal section such as a shallow transition from water to land via a replanted ecotone of indigenous flora. The vegetation helps to dissipate the energy of the storm surges while the slope and height of the recreated coastal transect provide flood protection. The intersection of this new landscape on the coastal edge and the typical urban development programme will mean a new urban form. The experience will be more akin to a park, walking through native vegetation that is responsive to certain water conditions: salty, brackish, clear.

Urban programme

Mapping historical and speculative pluvial flooding in a catchment as well as the effect of existing impervious surfaces in the catchment can also be used to help understand how flooding in an existing city might be ameliorated through a reconfigured urban/building programme. Removing building and impervious surfaces in the catchment will help to reduce flooding. In an existing city site, removal of affected buildings might not be able to be carried out immediately. Planning authorities can use this design process to undertake succession planning for removal of selected buildings over time. This will help allow for more pervious surface in the catchments to absorb water and to allow for detention zones. This new open space network can also be used as a new green space network for the city.

Faced with the evidence of future flooding both pluvial and coastal and increased stormwater pollution, the arsenal of remediatory measures needs to be thought about holistically. Adapting the proposed development plan to these measures will require the actual building programme of the development master plan be reconfigured. The mapping of overland flow paths and attendant remediation regimes can be used as the base development layer rather than the typical roading grid. The spaces 'left over' from the new remediatory landscape become the building sites, located alongside the new urban hydrological network. In the case of a massive all-encompassing flooding problem, especially for a greenfield site, the building programme could make use of a topographic manipulation of the flood plain to create safe spaces above the flooding, islands in effect, on which the different building programmes can be enacted.

All these measures help a city to become more resilient to the effects of climate change; however, they will have obvious spatial consequences: they will occupy space that would be used either for a transport infrastructure or a building site. These decisions will have financial consequences. An important component of the development plan is an expected GFA for the projects which is usually configured into a number of different FAR ratios according to the location of the building block within the master plan. By accepting the disruption of the environmental measures, the building GFA has to be retained if the original financial return is to be achieved. This can be achieved through 'clustering' (see chapter 2) the building programme, making denser, higher buildings that achieve the same GFA.

Greenfield case studies

To demonstrate how this design methodology might help build climate change resilience for urban development, six design case studies are presented. The case studies are a demonstration of the design method at a range of scales, for both brownfield and greenfield sites. The case studies located in the PRC, the UK, the USA and New Zealand.

Greenfield case studies

Introduction

Two greenfield waterfront developments, one in New Zealand and the other in the PRC, will be discussed.

The first project is a proposal for a new urban development located at Whenuapai, Auckland, New Zealand.

The second project is a waterfront development located at Furong, Guangdong, PRC. The two studies demonstrate the applicability of the design method in dealing with the environmental problems occasioned by urban development that will be exacerbated by the effects of climate change. The studies also demonstrate the ways in which these problems can be ameliorated through the use of a number of remediatory techniques.

Both projects share a common analysis: the identification of what environmental problems are likely to be engendered by the new urban development. In these two studies, the main environmental problem was identified as being the production and entry of contaminated stormwater into the existing hydrological system and thence into the receiving environment.

The remediation of this problem was threefold. The first technique was to increase the area of pervious surfaces. This will help decrease the amount of stormwater that will flow into the existing hydrological system. The Rational Method was used as a technique to understand the impact that the ratio of impervious to pervious surfaces within the catchment, before and after the development, would have on the production of stormwater.

The second technique was to protect the existing hydrological network from the entry of contaminated stormwater. The specific technique was to buffer the existing stream systems. This operation was carried out using GIS mapping and analysis to identify the existing hydrological network, the streams and overland flow paths, then, using the buffering function in ArcGIS, make protection zones around each OLFP and stream. The effect of this operation was to also increase the amount of pervious surface.

The third technique was to cluster the urban form. By acknowledging and buffering the existing hydrological system, the loss of development GFA was inevitable. Clustering the development GFA into a new urban form was a way of ensuring that the projected real estate programme didn't make for a financial loss.

The result for the urban design of the Whenuapai case study was to assemble the 'missing' GFA into apartment blocks at the intersection of the stream system with the littoral. In the case of the Furong waterfront, the waterfront building programme was clustered to form 'islands' within a new hydrological remediation landscape.

Whenuapai

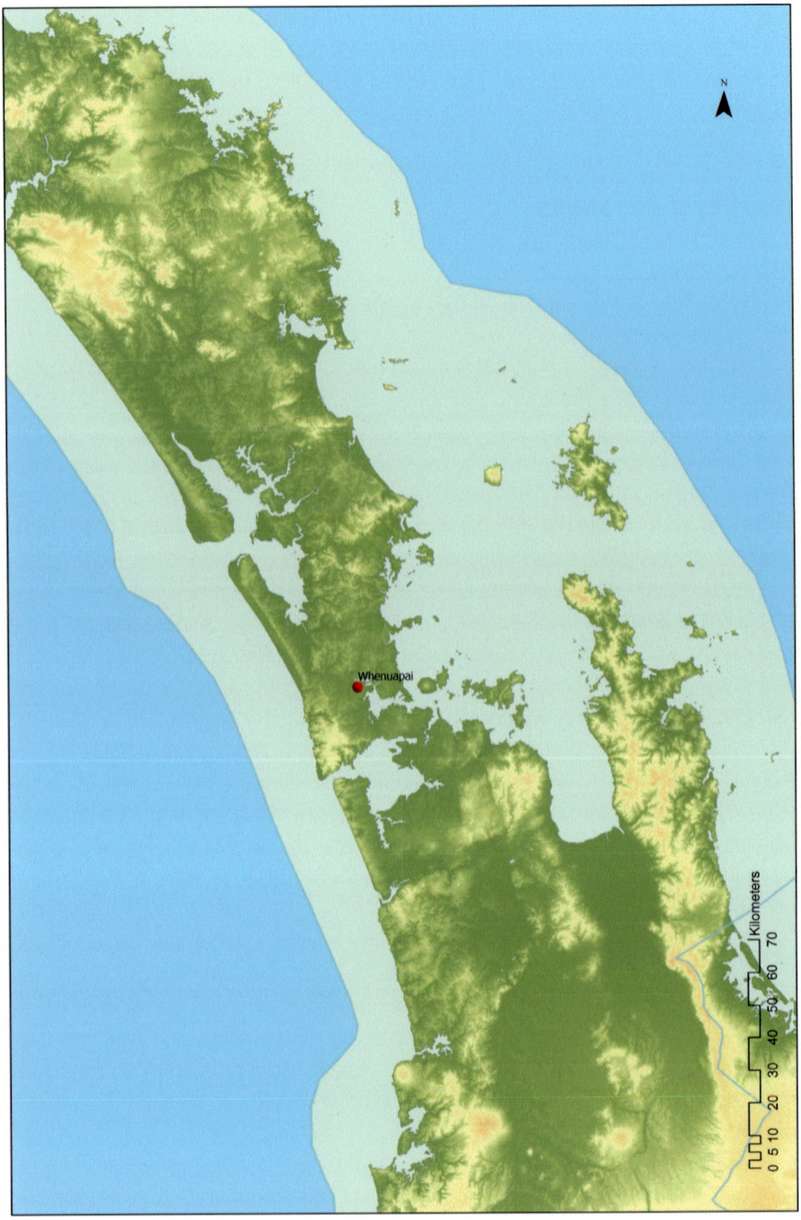

Figure 1 **Whenuapai aerial**

Introduction

Whenuapai is a new urban district planned to the west of Auckland, New Zealand.

Whenuapai site analysis

Whenuapai (Figure 1) is located on the southern side of the upper Waitamata Harbour, with Brigham's Creek forming a boundary to the west and State Highways 16 and 18 forming the southern and eastern edges of the site. The greater part of the site is a moderately flat plateau approximately 25 m above sea level. An airfield, the Whenuapai Aerodrome, dominates this plateau.

Hydrology

Whenuapai can be divided into four major catchments (Figure 2). These catchments are bisected by a number of streams: the Brigham, Rarawara and Waiarohei Creeks. Ten watercourses discharge into the harbour. The average annual rainfall in Whenuapai is 1333.5 mm, and the average monthly rainfall is 111.1 mm. The average rainfall in January, the driest month, is 79.3 mm. The wettest month is June, with an average rainfall of 147.8 mm.

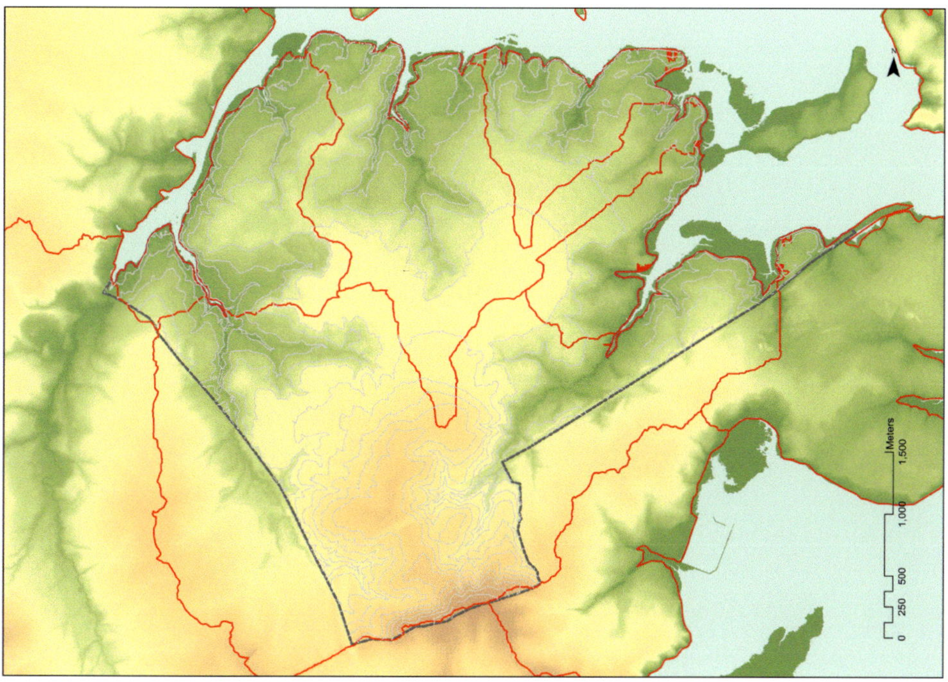

Figure 2 **Whenuapai catchments**

Aspect/slope

The aspect of Whenuapai is mostly northerly with an east-west division along the sides of the stream corridors (Figure 3). The slope of the majority of the site is flat (0 to 5 degrees); however, alongside some of the stream corridors the slope increases from 5 to 16 degrees (Figure 4).

Vegetation

The site was originally clad in New Zealand native coastal forest. The typical vegetation of the coastal edge of the Whenuapai catchment is characterised as belonging to the Kowhai-Kotare Harbour Coastline Ecosystem (Lucas & Head, 1997). The dominant tree species are pohutakawa, kowhai, kohekohe, purriri, kauri, karaka and titoki. Shrub species include karo, astelia, whārangi and ngaio.

Whenuapai structure plan

Auckland is undergoing rapid urban growth. More than 1,000,000 new citizens are expected to arrive in Auckland over the next 20 years. As a consequence of this growth there is an acute housing shortage. Whenuapai is located adjacent to SH16,

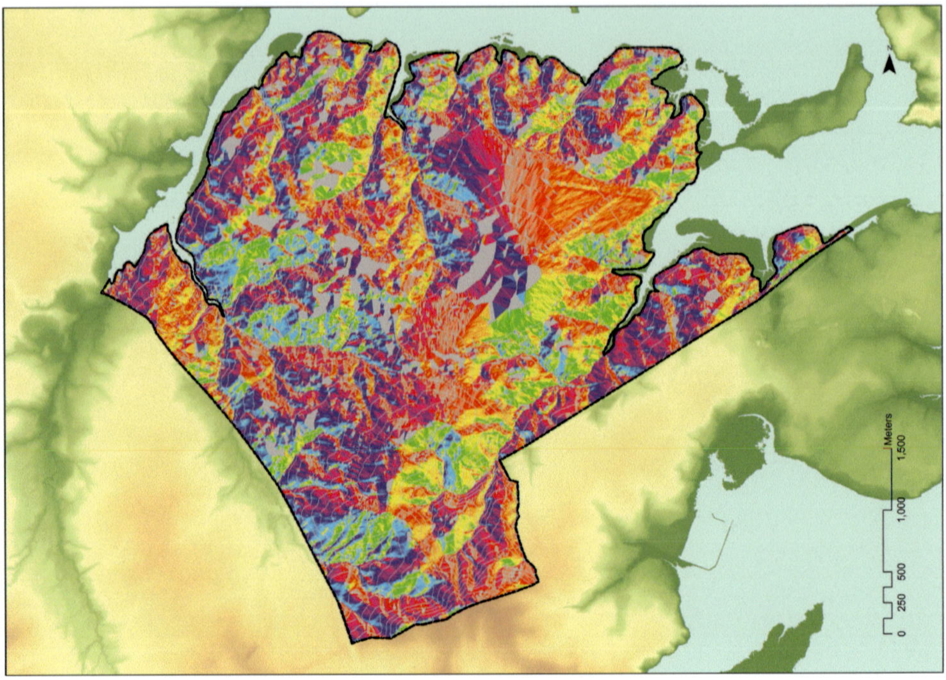

Figure 3 **Whenuapai aspect**

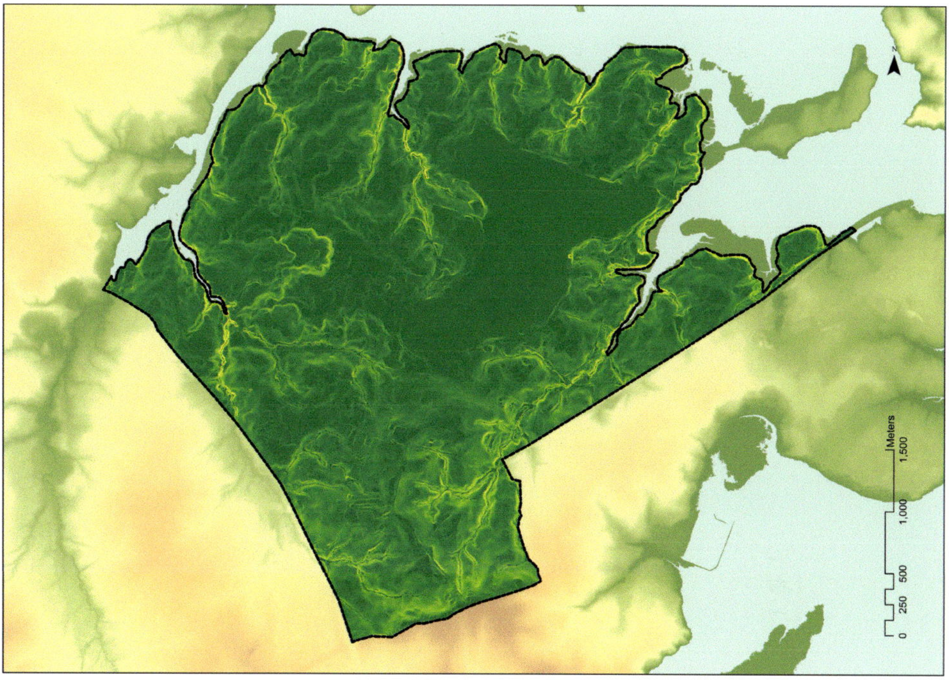

Figure 4 **Whenuapai slope**

an important motorway in the western growth corridor and near the new North-West Shopping Centre. Whenuapai also neighbours the successful Hobsonville housing development, making Whenuapai the next site for future urban development. To address the urban pressure Auckland is facing, the Auckland Council in 2016 (Auckland Council, 2016) developed an urban structure plan for Whenuapai to help conceptualise the shape of future urban development. The structure plan efficiently zones the available land according to proximity to infrastructure; industrial land and an apartment zone located adjacent to the main transport routes, SH16 and 18. Lower density housing zones are located nearer to the edge of the Waitematā Harbour. Single-storey housing with large sites are zoned for the coastal margin, while more intensive housing (medium density) is zoned between the coastal edge and the industrial zone (Figure 5).

The proposed structure plan will cause a number of environmental problems including an increase in stormwater contamination and flooding; these conditions will be heightened by the effects of climate change. To explore the impact of these effects, a sub-catchment of the larger Whenuapai catchment was chosen as a case study site. The selected site was the Rarawara sub-catchment to both understand the consequences of the proposed urban development and develop strategies to remediate the impact on the environment.

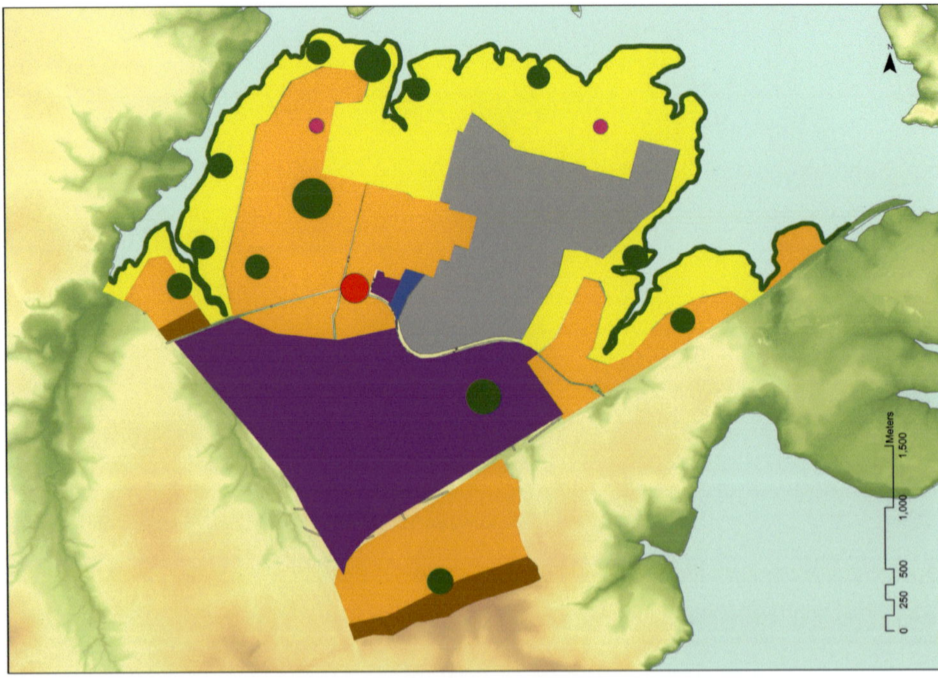

Figure 5 **Whenuapai council plan**

Rarawara catchment site analysis

The 324 ha Rarawara catchment is a moderately flat site bounded to the north by the Waitematā Harbour (Figure 6). To the west the site is defined by the Brigham Creek/Pitoitoi stream catchment, to the east by Whenuapai village and airfield and, to the south, by the intersection of SHW16 and 18.

Vegetation

The predominant vegetation in the catchment is grass, the result of the rural economy of the catchment. The other vegetation types are decorative gardens around the housing areas and shelterbelt species from the small horticulture and orchard blocks (Figure 7).

Hydrology

The catchment drains into the dominant stream, the Rarawara Creek (Figure 8). The creek runs roughly north-south and bisects the catchment. There are three sub-catchments. The stream exits into an estuarine mouth before connecting to Waitematā Harbour. There are smaller streams from the hinterland to the coast on either side of the Rarawara catchment (Figure 9).

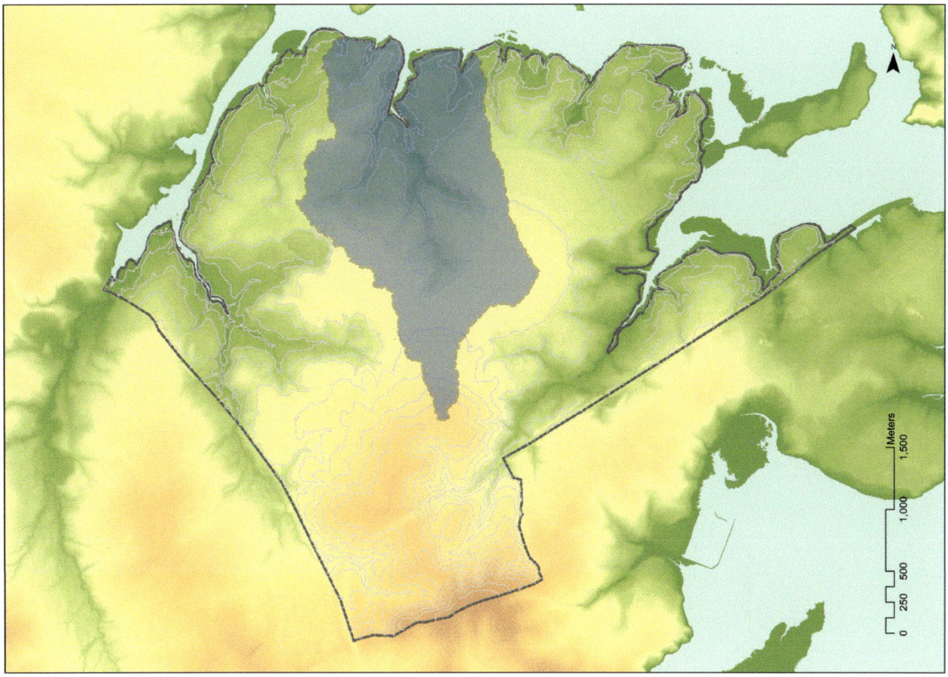

Figure 6 **Rarawara boundary**

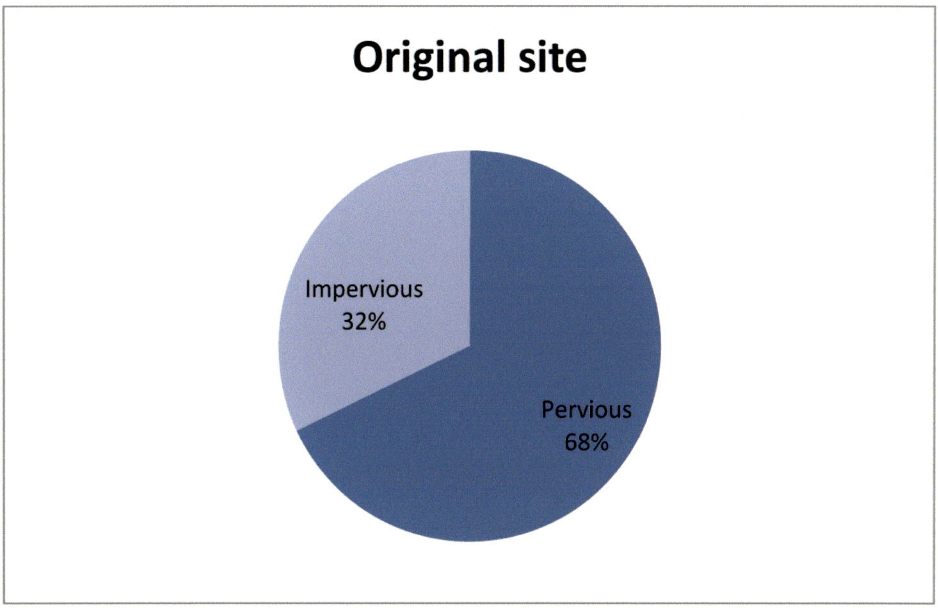

Figure 7 **pervious / impervious ratio**

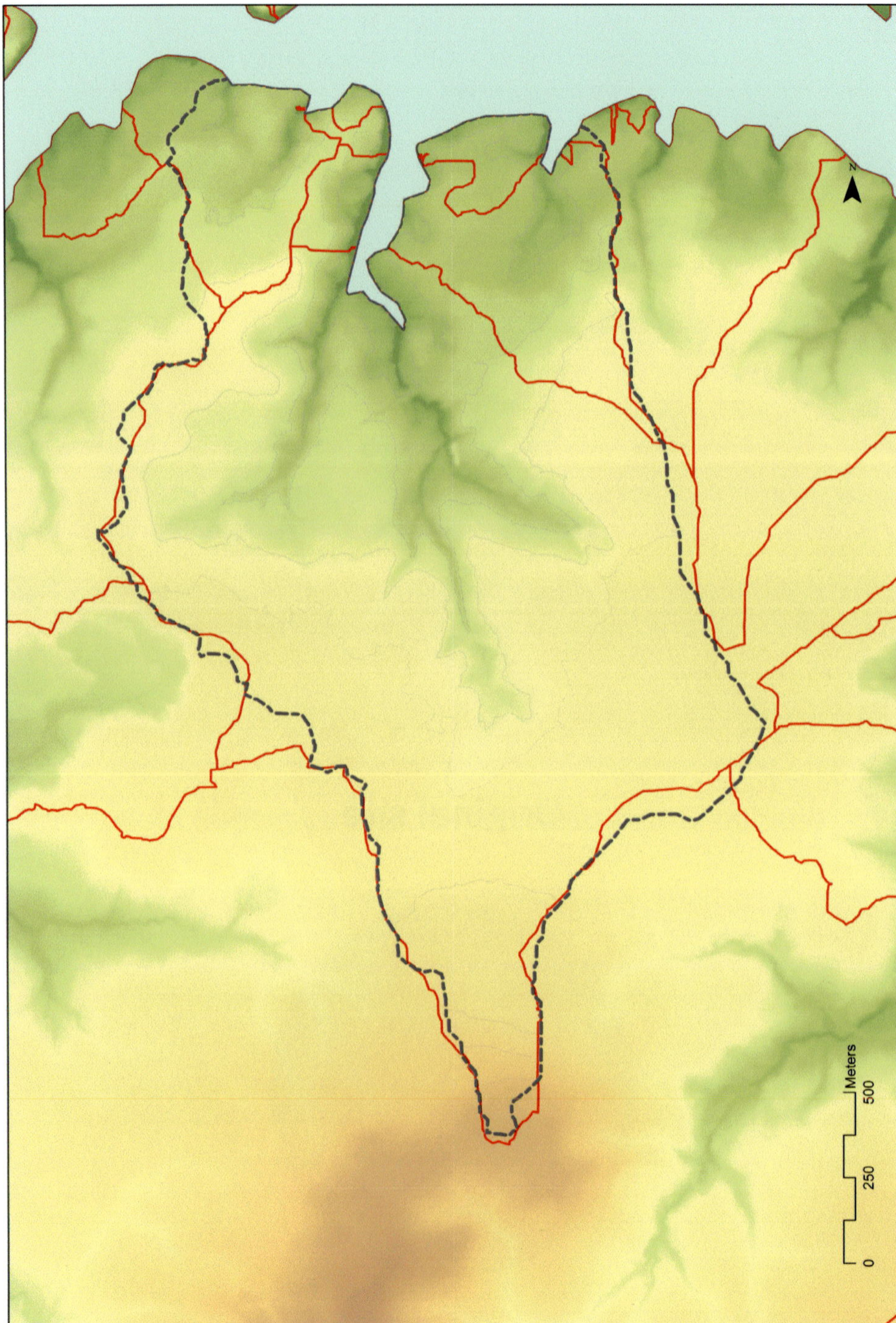

Figure 8 **Rarawara catchments**

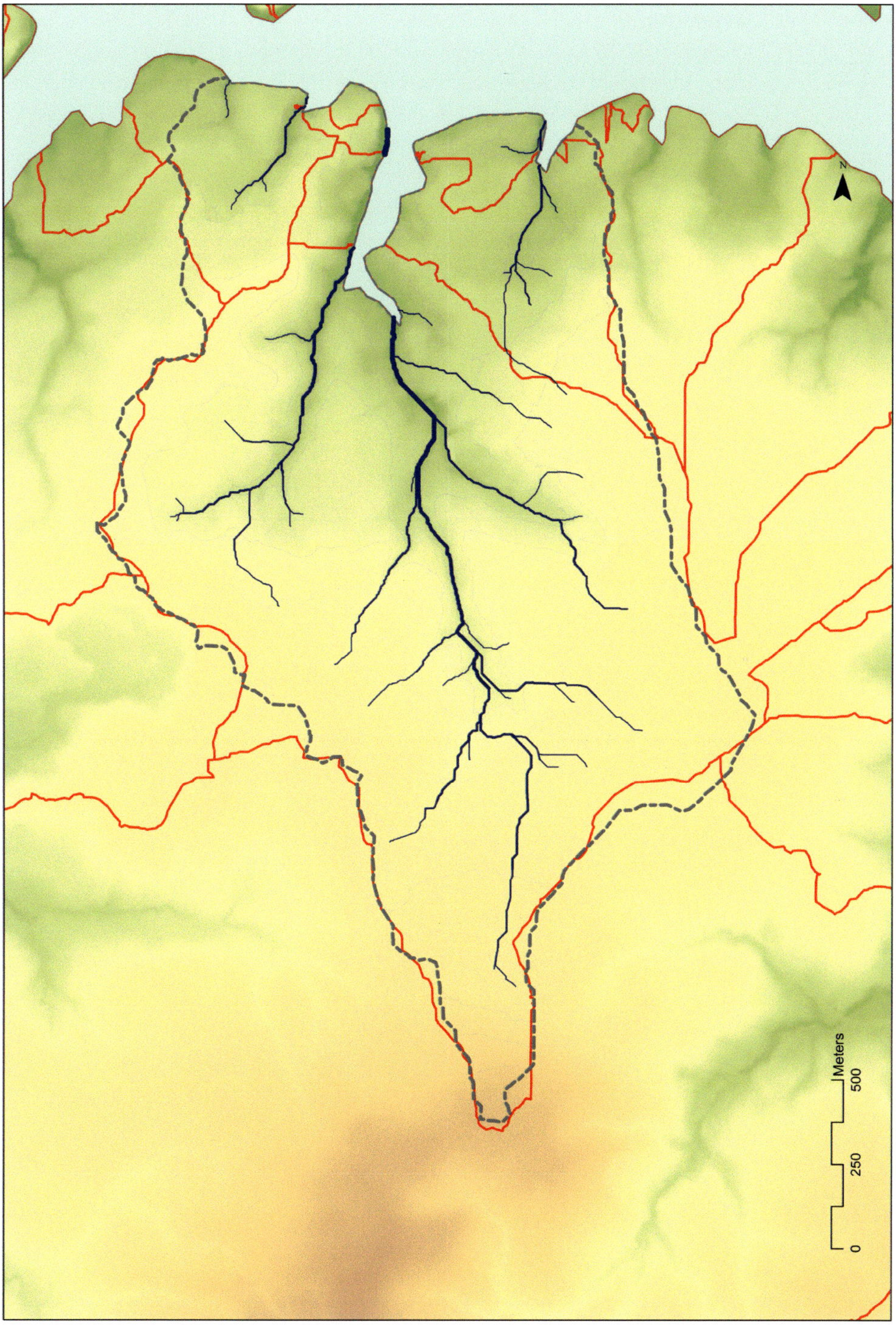

Figure 9 **Rarawara overland flow**

Aspect/slope

The aspect of the Rarawara catchment is mostly northerly with an east-west division along the sides of the stream corridors (Figure 10). The slope of the majority of the site is flat, 0 to 5 degrees, especially the aerodrome site (Figure 11). However, alongside the steam corridors the slope increases from 5 to 16 degrees.

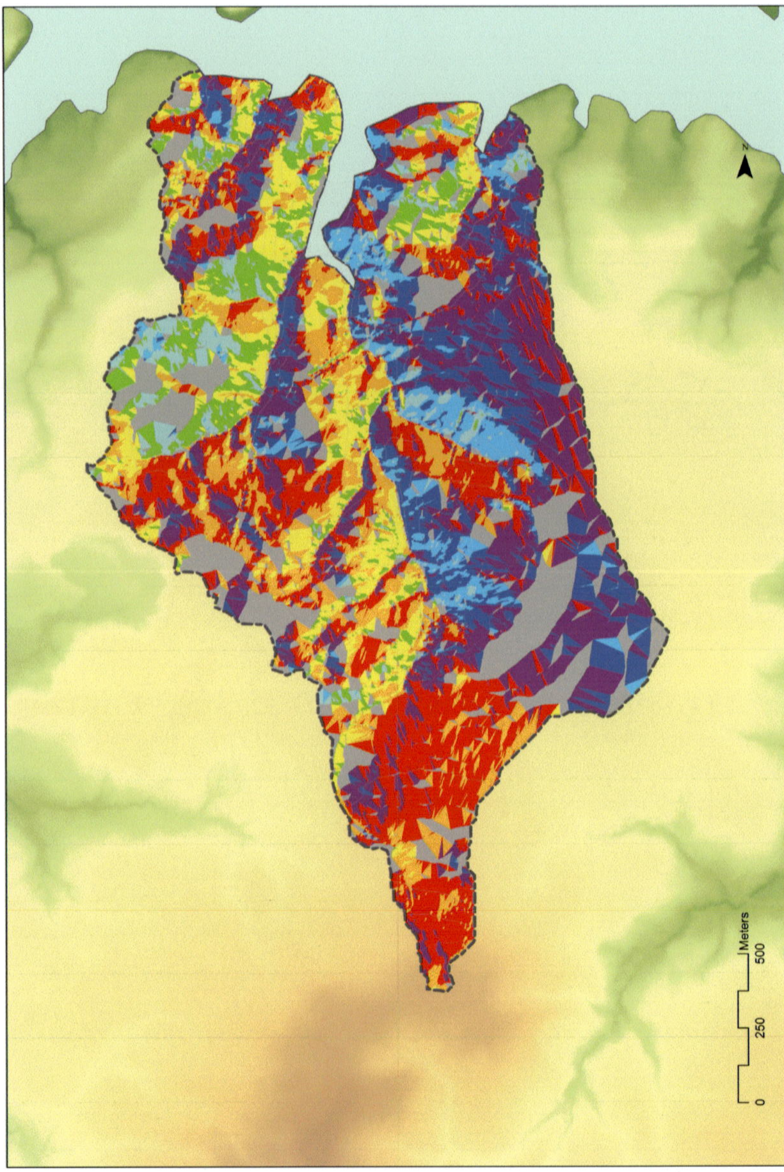

Figure 10 **Rarawara aspect**

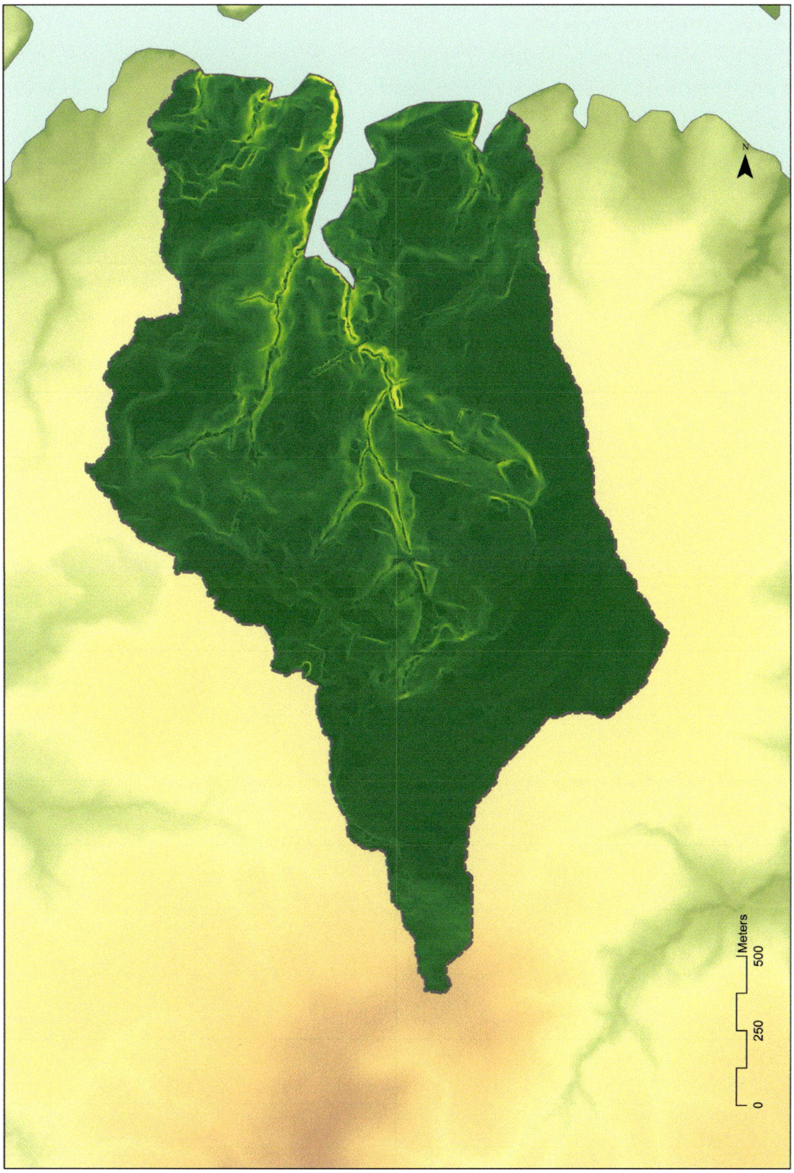

Figure 11 **Rarawara slope**

Land use

The land of the catchment is separated into two uses. The first is suburban housing, large lifestyle houses and sections on the northern coastal edge and a smaller subdivision to the west of the airfield. The rest of the catchment is made up of rural lifestyle blocks and small horticulture and orchard blocks.

Pervious/impervious ratio

Due to its mostly rural nature, the catchment is largely made of pervious surfaces (Figure 12). The impervious areas are the roading infrastructure and the airfield (Figure 13).

- The existing Rarawara catchment area is 324.1753 ha.
- The impervious surface area is made up of roads (81.8428 ha) and buildings (20.1004 ha).
- The total impervious surface area is 104.1488 ha.
- The total pervious surface area is 220.0265 ha.
- Giving a ratio of pervious to impervious of 2:11.

Figure 12 **Rarawara permeable**

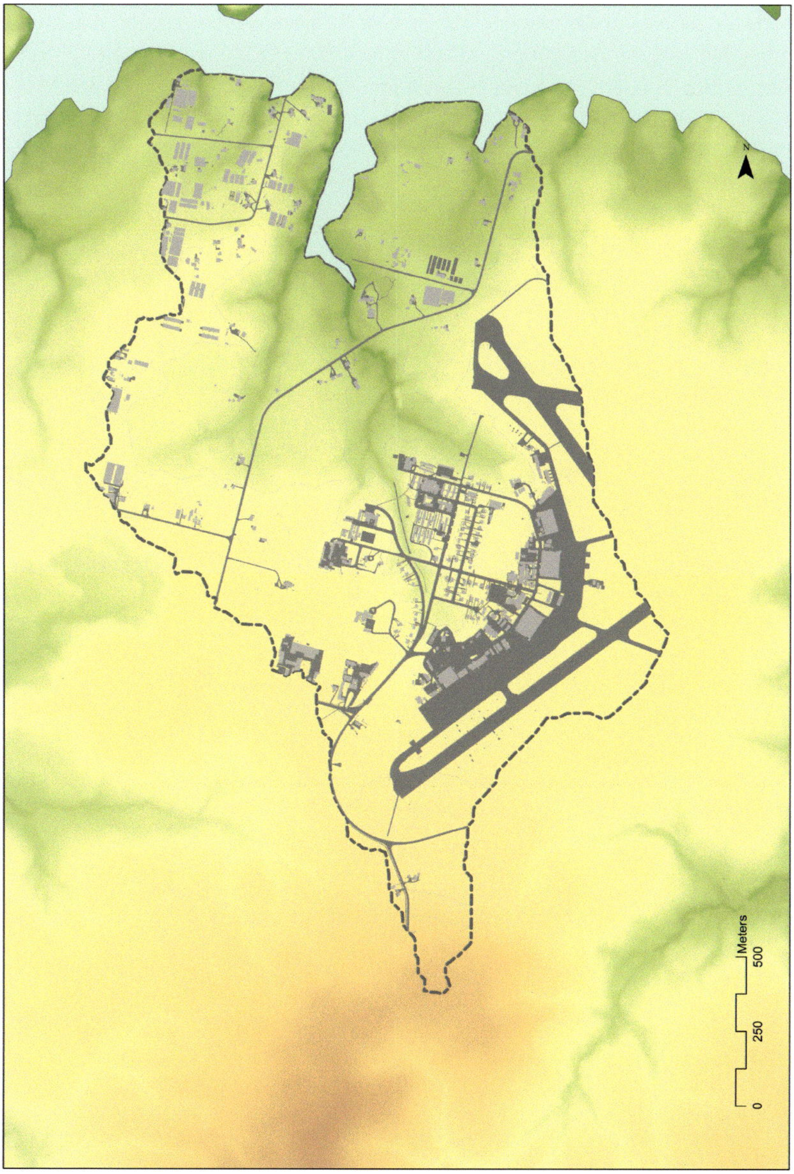

Figure 13 **Rarawara impermeable**

Rarawara structure plan

The effect of the Auckland Council's Whenuapai structure plan on the Rarawara catchment is to configure the catchment into four housing zones and an industrial zone (Auckland Council, 2016). The area closest to the coast is zoned for low-density, single-storey housing, along an approximately 100 ha coastal margin. Allowing for one dwelling unit (DU) per 500 m^2 gives 2,008 DUs, and 50 ha of impervious surfaces. A medium-density housing zone of 82 ha is planned behind the coastal zone. Allowing for one DU per 300 m^2 equals 2,743 DU, giving 61 ha of impervious surface. The remaining area is zoned industrial/commercial with two apartment zones to the east of the airfield zone. Three parks are proposed of approximately 35 ha in total. Roads and proposed and existing housing make up 212 ha of impervious surface (Figure 14).

Figure 14 **Rarawara council plan**

Rarawara catchment: environmental problems

With the construction of the new housing and the associated infrastructure, the hydrological pattern of the existing territory will be irrevocably changed; increased runoff with increased sedimentation will add to already high levels of sedimentation in the upper Waitematā Harbour. Runoff will also be polluted from roading contaminants and roof debris.

Pervious/impervious ratio

In the Auckland Council structure plan the impervious surface in the Rarawara catchment will increase markedly.

- The existing Rarawara catchment area is 324.1753 ha.
- The impervious surface area is made up of road (81.8428 ha), and buildings (206.9095 ha).
- The total impervious surface area is 288.7523 ha.
- The total pervious surface area is 35.423 ha.
- Giving a ratio of pervious to impervious of 8:1.

If this plan were built, then the result of this high degree of imperviousness would be a large amount of contaminated stormwater runoff discharging into the harbour.

To calculate the volume of stormwater that would be discharged from the catchment under the new structure plan, the Rational Method can be used (Thompson, 2007). To calculate the required volume for the construction of a storage and treatment wetland, TP10 (Auckland Council, 2003) is used.

- The runoff discharge flow rate over two years (m^3/sec) would be 5.95 m^3/sec.
- The required storage and treatment wetland for this runoff is sized at 32,140.04 m^3.
- For a ten-year runoff discharge flow rate of 8.71 m^3/sec,
- The required storage volume is 47,019.68 m^3.
- For a 100-year runoff discharge flow rate of 13.95 m^3/sec,
- The required storage volume is 75,350.53 m^3.

Rarawara catchment: environmental remediation: design process

To ameliorate the effects of urbanisation on the coastal receiving environment, an understanding of the hydrological behaviour of the catchment is necessary. The first step is to determine the structure and shape and size of the catchment on the site through mapping with ArcGIS. This data can be manifested as a series of maps showing catchment boundaries and a network of overland flow paths. From this mapping the size of the catchment and the ratio of impervious to pervious surface can be determined. Using the Rational Method, an understanding of the amount of increased rainfall runoff with the expanded site can be gained. By measuring the increase in impervious surface due to the number and type of housing zones, the increase in stormwater runoff can be calculated. Once the connection of housing density to the impervious/pervious surface ratio is established, the different zoning densities and associated impervious/pervious ratios can be manipulated to allow for greater permeability, while at the same time ensuring that the planned number of dwelling units remains the same.

Hydrology

The environmental damage from an increase in stormwater discharge into the upper Waitematā catchment can be ameliorated through decreasing the amount of impervious surfaces. The removal of infrastructure such as roads and housing will lead to an increase in the amount of pervious surface, leading to an increase in the absorption of stormwater runoff.

One way to increase the pervious surface of the catchment is by protecting and enhancing the existing stream network by establishing a protective buffer zone of at least 25 m around the stream and overland flow paths (Figure 15). Protection

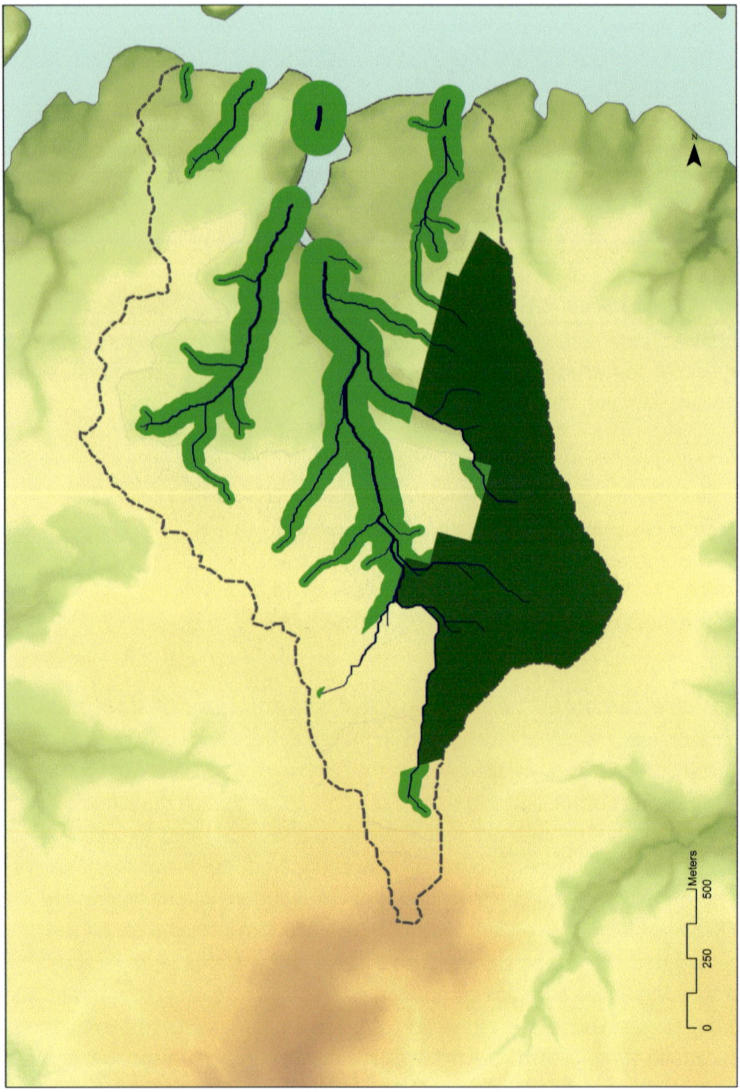

Figure 15 **Rarawara buffer OLFP**

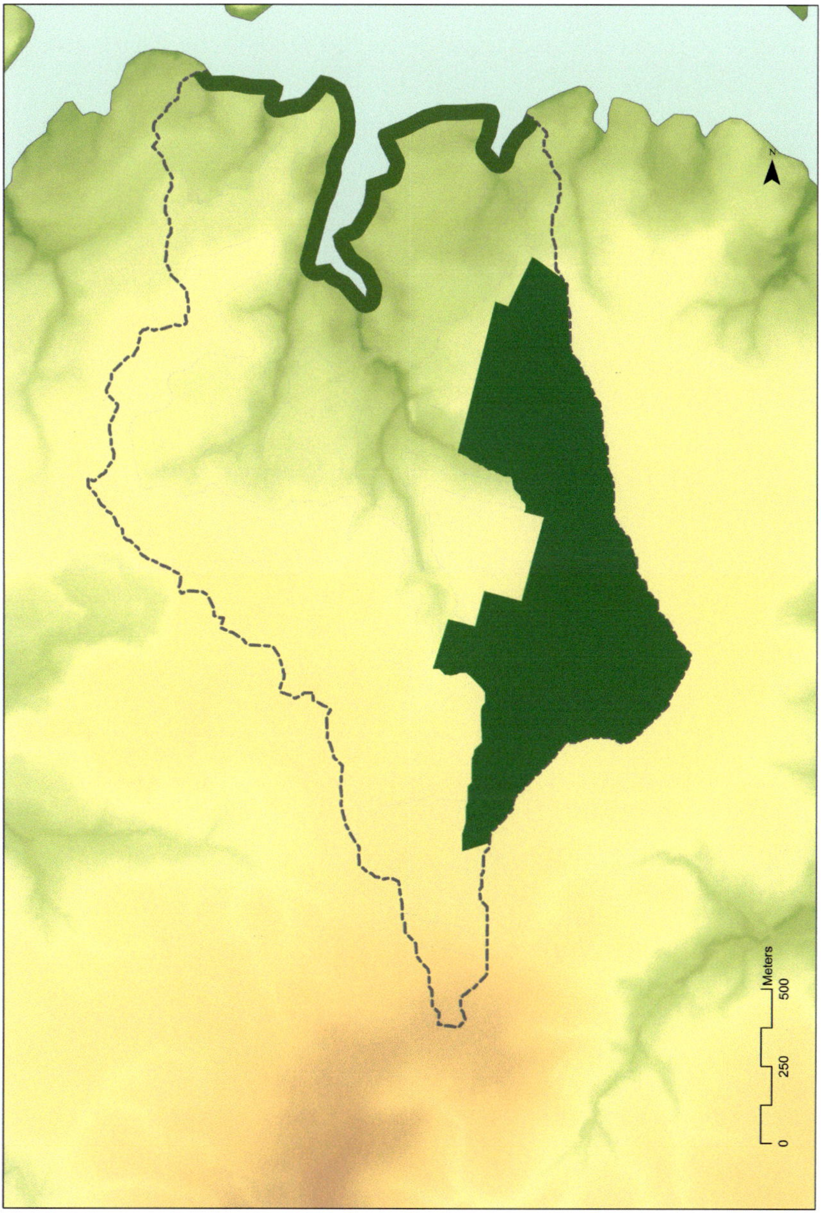

Figure 16 **Rarawara buffer harbour edge**

of the coastal edge is another important environmental measure; a buffer of 30 m would give a zone of 43 ha (Figure 16). These two measures increase the area of pervious surfaces within the catchment by 128 ha. This intervention also has the effect of developing a new park system along the stream corridors and the waterfront coastal edge (Figure 17).

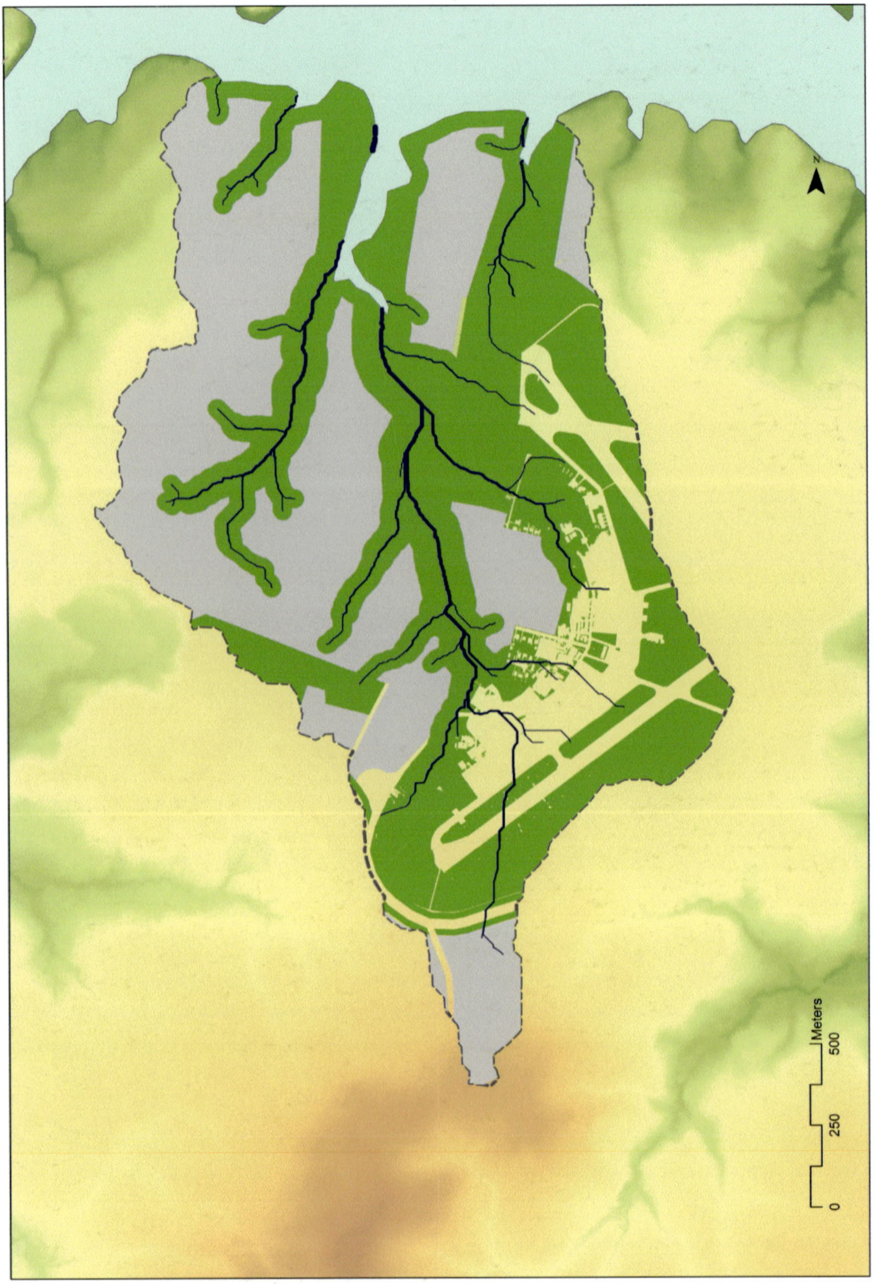

Figure 17 **Rarawara buffer stream**

Accommodating these two measures necessitates a change in the housing footprint. This is accomplished by decreasing the low-density zone from 100 ha to 23 ha, and decreasing the medium-density zone slightly, from 82 ha to 74 ha.

Rarawara catchment: urban design

To accomplish the increase in pervious surfaces and the consequent decrease in stormwater discharge means a loss of housing units. Under the Auckland Council structure plan the number of low-density DUs in the catchment is 2008 and medium-density is 2,743, equalling 4,752 DUs (with no provision for high-density units). By enlarging the pervious surface area, the number of DUs in the low-density zone will drop to 473 DUs and in the medium density zone to 2,471 DUs. The shortfall in DUs will be 1,827.

One solution to this real estate shortfall is to substitute apartments for the missing lower density DUs. This solution will increase the number of DUs to 1,468, making a total of 4,420. By increasing the number of apartments by making the building denser or higher, the shortfall of 1,827 DUs could be matched or even surpassed to give a better real estate return (Figure 18).

The new apartments could be located in the coastal zone around the existing stream mouth; an area of 8.8 ha would provide two high-density apartment zones within the low-density area.

Pervious/impervious ratio

- The Rarawara catchment area (324.1753 ha).
- Impervious surface of 196.1642 ha, roads (65.9289 ha) and buildings (130.2353 ha).
- Pervious surface, 128.001 ha.
- Giving a ratio of pervious to impervious of 2:3.

Using the Rational Method, the effect of the new pervious surfaces will lead to a two-year runoff discharge flow rate of 29,304.15042 m^3, compared to the discharge of 26,468.26489 m^3 from the original site and 32,140.03594 m^3 discharge with the proposed Auckland Council structure plan.

In the ten-year runoff discharge, the flow rate of the new plan is 42,870.88672 m^3, compared to the discharge of 38,722.09123 m^3 from the original site and 47,019.68221 m^3 from the proposed Auckland Council plan.

In the 100-year runoff discharge, the flow rate of the new plan is 68,701.95265 m^{3,} compared to 62,053.37659 m^3 in the original site and 75 350.52871 m^3 in the Auckland Council proposed plan (Table 4.1).

Figure 18 **Rarawara new master plan**

Table 4.1 **Rarawara catchment runoff**

Plan	Two-year runoff	Ten-year runoff	100 years
Present catchment	26,468.26489 m^3	38,722.09123 m^3	62,053.37659 m^3
Auckland City structure plan	32,140.03594 m^3	47,019.68221 m^3	75,350.52871 m^3
New plan	29,304.15042 m^3	42,870.88672 m^3	68,701.95265 m^3

Rarawara catchment: environmental implications of the design process

Stream network

A buffer zone around the revealed hydrological network will enable the stream corridors to be revegetated with native species. The zone also gives the opportunity to allow for the location of structural stormwater cleaning instruments – in particular, wetlands and a rain garden – which can all be installed within the new zone. This stream zone can form a deep connection from the coastal edge to the hinterland, creating an ecological corridor.

Having housing adjacent to the new river zone will also help to increase real estate values. By locating medium-density housing along the edges of the new stream parks, owners can enjoy views of the water and native vegetation. The nature of the new river zones and the link from the coast to the hinterland provide the opportunity for owners in the centre of the development to have access to the coast.

Coastal zone

Establishing a coastal buffer zone means that the critical environmental conditions in this zone will be protected. Critical riparian ecologies can be restored and protected, and damage from building in this zone can be ameliorated.

Urban design

Establishing a protective buffer zone around the coastal and stream hydrological networks will increase the ability of the Rarawara catchment to absorb rainfall, rather than add to runoff into the upper Waitematā Harbour. To ensure the same economic return is met – that the same number of DUs are constructed as specified in the Auckland Council structure plan – the loss of low- and medium-density housing is met by a greater number of apartments with a smaller footprint. The result will be a low-rise domestic landscape of gardens and houses broken by apartment towers that emphasise the unique stream system.

One criticism of this urban design proposal might be that building apartments in the coastal zone is an urban typology that is hostile to the Auckland suburban ethos. However, there are many existing examples of residential apartments in Auckland coastal suburbs such as Kohimarama, Herne Bay and Takapuna. These examples demonstrate the possibility of coexistence between low-density, two-storey, single family housing on the coastal edge with apartment dwelling. A new 14-storey apartment building has also been recently proposed for the neighbouring suburb, Hobsonville Point (Gibson, 2018).

Whenuapai catchment: environmental implications of the Rarawara case study

The new development plan (Figure 18) shows how the coastline and stream corridors are protected through buffering. There are three consequences of this action.

The first is that the vegetative buffers have the effect of protecting the hydrological network by protecting the streams from the influx of contaminated stormwater. The second effect is that the ratio of impervious to pervious surface is relaxed, ensuring that more rainfall is able to be absorbed by uncovered ground. A social consequence of this new green network is the establishment of a new path/park system that links the hinterland of the subdivision with the coast. The third consequence of this action is the clustering of the GFA that has been displaced by the new stream/buffer stream network into a series of apartment towers located at the intersection of the stream networks and the coast. All these measures will help build future resilience as the environmental effects of climate change become more and more persistent. Two of the Te Aranga principles, Mauri Tu and Taiao, are manifest, in particular an understanding of how existing water systems will be affected by the proposed urban development. The design strategy advances a holistic way of understanding the site to ensure that any damage is remediated through an understanding of the interrelatedness of wai water, whenua land and ngāhere vegetation. Connecting to the original flora and fauna through a revegetation programme helps to rebuild the biodiversity of the site through the uses of the stream system as an ecological corridor

Furong New Town

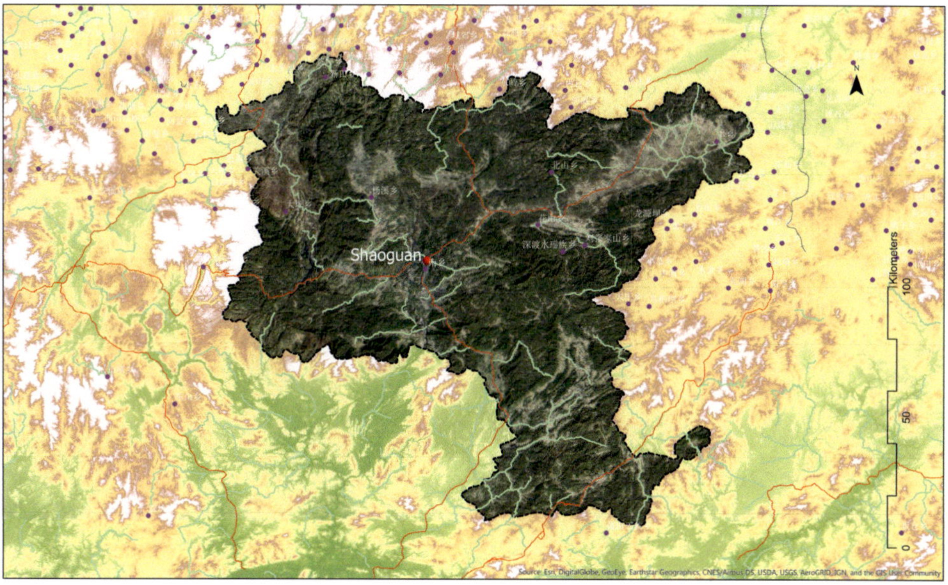

Figure 19 **Shaoguan location in Guangzhou**

Introduction

Furong New Town is a new city to be constructed adjacent to Shaoguan in northern Guangdong Province, PRC.

Shaoguan region site analysis

Shaoguan is a prefecture-level city located in the north of Guangdong province in the upper reaches of Beijiang River Basin (Figure 19). The city lies to the south of the Nanling Mountains, which form a boundary between southern and central China (Figure 20). The city of Shaoguan is located in an important pass linking Hunan in the north with Guangzhou in the south.

Hydrology

The major rivers in the Shaoguan region are the Zhenjiang, the Wujiang, the Mojiang, the Jinjiang, the Nanhuaxi, the Nanshui, the Wengjiang, the Beijiang and Xinfeng Jiang (Figure 21). Shaoguan City is located on the confluence of two rivers, the Zhen River from the northeast and the Wu River from the northwest. The two rivers connect, becoming the North River, or Beijiang, linking Shaoguan to Guangzhou. There are five major catchments in the region. The average annual rainfall in Shaoguan is 160.4 days, and 1,583.5 mm. The average rainfall over 100 mm is in the months of February to August; the month with maximum rainfall is May (253.2 mm), and the second heaviest rainfall is in April (230.3 mm).

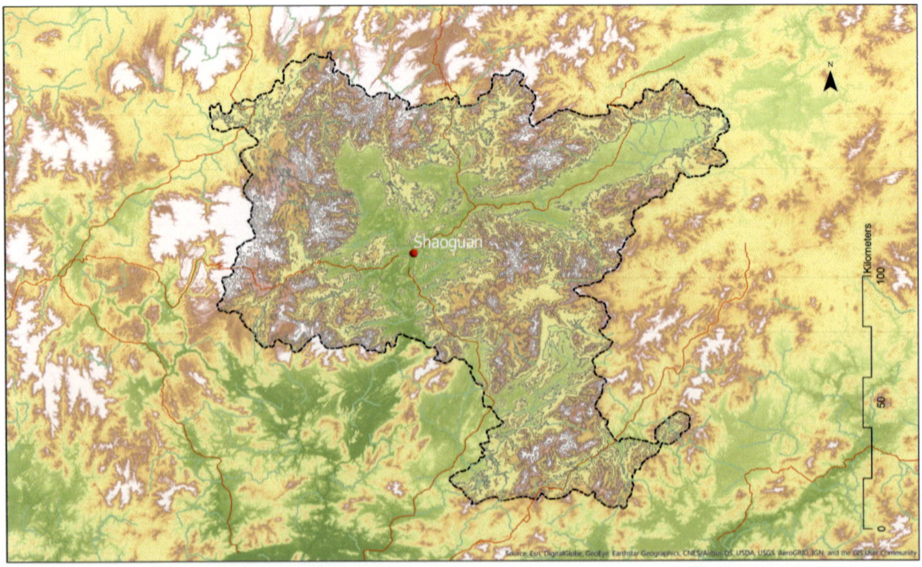

Figure 20 **Shaoguan contours**

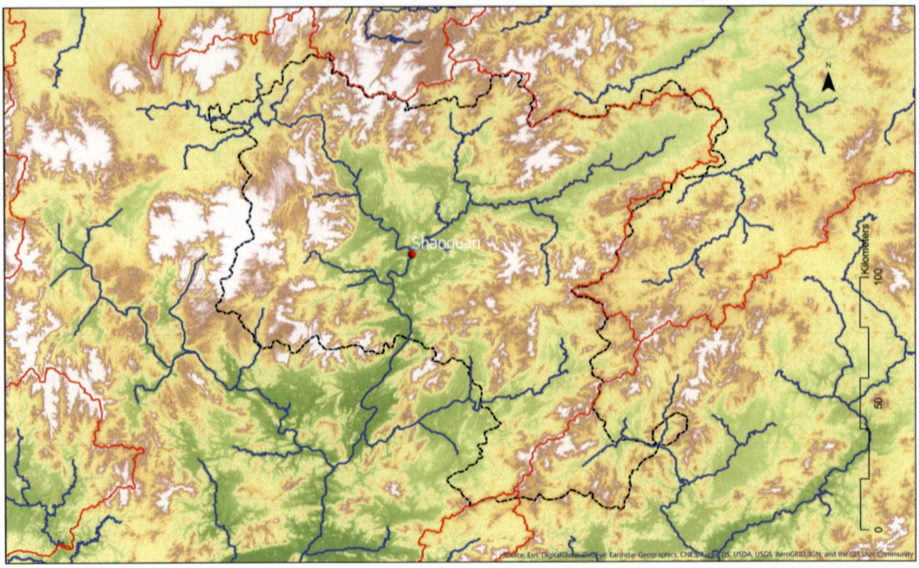

Figure 21 **Shaoguan overland flow**

Topography

Shaoguan is located in the southern foothills of the Nanling Mountains, which run in an east to west direction. Shikengkong is the highest point of Guangdong Province, at 1,902 m. The lowest point is Shaoguan City, at 35 m. The rapid growth of Shaoguan is constrained by its location on the confluence of the two rivers and the topography of the surrounding hills. To address these issues, a new city is being built in a 2,500 ha valley to the south of the existing city. A new high-speed rail station is located in the valley as is the new Jingzhu expressway from Beijing to Zhuhai. This new city, Furong New Town, will help link Shaoguan with the rest of China.

Furong New Town: site analysis

The site of the new city (Figure 22) is a large valley orientated north to south adjacent to the old city of Shaoguan, northern Guangdong Province. The catchment area is approximately 2,086.69 ha, surrounded on three sides by hills, including the Furongshan National Mining Park (Figure 23). The southern boundary of the valley is demarcated by the Beijiang River and the large island of Chetouzhou (Figure 24).

Vegetation

The existing landscape can be divided into two types: productive agricultural land, mostly paddy fields and fishponds, and remnant native vegetation. The surrounding hills are not cultivated and are colonised by broadleaf rainforest species, plus exotic species such as pine and eucalyptus (Figure 25).

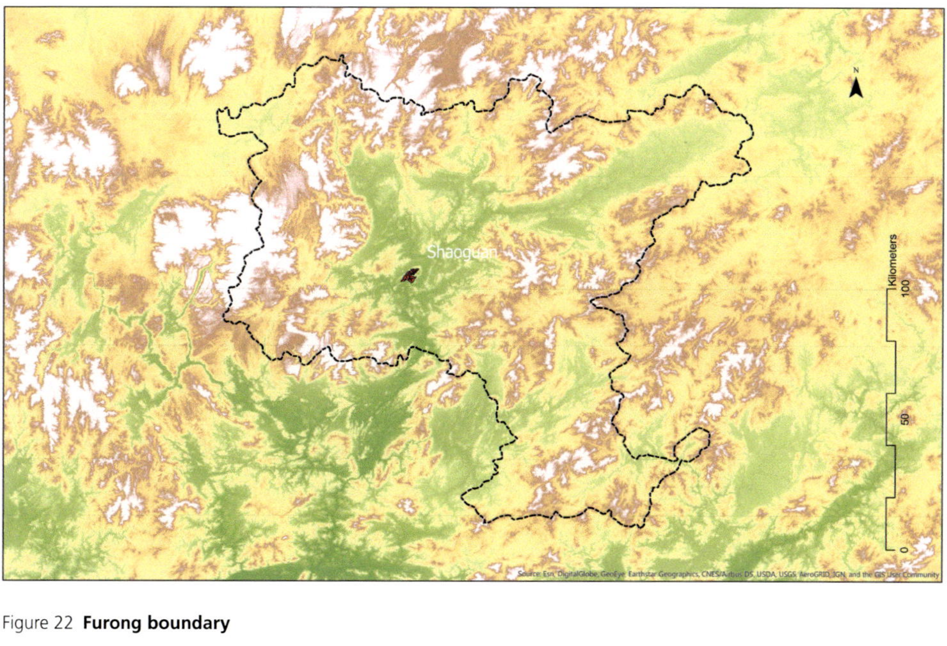

Figure 22 **Furong boundary**

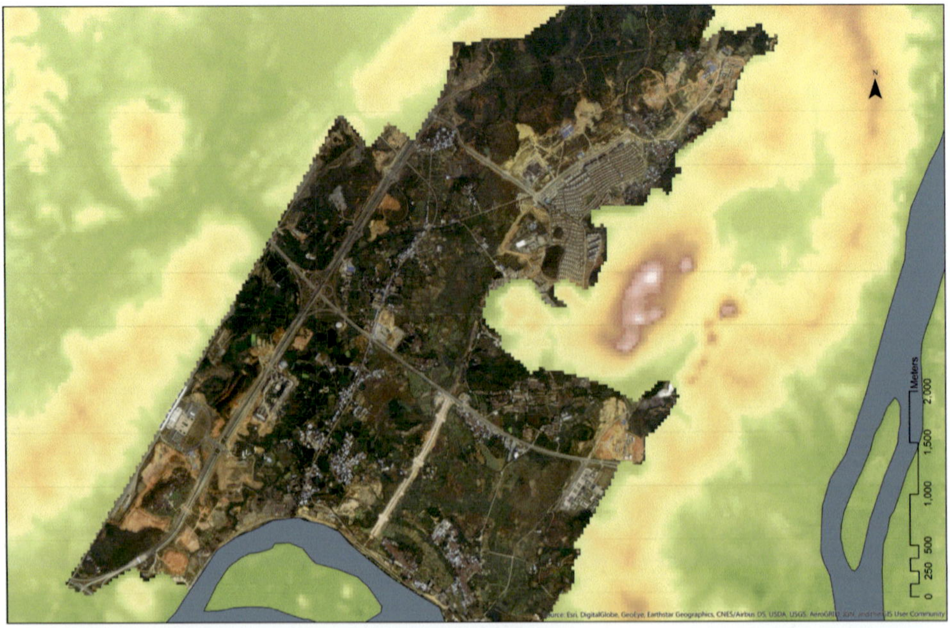

Figure 23 **Furong aerial**

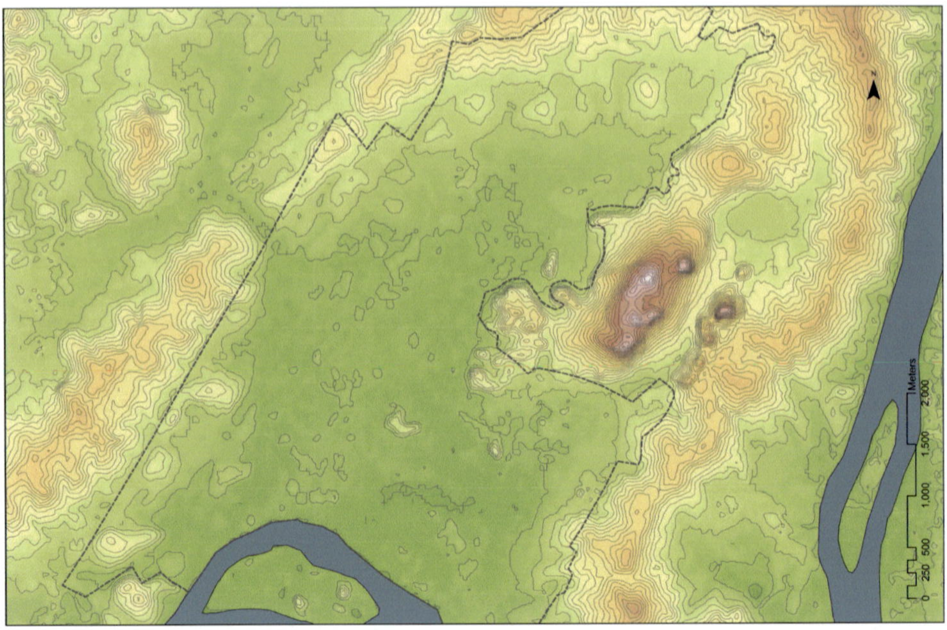

Figure 24 **Furong contours**

Figure 25 **Furong green space**

Hydrology

The city site occupies two catchment systems (Figure 26). The major catchment system occupies about two-thirds of the city site, from the surrounding hills to the river. The other catchment system is on the western edge of the city plan and encompasses the discharge point of the neighbouring catchment. Each catchment has a major stream system, with associated overland flow path networks. The northeast system is the most fully developed with an extensive network stretching deep into the catchment. The two catchments discharge into the Beijiang River, the outlets are located close to one another (Figure 27).

The existing hydrological system retains the natural hydrological pattern in the surrounding hills, but has been completely modified in the valley by manmade interventions – agricultural fishponds and paddy fields. Recent flood control measures along the Beijiang includes a concrete flood protection wall along the river and a large dam located upstream of the site.

Aspect and slope

The aspect of the site is north-south, aligning with the surrounding hills (Figure 28). The slope of the site is mostly 0 to 5 degrees, with higher elevation in the hills (Figure 29).

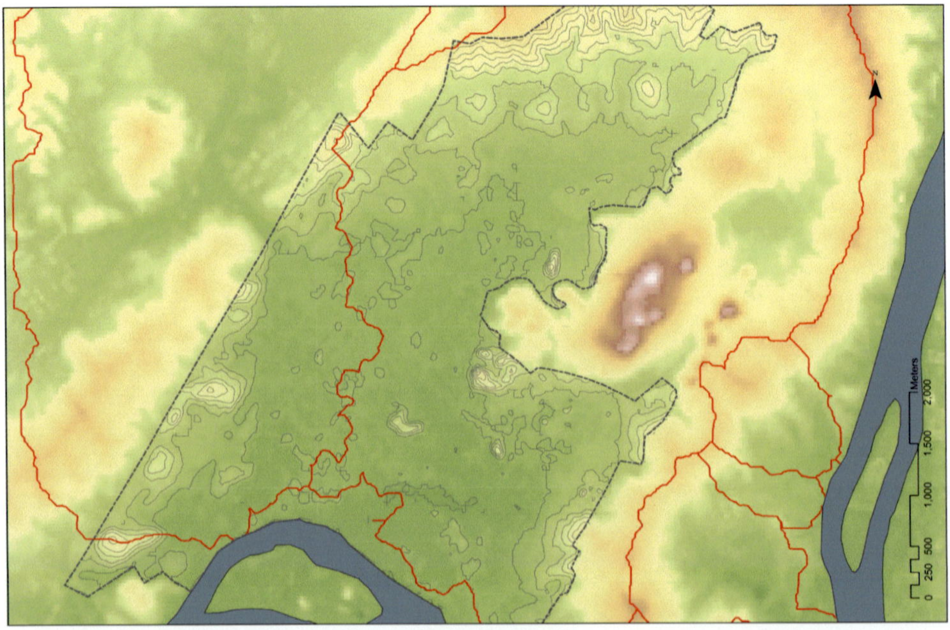

Figure 26 **Furong catchments**

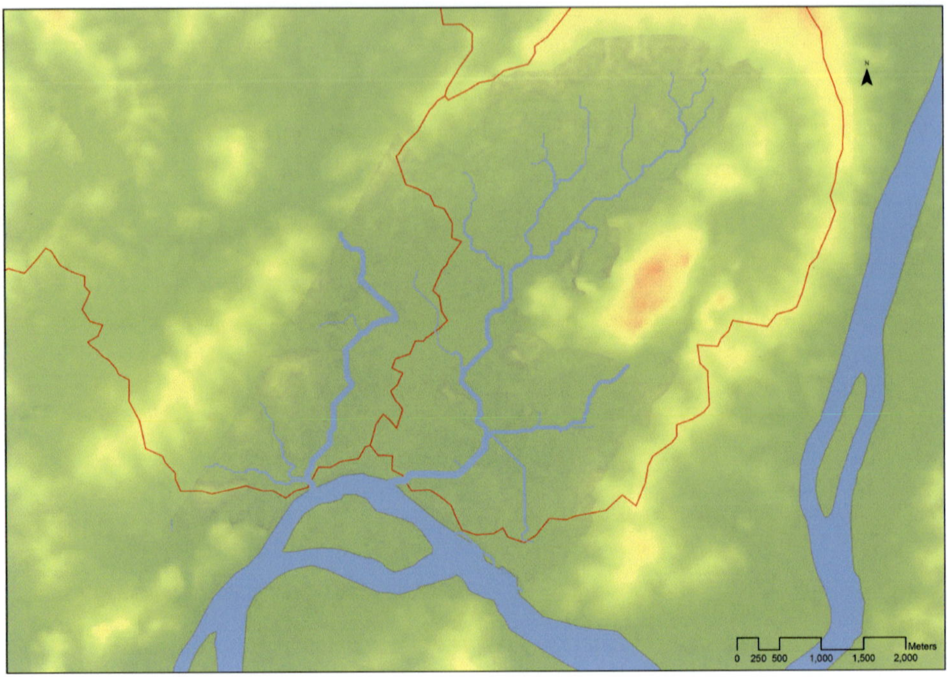

Figure 27 **Furong stream**

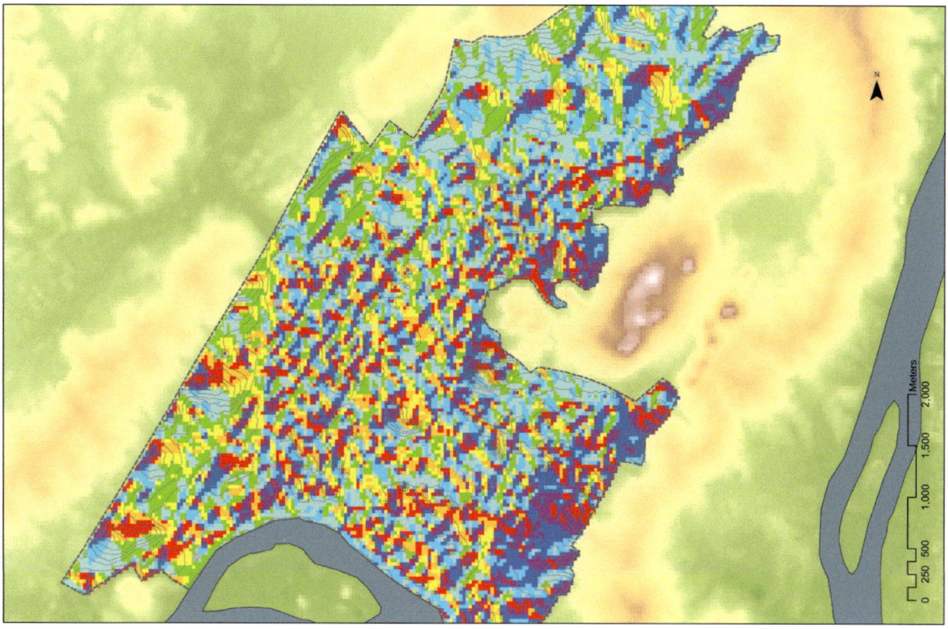

Figure 28 **Furong aspect**

Figure 29 **Furong slope**

Pervious/impervious ratio

The Furong catchment covers an area of 2,086.69 ha, of which the vast majority is pervious surface (Figure 30). The small amount of impervious surface is made up of buildings, roads and farm infrastructure.

Furong New Town master plan

The new city master plan occupies 1,654 ha of the 2,086.69 ha catchment. Buildings and infrastructure occupy 565 ha of the site, while the remaining parks and reserves occupy 1,089 ha.

The new city plan is laid out in a grid pattern. The new freeway infrastructure forms a rough cross-shape within the urban plan. The northern arm of the cross, Shaoguan Avenue, runs along the western side of the city to Shaoguan. The eastern arm, Baiwang Road, runs west to east through a tunnel on the eastern edge of the catchment hills to a new administration district to be built on the bend of the Beijiang River. A railway station for the high-speed train has been built on the western side of the city adjacent to Shaoguan Avenue.

The zoning pattern of the new city is broadly determined by the new road infrastructure. To the south of the new freeway, the city is zoned for government, cultural and commercial use. The area north of the new freeway is mostly designated for residential use, with a thin corridor for commercial use running north-south. Public space and parks are allocated to blocks within the new city grid. The existing stream network is channelled into a single, central water stream that runs down the centre of the valley.

Figure 30 **Furong permeable**

Furong waterfront

The river edge of the new city is zoned as a public space (Figure 31). The waterfront is approximately 2 km long and 500 m wide, occupying a broad concave bend in the river, encompassing two stream outlets from the larger catchment (Figure 32). The proposed waterfront architectural/urban programme is for the construction of

Figure 31 **Furong waterfront aerial**

Figure 32 **Furong stream system**

four building groups, running west to east: an open-air shopping mall, a convention centre, the preservation and restoration of an existing village and a resort/hotel. The remainder of the site is zoned as a public park.

Furong New Town waterfront: environmental problems

Stormwater

The construction of the new city will particularly affect the proposed waterfront development. The increase in impervious surfaces causes an increase in contaminated stormwater which will be discharged into the Beijiang River (Figure 33).

Pluvial flooding

The increase in pervious surfaces will also cause pluvial flooding in the city that will gather at the river's edge.

River flooding

In addition to these problems the Beijiang River is likely to flood (Figure 34). With the impetus of climate change, all three environmental problems will be aggravated.

Figure 33 **Furong stormwater infrastructure**

Figure 34 **Furong river flooding**

Furong New Town waterfront: environmental remediation: design process

There are a number of remediation solutions to these problems.

Stormwater

By situating structural water-cleaning devices in the public space of the new waterfront, stormwater can be cleaned before being discharged into the Beijiang River. Devices could include a swale, located at the junction of the city grid and the waterfront site, to accept, attenuate and treat contaminated stormwater from overland flows from the city (Figure 35). Buffering the OLFP/stream network helps to delineate a space in the waterfront development for remediation measures (Figure 36).

River flooding

In a similar way, buffering the riverfront also helps to allocate space for the necessary remediation measures (Figure 37). A raised stop bank planted with indigenous flora could help both protect the site from flooding and help to build biodiversity.

Combining the buffer zones indicates a space in which remediation of stormwater and pluvial flooding can take place (Figure 38). A constructed wetland, occupying most of the public space of the waterfront site, could take stormwater

Figure 35 **Furong swale**

Figure 36 **Furong OLFP buffer**

Figure 37 **Furong river buffer 100 m**

Figure 38 **Furong all buffers**

from the two existing streams and the new piped infrastructure, and subject the contaminated water to cleaning before discharge into the river. The wetland can also be planted with vegetation that is indigenous to the area, to help build biodiversity. The constructed wetland could also double as a detention zone for pluvial flooding from the new city.

The public space of the waterfront would then become a shifting temporal landscape that displayed various hydrological conditions according to the seasons: a dry landscape in winter, a wet landscape in summer.

Urban design

The new, environmentally-driven process creates 'leftover spaces', outside of the remediatory measures. These spaces become a set of 'islands', surrounded by different water conditions according to the seasons (Figure 39). The building programme – the mall, convention centre, hotel and village – could be treated as a self-contained entity. This hermetic quality of the islands can be emphasised topographically by locating each building group on each of the islands. If the new islands are unable to accommodate the proposed building programme, then the FAR of the development might need to be reconsidered to allow for a taller, more intensive use of the site.

Figure 39 **Furong building zones**

Furong New Town waterfront: environmental implications of the Furong case study investigation

The new waterfront development plan shows how the new city of Furong could be protected from the consequences of a massive change to the hydrological pattern of the existing catchment, a change that will be worsened with the impact of climate change. Rethinking the typical waterfront development model to a remedial landscape has a number of consequences for the urban development of the city. The waterfront becomes a literal buffer to the effects of river flooding, and a site to absorb pluvial flooding and to remediate contaminated stormwater.

Brownfield case studies

Introduction

Four brownfield urban developments located in New Zealand, the PRC, the USA and the UK are discussed.

The first project is a proposal for the design of a waterfront park in the Wynyard Quarter in Auckland, New Zealand. The second project explores how to build resilience to flooding in a dense urban catchment in Jinan, PRC. The third project demonstrates how urban resilience can be built through mapping both river and pluvial flooding for a brownfield development site in Pittsburgh, USA. The fourth study explores how to build on a flood-prone site in Oxford, UK. All four case studies demonstrate different ways in which to develop an urban programme that is resilient to effects of climate change.

Wynyard Quarter, Freemans Bay, is an inner-city waterfront development in Auckland, New Zealand, on an existing reclaimed site, partially developed. The case study looks at how an alternative urban form might be developed. GIS mapping is used to identify the natural hydrological patterns of the site. The coastal edge and overland flow paths are identified and protected from development. A new urban park is proposed for Wynyard Point. To achieve an increase in pervious surface, the existing master plan is reconfigured through an amalgamation of building uses and an increase in building height. The proposed development master plan is radically redefined to allow for an increase in pervious surfaces through a manipulation of the required building FAR. The result is a new kind of urban development within a new urban park that connects citizens to the natural world while ameliorating environmental problems.

The second case study is from Jinan, PRC. The case study starts with acknowledging a real problem, the previous flooding of the centre of Jinan. GIS mapping identifies the existing topography and the urban catchments that have contributed to the flooding. A hydrological analysis reveals the overland flow paths that confirm the location of the flooding at their nexus. The study identifies existing green areas in the catchments that could be used as detention zones. Planners can use the study as a document to guide the future urban development of the catchment. In this way, increasing the amount of green space in the catchment will reduce the likelihood of flooding in the future.

The third case study is Hazelwood Green, located in Pittsburgh, USA. The site, an ex-steel mill alongside the Monongahela River, has been planned for an extensive urban development (ReMake Group, 2018). Through mapping the existing hydrological conditions, especially river flooding and overland flow paths, an alternative urban development plan starts to emerge. By protecting these conditions, environmental resilience to the increase in storm events as a result of climate change can be engendered, thus helping the development stakeholders to safeguard the site.

The last case study is located at Osney Mead, Oxford, UK. The site is a mid-century industry estate to the west of Oxford. Oxford University is proposing to redevelop the site to provide new research and graduate accommodation. The site is locating in the upper Thames flood plain, a problem that is quickly revealed by preliminary analysis. By mapping the dry ground after flooding, a new development plan can be developed that ensures safety from flooding while at the same time realises the ambition of the development plan.

Wynyard Quarter

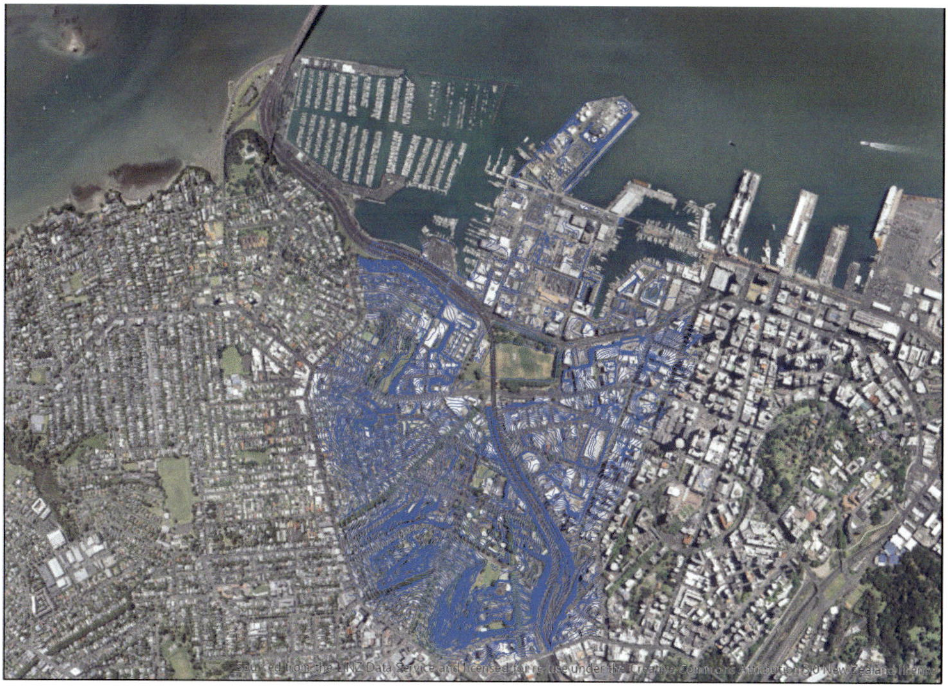

Figure 40 **Freemans Bay contours**

Introduction

The Wynyard Quarter is a new urban waterfront being built in the Freemans Bay catchment, Auckland, New Zealand. The size of catchment is 244 ha.

Freemans Bay catchment: site analysis

Freemans Bay is located in the centre of Auckland City. Auckland/Tamaki Makaurau is situated on an active volcanic field located on an isthmus between the Pacific Ocean and the Tasman Sea. This unique landscape is made up of over 50 volcanic vents that form a unique topography, both watery and hilly. Lakes and basins were formed where water and a volcanic eruption joined together. Auckland's unique landform, the volcanic cones, were created from eruptions, building hills of magma.

Topography

Freemans Bay is made up of two parts, an inner-city suburb in the centre of the city (Figure 40) and a large area of reclaimed land. The original landscape is made up of a number of valleys that run in a north-south direction. Ridges that are now roads define the edges of the suburb: to the west, Shelly Beach Road, Jervois Road and

Ponsonby Road, then K Road to the south and Hobson Street on the eastern side. The original shoreline is defined by three roads: to the west, Beaumont Street and Victoria Street and then Halsey Street on the eastern side.

Freemans Bay is one of a series of three large urban valleys running north-south that form the core of the Auckland Central Business District. These three valleys and headlands once opened onto five bays: Freemans Bay/Waiatarua, Smales Point/Ngauwera, Commercial Bay/Te One Panea, Point Britomart/Te Rereanga-Orati and Official Bay/Te Hororoa.

The second part of the catchment is reclaimed land. This reclamation was carried out in two parts. The first was the filling of Freemans Bay and the construction of Victoria Park in the early 20th century. The second was the construction of the Wynyard Quarter reclamation in the early 20th century as a warehouse/industrial port zone.

Hydrological pattern

Historically the Freemans Bay catchment was dominated by two streams; the first is the Waikutu on the southwest side of the catchment, discharging into Freemans Bay near to where Collage Hill starts the ascent to Ponsonby. The other stream, the Tunamau, was located on the southeastern side of the catchment, where the present Western Park is located. The Tunamau discharged into the bay where Franklin Road starts the ascent to Ponsonby Road. The hydrological pattern, the streams and associated overland flow paths make up 29 sub-catchments within the greater catchment (Figure 41). However, the native hydrological system has long since been subsumed by a conventional piped network that now discharges into the sea from a single point at the end of the Wynyard Quarter.

Figure 41 **Freemans Bay OLFP flood**

The aspect of the catchment faces north with a series of valleys running in this direction with faces opening to the east and west (Figure 42). The average slope in the catchment is 5 to 10 degrees but some slopes are up to 40 degrees (Figure 43).

Figure 42 **Freemans Bay aspect**

Figure 43 **Freemans Bay slope**

Vegetation

Freemans Bay has two important parks. The first one is Western Park, one of the earliest parks built in Auckland in 1873. It was planted as an arboretum with a selection of mostly European tree species. The park is 8 ha, running in a north-south direction, and encompasses one of the major valleys in the catchment. The other park is Victoria Park, 12 ha, built on reclaimed seabed in 1905. This park was designed for a more active programme with sports fields and a large playground and kindergarten.

Pervious/impervious surfaces ratio

The Freemans Bay catchment covers an area of 244 ha, of which 72.7 percent is impervious surface (178 ha). The impervious surfaces are made up of buildings, roofs (64 ha), roads, driveways and footpaths (114 ha) (Figure 44). 27.3 percent (66 ha) is a pervious surface made up of park and domestic gardens (Figure 45). The result of this high degree of imperviousness is a large amount of contaminated stormwater runoff discharging into the harbour.

History of the site

From the mid 17th century, Ngāti Whatua were the dominant iwi in Tamaki. They settled on and around the great volcano/maunga of the Auckland isthmus. Waiatarua / Freemans Bay was used for fishing and shellfish gathering as evidenced by the alternative names for the bay, Wai Kototoa (the place where cockles are found) and Te Koranga (the scaffold or the drying racks where fish can be preserved by drying). The Treaty of

Figure 44 **Freemans Bay impervious surface**

Figure 45 **Freemans Bay pervious surface**

Waitangi, an agreement between Captain Hobson and Maori leaders was signed in 1840 at the Bay of Islands. Later that year, Āpihai Te Kawau, the Ngāti Whatua leader, gave Governor Hobson 3000 acres, including Waiatarua /Freemans Bay, as a gift. Over the next 150 years Ngāti Whatua gradually lost all their ancestors land in Tamaki until by the 1950 they were left with a small urupa in Okahu Bay (Stone, 2001).

Under European occupation, the Bay became an early industrial area for saw milling. Native trees were floated in log rafts from as far afield as the Coromandel to be sawn into timber. Workers were accommodated in fairly rudimentary dwellings close by the sawmills. The industrialisation of the Freemans Bay area continued in the 19th century with the construction of brickworks, shipyards and a foundry. The bay was also the location for municipal services, a morgue, a night soil dump and the council rubbish incinerator, built in 1905.

Wynyard Quarter

Land use

Wynyard Point (rebranded as Wynyard Quarter in the 1990s) is the northern point of the Freemans Bay reclamation, situated between the Westhaven Marina and the Viaduct Harbour. Wynyard Quarter was used for warehousing, the fishing industry and most importantly as an industrial fuel store. The fuel store or tank farm was a major feature of the site. Over the last 20 years Wynyard Point has been undergoing a slow redevelopment from an industrial wharf and tank farm to a new consumerist waterfront development.

Site analysis

The Wynyard Quarter is a flat site, built of reclaimed material, 2 m above sea level (Figure 46). The site is made up of two parts. The first is a square-shaped 450 x 580 m block, oriented north-south and bounded by Fanshawe Street to the south and Hamer Street and the Westhaven Marina to the west. Most of the yacht, black boat hauls out and maintenance facilities are located on this edge. Halsley Street runs along the eastern edge with the old America's Cup bases and the Viaduct Basin development. Jellicoe Street defines the northern edge with the new North Wharf development.

The second part of the reclamation veers towards the northeast in a rough 480 x 170 m parallelogram. The site is bounded by an extension of Hamer Street to the west side and Brigham Street on the east running parallel with the Wynyard Wharf. This site is where most of the existing bulk storage tanks are still located. As a reclaimed site, the topography is mostly flat with some small local declinations.

Vegetation

Wynyard Quarter has no vegetation; indeed after a number of years of use as an industrial tank farm with many spillages, the ground is highly contaminated, making it impossible even for the growth of adventurous vegetation.

Figure 46 **Wynyard Quarter contour**

Hydrological pattern

Wynyard Quarter is a highly impervious industrial site. The overland flow path network (Figure 47) is confined to the periphery of the site with a series of overland flow paths from the interior to the littoral. The paths form a series of 12 sub-catchments.

Aspect/slope

Since the site is for all intent and purposes flat, the aspect and slope of the site is negligible (Figures 48 and 49).

Figure 47 **Wynyard Quarter OLFP**

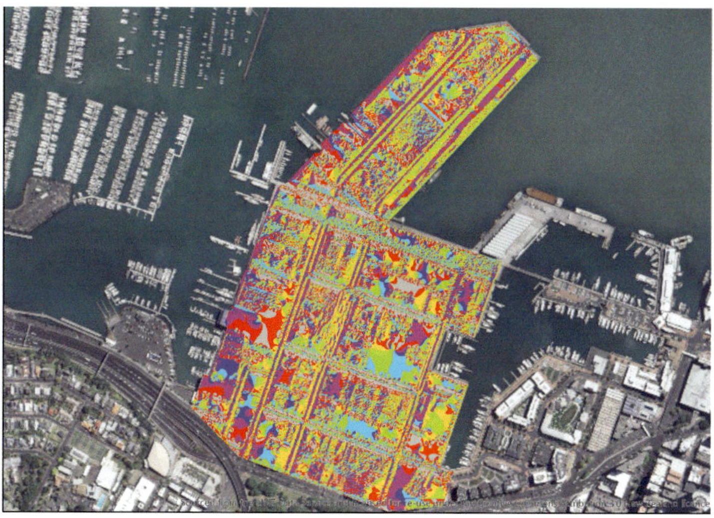

Figure 48 **Wynyard Quarter aspect**

Figure 49 **Wynyard Quarter slope**

Figure 50 **Wynyard Quarter impervious surface**

Impervious/pervious surface ratio

The site is highly impervious. The catchment area is 38.8 ha, all the roads and building occupy 35 ha (Figure 50), leaving 3.8 ha of the site as pervious surface (Figure 51), a ratio of 90 percent impervious to 10 percent pervious. The result for the two-year runoff discharge flow rate from the existing WQ site is .82 m/sec; the storage volume to treat this is 4412.29 m^3.

Figure 51 **Wynyard Quarter pervious surface**

Wynyard Quarter master plan

Like many industrial waterfront's zones around the world, the Wynyard Quarter is being transformed into a consumerist wonderland powered by conventional real estate imperatives.

Peter Walker, an American landscape architect, was commissioned in 2003 to develop a master plan to develop Wynyard Point. The master plan encompasses approx. 38.8 ha. Of this area, 5.8 ha is to remain as a base for existing marine-related industries, mainly on the Westhaven marina side. The main body of the site is a development zone of approximately 21 ha. The conceptual basis of the master plan was the establishment of two axes that connect the Wynyard Quarter to the city.

The first axis is north-south from the existing Victoria Park to the northern tip of the Wynyard Quarter. The second axis runs west-east, from the Wynyard Quarter to the CBD via Quay Street. This plan was modified in 2007 by a local Auckland architectural practice, Architectus (2007).

The master plan for the new development breaks the site into three zones. The first is the Point Precinct at the northern end of the site. Four large blocks are proposed to occupy the southeast part of this site with three smaller ones on Wynyard Wharf. The ground floor of these blocks is devoted to entertainment/retail with commercial use on the first floor. Residential use is proposed for the upper storeys of the larger blocks; commercial use is proposed for the upper storeys of the smaller blocks. The resulting build-out is entertainment and retail, 17,010 m^2 commercial, 22,230 m^2 and residential 18,6400 m^2.

The middle zone, the Jellicoe Precinct, has a more complex social and building programme that relates to its role in the master plan as part of an urban axis linking the Wynyard Quarter to the CBD. Jellicoe Street is lined with two rows of buildings: the northern blocks are repurposed warehouses; for the southern side of the road, blocks of up to 52 m high are proposed. The GFA of this zone is 22,566m^2 devoted to entertainment and retail, 49,105 $m^{2'}$ for commercial and 13,8386 m^2 for residential.

The Central Precinct is the largest zone from Jellicoe Street to Fanshawe Street; a third of this site is owned by another party, Viaduct Holding Group. This zone is devoted to mostly residential and commercial use with a small percentage of retail use. The proposed build-out is 37,125 m^2 for entertainment/retail, 515,250 m^2 for commercial and 138,386 m^2 for residential.

The total GFA for the Wynyard Quarter is residential/retail 76,701 m^2, commercial 586,585 m^2 and residential 453,661m^2, giving a total build-out of 1,115,947 m^2.

Public space

The two main areas of public space in the waterfront development of the Wynyard Quarter master plan are the North Wharf, located at the end of the west-east axis linking the site to the city, and Point Park, at the northern end of the north-south axis, linking the site to Victoria Park. The North Wharf zone is configured as two east-west thoroughfares; the northern one is a pedestrian promenade running alongside the harbour. The southern one, Jellicoe Street, sandwiches an active zone of restaurants, bars and public spaces. The other major public space is Point Park. This is a proposed large park located at the tip of the Wynyard Quarter; work is due to start on this project in 2025 when the current tank storage tank leases expire.

Stormwater remediation

The Wynyard Quarter master plan proposes the construction of over 1,000,000 square metres of new buildings, infrastructure and associated public space. The result will be a densely urbanised zone with a high degree of impervious surface producing a large amount of contaminated runoff.

To remediate this problem, a structural stormwater treatment strategy has been adopted. Two specific techniques have been introduced to ameliorate the production of contaminated runoff. The first is a linear rain garden running between the streets and the pedestrian footpath. These vegetated strips have been intensively planted with a selection of coastal native species, from ground covers to shrubs to trees. The road gradient is constructed to direct runoff into the rain gardens through a constructed filtration layer before being discharged into a conventional stormwater drainage system. However, the rain garden runoff in Jellicoe Street undergoes a further cleaning through a constructed wetland that is part of the North Wharf public space programme. The treated runoff is then discharged into Westhaven Marina.

Impervious/pervious surfaces ratio

The impervious/pervious surface ratio is 69 percent impervious to 31 percent pervious. The result for the two-year runoff discharge flow rate from the completed Wynyard Quarter development will be .72 m/sec; the storage volume to treat this is

3,903.36 m^3. The decrease in runoff is mainly due to the design of the Point Park, a large area of pervious surface that will help absorb some of the stormwater runoff.

Social issues

At the time of writing, Auckland is undergoing a housing crisis, or to be more accurate, a housing shortage crisis. Reasons for this crisis are varied and complex, but involve a combination of speculative pressures from the macroeconomic setting since the Great Financial Crisis that include quantitative easing and very low interest rates which have led to the availability of easy credit. Combined with a sustained growth in immigrants to New Zealand and especially Auckland, these factors have led both to a shortage in housing and perhaps more importantly a shortage of affordable housing. The Wynyard Quarter development has deliberately included a high proportion of residential space as part of the master planning. However, the provision of social housing, or affordable housing, in the residential section has been deliberately elided. The residential component of the housing has been consciously aimed at the top end of the market.

Wynyard Quarter: environmental problems

There are a number of specific environmental problems in the Wynyard Quarter sub-catchment. These are pluvial flooding, marine flooding caused by sea-level rise, contaminated stormwater discharge into Waitamata Harbour from Freemans Bay and a lack of local biodiversity.

Stormwater

The central Daldy Street trunk pipe is the main conduit for the Freemans Bay catchment. The pipe is 2,750 mm in diameter and runs from Pakenham Street to Jellicoe Street as part of the Daldy Street linear park construction. This pipe terminates at the Daldy Street sea wall, discharging contaminated stormwater from the Freemans Bay catchment into Waitamata Harbour.

In particular, organic and inorganic contaminates are being discharged into the harbour from the North Wharf outfall. Sewage contamination is one part of the problem. 'The worst of the 6 Combined Sewage Overflows discharging to the Daldy Street trunk storm water pipe are at Scotland Street, spilling 49 times with a total of 30,000m3 per year, and Wellington Street, spilling 38 times with a total of 40,000m3 per year. This issue remains a significant risk to public health and perception' (Smedley, 2011). Inorganic contaminants are made up mainly of a number of heavy metals from road runoff and are also being discharged untreated into Waitamata Harbour.

With the continuing construction of the Wynyard Quarter master plan, a new underground stormwater network has been installed. There are three local stormwater pipes that travel in a north-south direction linking to Beaumont, Daldy and Halsey streets. This piped network discharges local stormwater into the Viaduct Basin and at the end of Hamer Street.

Pluvial flooding

Wynyard Quarter sees regular flooding in two- to five-year storm events due to a combination of highly impervious surfaces and a low gradient. Typically this flooding takes the form of surface and road flooding. However, heavy flooding in a 50-year storm event has led to the inundation of ground floor premises (Smedley, 2011).

There are seven areas in the Wynyard Quarter that are marked as being flood-prone. The first is bounded by Beaumont Street, Gaunt Street, Fanshawe Street and Hawley Street. The second is between Halsley Street and the Lighter Basin. There is a smaller area in the middle of Pakenham Street. The largest flooding zone occupies the whole of Jellicoe Street and the North Wharf area. The last zone is along the Brigham Street axis.

Flooding has occurred along streets mainly to the southern end of the development: Fanshawe Street, Gaunt Street, Daldy Street, Halsley Street and isolated flooding in upper Jellicoe Street and at the intersection of Hasley and Jellicoe streets. With increasing and more violent storm events as a consequence of climate change, more pluvial flooding is expected to occur (Figure 52).

Coastal flooding

Because of the low-lying and mostly level topography, the Wynyard Quarter is vulnerable to coastal flooding. The dark blue zone shows which areas of WQ will be affected by a 2 m rise in sea level. These areas are relatively negligible and confined to the coastal margin. However, if the sea level rises by 3 m (as shown by the light blue colour), then most of the Wynyard Quarter will be underwater (Figure 53).

Figure 52 **Wynyard Quarter flooding**

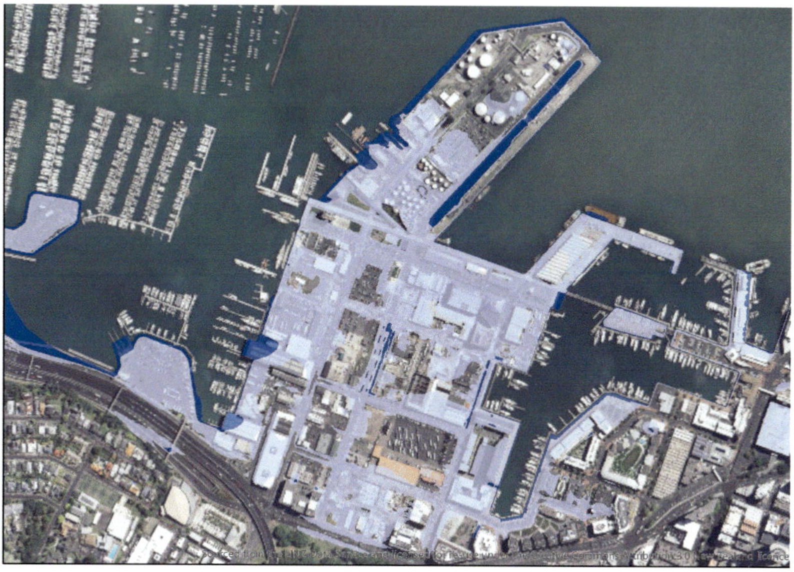

Figure 53 **Wynyard Quarter sea-level rise**

Summary and discussion

There are three major environmental problems in the Wynyard Quarter sub-catchment: contaminated stormwater from the larger Freemans Bay catchment, pluvial flooding from the Wynyard Quarter sub-catchment and the threat of coastal flooding. These three conditions will be intensified by an increase in the size and frequency of storm events due to climate change (Intergovernmental Panel on Climate Change, 2014). While localised Wynyard Quarter stormwater remediation services have been installed, they are not large enough to treat all the contaminated water from the Freemans Bay catchment. In a similar way, as the intervals between storm events decrease due to climate change, pluvial and coastal flooding will increase. The densely gridded, impervious Wynyard Quarter master plan does not provide an opportunity to provide any of the remediation measures necessary to address these issues.

Wynyard Quarter: environmental remediation: design process

Stormwater

There is a considerable amount of untreated stormwater discharging into Waitamata Harbour from the Daldy Street outfall. A number of different options to treat, remediate and retain the stormwater production have been canvassed. One option to remediate the stormwater from Freemans Bay is to place a large remediation wetland at the end of the Freemans Bay discharge outlet. Using TP10 (ARC, 2003), the size of wetland can be calculated to treat the runoff from Freemans Bay. During a two-year storm event, the impervious surfaces of the Freemans Bay catchment produce

132,940 m^3 of water runoff in 24 hours. For a wetland to effectively treat the 41,636 m^3 of water runoff from the Freemans Bay catchment during a two-year storm event, the wetland must be approximately 5.4 ha.

Pluvial flooding

The pattern of the overland flow paths and the associated flood zones in the Wynyard Quarter is revealed in the GIS mapping of the area. One of the recommended techniques for the control of pluvial flooding is to allow for the conveyance of flooding to the nearest discharge point, a stream or harbour. When the successful discharge of flooding is not possible, for example, when high tides would prevent the successful discharge of flooding into a harbour, then the provision of a detention zone where floodwater can be retained is recommended.

The mapping of OLFP clearly demonstrates the path of flooding to the nearest discharge point. Utilising these paths as conveyance channels (Maksimović et al., 2009) ensures the speedy clearing of urban flooding. Correctly sizing the conveyance channels can be accomplished through increasing the width of the OLFP. This can be achieved by using a specific mapping technique, buffering and using ArcGIS; in this case study the OLFP is buffered by a 10 m margin.

The flooding zone of the Wynyard Quarter was found via the AC Geomaps site. By amalgamating both the overland flow paths and the flood zones and buffering these combined areas using the GIS function, a zone is created which can be used to both relieve and ameliorate pluvial flooding. The zone could be used to both detain flooding or, in dire circumstances, the zone could be used to hasten flooding through the protected overland flow paths to discharge into the nearest receiving environment (Figure 54).

Figure 54 **Wynyard Quarter OLFP flood buffer**

Coastal flooding

The predicted coastal flooding map of the Wynyard Quarter indicated a 2 m sea-level rise and a 3 m sea-level rise. The 2 m rise was confined to the littoral and does not seem particularly calamitous, but planning to accommodate this rise would seem desirable.

For the Wynyard Quarter waterfront, the chosen remediation strategy is developing a soft-engineered littoral zone that restores the indigenous Auckland coastal edge (Morton, 2004). The typical wharf/water edge, an abrupt transition from the wharf infrastructure to water, can be reformed by establishing a new topography, a gradual shelving from land to sea. The coastal edge can then be reconstructed as a native littoral zone using indigenous plants. The new littoral will have a series of distinct ecological zones based on the transition from salty to brackish to stormwater. Along this hydrological gradient are planted the appropriate plant ecotones. This soft-engineering approach represents an opportunity to restore Auckland's rare salt meadow habitat. To demarcate the zones, the ArcGIS buffer function can be used to form a 30 m buffer zone (Figure 55).

The altered topography has the effect of lessening the effect of storm surges and allowing for flooding on the coastal edge (New York State Department of Environmental Conservation, 2014).

These remediation measures will have the least spatial impact on the proposed master plan; however, the new coastal zone does alter the urban nature of the typical waterfront promenade. This is usually a hard, urban space (West 8, 2015). This remediation measure is a new kind of public space, a restored native littoral condition that helps to build resilience to sea-level rise.

Figure 55 **Wynyard Quarter coastal buffer**

Biodiversity

A fourth environmental problem is also present. The biodiversity rating for Wynyard Quarter is very low (Myers, 2014). The benefits of improving biodiversity within the city are numerous.

An important technique for encouraging an increase of biodiversity is the planting of indigenous species to ensure the ecological health of the planting, the creation of an ecopatch. An ecopatch is where the planting forms a distinctive 'island', a separate, distinct and ecological homogenous zone. The health of this zone is dependent on two factors: the number of species and the size of the planted areas. The viability of the zone is then dependent on the distinction between these islands. New Zealand scientists Meurk and Hall (2006) suggest that the appropriate size for a viable ecopatch is 6.5 ha. The health of the ecopatch also depends on the distance to the next ecopatch. Meurk and Hall suggest that a maximum distance is 5 km.

Summary

Four environmental problems, stormwater contamination discharge, pluvial flooding, sea-level rise and a lack of biodiversity, were identified. The remediation solutions proposed were a 5.4 ha remediation wetland, a network of flood retention zones and flood conveyance paths, a 30 m wide littoral sacrificial zone, and a 6.5 ha ecopatch. Using ArcGIS mapping, the dimensions of the four interventions can be articulated. This mapping clearly shows the serious spatial implication of enacting any of the remediation measures necessary to address the critical environmental problems.

Combining the coastal buffer and the pluvial flooding detention and the conveyance network can be shown (Figure 56). Amalgamating these remediation measures demonstrates the development of a new kind of public space on the Wynyard Quarter waterfront (Figure 57). This new green network embodies two important Te Aranga principles, Taiao and Mauri Tu. The original vegetation of Waiatarua is

Figure 56 **Wynyard Quarter flood OLFP coast**

Figure 57 **Wynyard Quarter park**

used to carry out a range of tasks, to help buffer the coastal edge, retard and detain overland flooding, clean contaminated stormwater and help build biodiversity. Through these processes the environmental health of the new urban quarter is rebuilt, rediscovering the mauri of the site. The wellbeing of the new citizens is increased through an engagement with the natural world.

Wynyard Point case study

Introduction

This investigation starts with an in-depth design inquiry into the implication of using Wynyard Point as the location of the remediation wetland. The design deepens the investigation by using the design process developed in the previous section to build up a new master plan for the WP site.

Site analysis

Wynyard Point is at the northern end of the Wynyard Quarter (Figure 58). At present it is occupied by an industrial tank farm. The tanks are still leased by a number of petrochemical companies (the leases don't expire until 2025). The size of Wynyard Point Park is approximately 8 ha. The proposed real estate development area in the Wynyard Point Zone is four blocks confined to the southeast corner of the site, at the intersection of North Wharf and Brigham Street. The rest of the site is zoned for public space and an 'iconic' public building at the northern end of the point. Each block site has an accumulative footprint of 60 x 60 m^2 (Architectus, 2007), giving a total site footprint of 14,400 m^2. The FAR is 3.61, giving a GFA of 12,996 m^2. The maximum building height is eight floors, giving a typical floor area of 1,624.5m^2. There are four sites, giving a total GFA of 51,984 m^2.

Figure 58 **Wynyard Quarter WP site**

Wynyard Point: environmental remediation: design process

Hydrology

The first step in the analysis is a specific mapping of the hydrological condition of Wynyard Point including a more precise map of the OLFP network. This network demonstrates how surface water is flowing on the site and especially where it discharges into the harbour (Figure 59).

Stormwater

To remediate the stormwater water from the Freemans Bay catchment will require a wetland of 5.4 ha. Rather than constructing a single wetland, the option of constructing a series of smaller, interconnected remediation ponds is explored. To size and locate the network of stormwater-cleaning wetlands, the OLFP network was increased in size through a buffering operation and amalgamated. In this way, the space required for the Freemans Bay stormwater treatment operation was accommodated while connecting to the existing hydrological network.

The OLFP network was buffered by 25 m and amalgamated with the map of the original network (Figure 60). This forms a total area of 51706.177 m^2. (The area required for the treatment of stormwater from the catchment is 5.4 ha.)

Figure 59 **Wynyard Point OLFP**

Figure 60 **Wynyard Point OLFP 25 m buffered**

However, rather than one large single wetland, the buffered overland flow path network gives a more nuanced design outcome. The result is a hydrological pattern that would become a collection of both large and small wetland remediation ponds directly connected to the littoral (seven ponds along the Westhaven Marina side with six ponds on the Wynyard Bay side). These ponds would be fed by the existing Freemans Bay outlet, currently located at the junction of North Wharf and Daldy Street.

Coastal flooding

To accommodate the expected sea-level rise and the associated storm surges, a 30 m buffer around the edge of Wynyard Point is set aside to protect the interior (see Figure 61). The combination of the two environmental remediation measures, the storm surge buffer and the stormwater remediation wetlands, with the overland flow paths form an integrated green infrastructure (Figure 62).

Urban design

The 'leftover' areas, the zones that are not directly used for stormwater remediation and the littoral zone, are set aside for the building programme (Figure 63).

To accommodate the necessary building programme on the 'leftover space', a tower block model is explored. The blocks are positioned on the 'leftover' building zones clear of the coastal protection buffer (Figure 64). The building programme is speculatively divided into four blocks. The total Wynyard Point GFA of 51,984 m^2 is divided into the four footprints; these blocks are then extruded to accommodate the total GFA, giving four 11-storey-high blocks (Figures 65, 66 and 67).

Figure 61 **Wynyard Point coastal buffer**

Figure 62 **Wynyard Point coast OLFP**

Figure 63 **Wynyard Point leftover space**

Figure 64 **Wynyard Point towers**

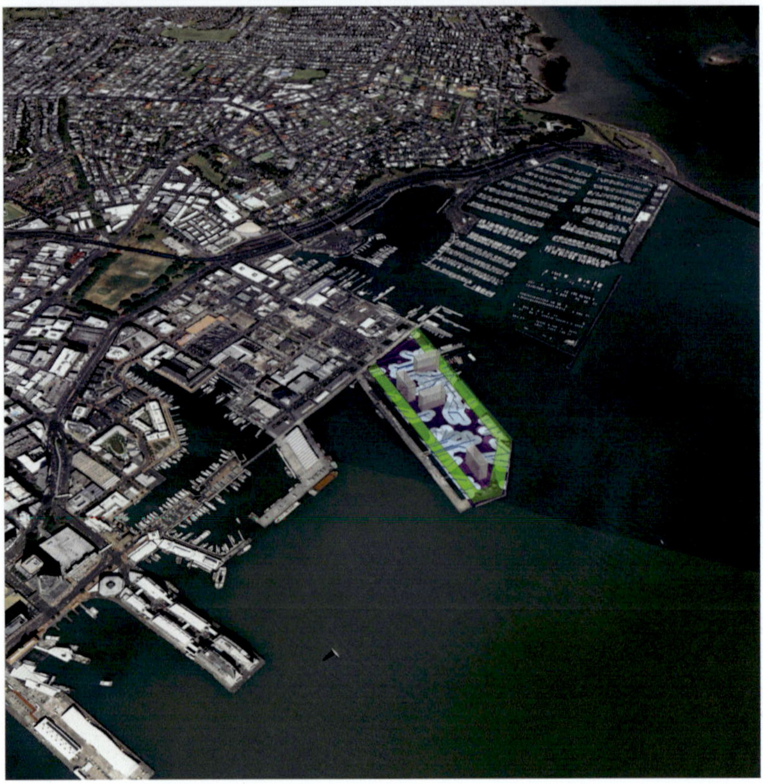

Figure 65 **Wynyard Point towers 1**

Figure 66 **Wynyard Point towers 2**

Figure 67 **Wynyard Point towers 3**

Wynyard Point: environmental implications of the design process

The maps represent the testing of a design process based on accommodating the necessary remediation regime to ensure the environmental resilience of the Wynyard Point waterfront development, while at the same time satisfying the necessary real estate return. The following comments are a series of speculative possibilities for the different designated zones.

Using the new remediation wetlands to treat the stormwater from the Freemans Bay catchment would require an extension of the existing Daldy Street trunk line. The stormwater treatment zone is generated by a buffer and the amalgamated OLFP network. The result is a series of smaller wetlands that discharge the cleaned stormwater directly into the harbour. The wetlands would be excavated to below the mean tide level where applicable. The local high tide rises to 1.5 m above Mean High Sea Level so each wetland can be excavated to a lowest level of 2.0 m. Some of the wetlands discharge points are excavated to below the high tide level to contribute to the coastal ecological restoration of the 30 m buffer zone. This zone would be characterised by a mix of topographic modification and the restoration of indigenous coastal species. Approximately 60 percent of the excavated zone area would be a stormwater wetland. The stormwater wetland ground level is at 2.5 m, with 1 m deep pools excavated to 2.0 m. This is high enough to prevent the tide flowing into the wetlands, though with sea-level rise these environments may become brackish rather than fresh water.

Wynyard Quarter: environmental implications of the Wynyard Point case study investigation

The Wynyard Point design study demonstrates a new design process. The GIS mapping and analysis of the remediation measures has scale and a dimensional reality, with a clear relationship between water, land and building. However, the mapping lacks a material reality. The remediation zones are areas in which certain activities could take place: a building, a wetland, a coastal buffer. The Wynyard Point study is a demonstration of a design process which is not fixed like a conventional master plan. The process is elastic enough to be able to be modified while retaining the primacy of the environmental remediation regimes, their size and position intact. The next stage would be a more conventional design process where the material consequences of the wetlands planting, the building shapes and specific infrastructure requirements could be explored.

The outcome of the design process clearly demonstrates two of the Te Aranga principles: Mauri Tu and Taiao. Through a holistic understanding of the urban catchment, damage to wai water, whenua land and ngāhere vegetation can be clearly understood. The remediation of these problems is not just confined to an isolated singular device but part of an integrated system. This system is linked back to the original environment through the return of indigenous flora. The biodiversity of this vegetation is nurtured through a series of connected remediatory regimes.

Xinglong

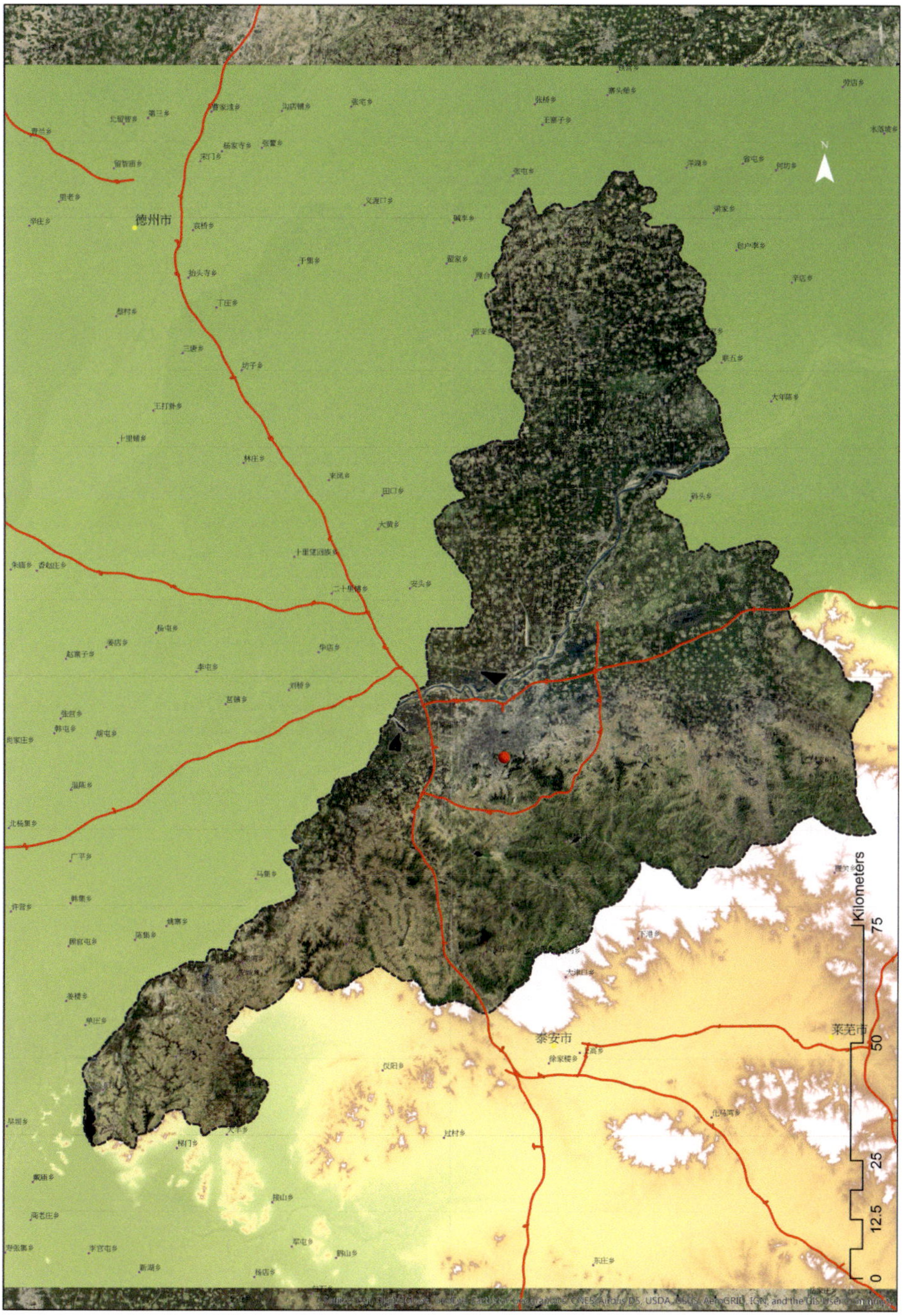

Figure 68 **Jinan aerial**

Introduction

Jinan is the capital of Shandong province. Jinan is a sub-provincial city in the PRC. The size of the Jinan region is 8,177.21 km^2.

Jinan site analysis

Jinan City is located in Northern Shandong province (Figure 68). It is in a transition zone between the Taishan Mountain foothills and the Huang He River plain. The terrain of the city can be divided into three zones: an alluvial plain zone to the north, a piedmont zone in the middle and a mountain range zone to the south. (The total area of Jinan city is 81.77.21 km^2; about 40 percent of the city is located on the alluvial plain while the rest, 60 percent, is in the foothills of the Taishan range [Figure 69].)

Hydrology

Jinan has a semi-humid continental climate with four well-defined seasons. The rainy season is in summer; rainfall in Jinan is more than in other cities in northern China. Due to the particular topography, Jinan is surrounded by hills in three directions, and hot air flows accumulate within the city. This causes high temperatures and humidity in summer.

The major permanent rivers in Jinan are the Huang He, the Xiaoqing River and the Tuhai River. Major seasonal rivers include the Jinyangchuan and the Jinxiuchuan in the mountains. There are four major catchments (Figure 70).

Jinan lies on a Karst aquifer. Water flows from the southern mountains into an underground system. When blocked by an impervious diorite layer, the underground water comes to the surface as springs in the city and surrounding regions. This phenomenon has given rise to the city's sobriquet, the Spring City. The four main groups of springs are the Baotu, Heihu, Wulong and Zhenzhu.

To ensure a constant urban water supply and maintain the flow of the springs, Jinan has closed many of the groundwater wells and uses surface water as a water resource. Large reservoirs have been built to the south, west and north of the city to ensure fresh water supply all year round.

According to the climatic average data from 1951 to 2015, the average rainfall days in Jinan are 72.8 days. The annual average rainfall is 672.7 mm. The monthly average rainfall that is over 50 mm is from June to September. The maximum rainfall month is July (201.3 mm); the second is August (170.3 mm).

Aspect/slope

The topography of Jinan slopes from the south to the north, with an elevation difference of 260 m.

The aspect of the site is mostly northerly with a marked east-west orientation of the surrounding foothills (Figure 71). The slope of the site is mostly from 0 to 5 degrees except for the foothills (Figure 72).

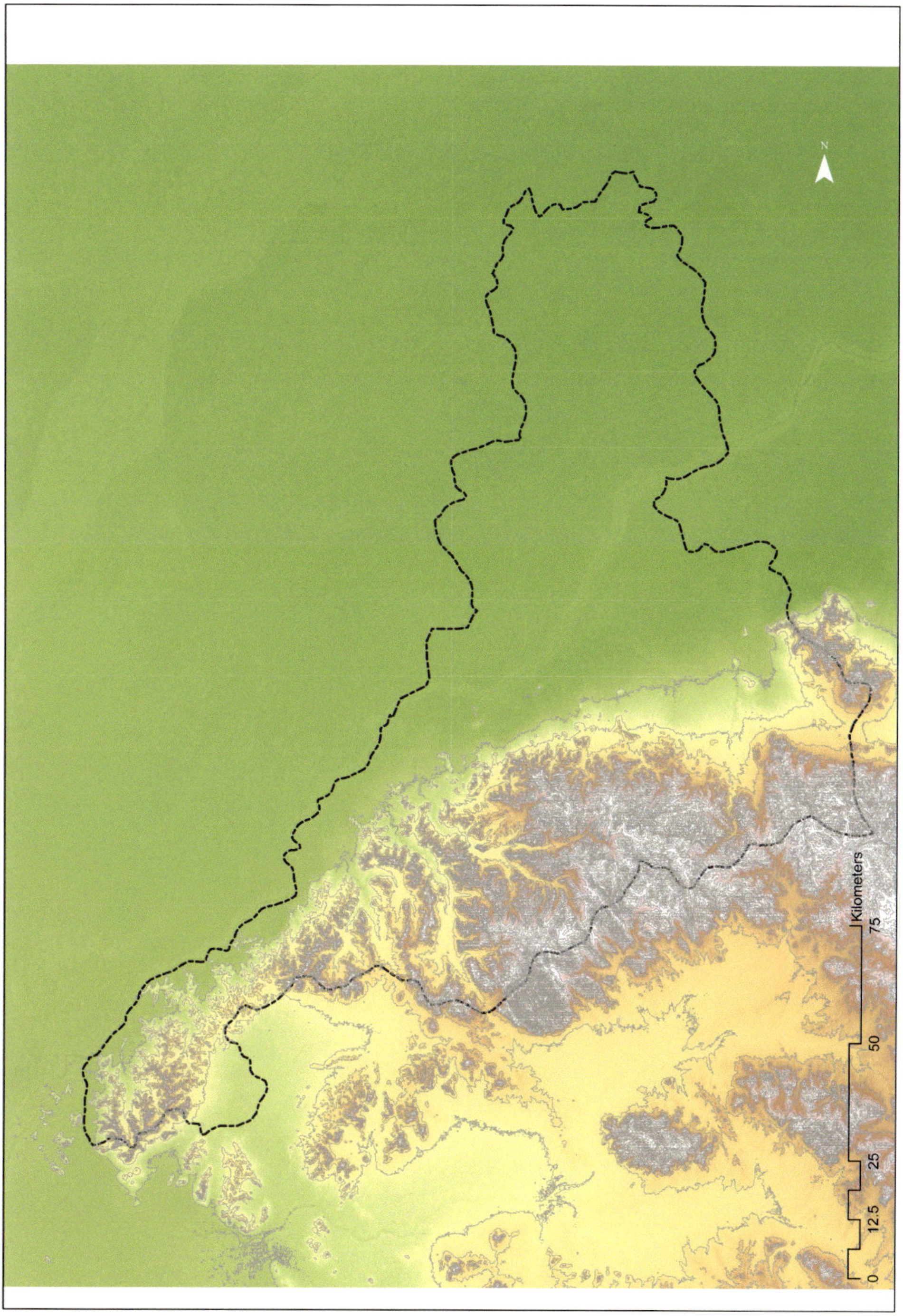

Figure 69 **Jinan contours**

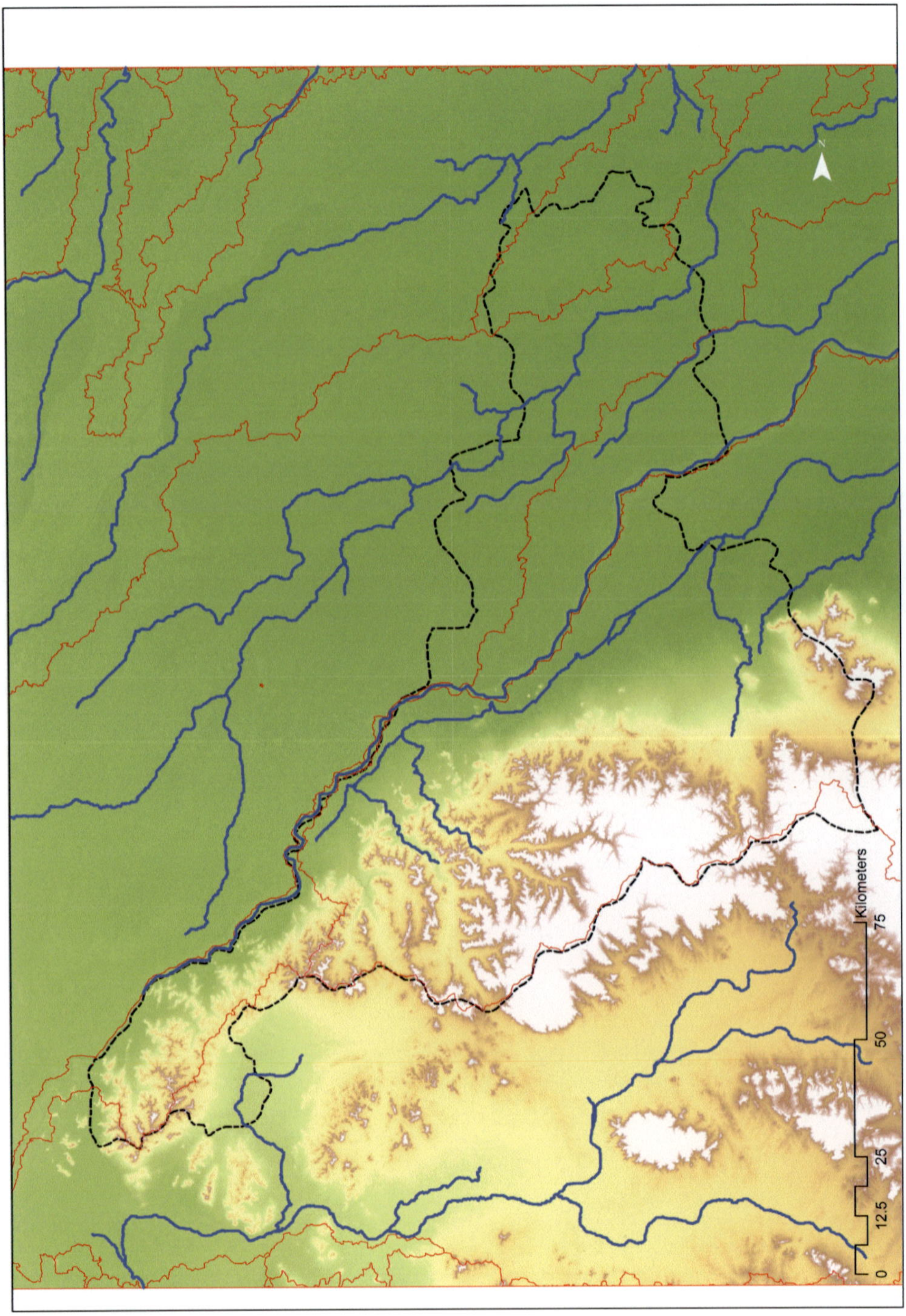

Figure 70 **Jinan overland flow**

Figure 71 **Jinan aspect**

Figure 72 **Jinan slope**

Vegetation

The native vegetation in the mountainous areas of the province is very sparse due to many centuries of deforestation. The main species in the lower slopes of the mountains are a typical mixture of deciduous and evergreen species such as oak, maple, ash, chestnut and elm, with thuja and platycladus and cotinus species.

History

Early settlement in Jinan can be dated back 4,000 years. Jinan became the capital of the region in the Han dynasty (206 BCE–220 CE), and grew to become an important cultural and economic centre in northern China. In 1994 Jinan was upgraded to a sub-provincial city, and contains ten county-level divisions and 146 township divisions (Yu, Lei, & Dihua, 2008).

Land/use urban pattern

The urban pattern of Jinan City follows the urban typology of many cities in the Huang He delta. The old city was surrounded by an artificial moat on three sides with the Daming, a large lake, located at the northern side of the city. This water boundary acted as a flood control mechanism from flooding from both the Huang He and the Taishan mountains.

In 1904 Jinan was opened to foreign trade through the building of the Jiaoji (Jinan to Qingdao) railway and Jinpu (Tianjin to Pukou) railway. A commercial zone was constructed to the west of the existing city around the new railway station. A model city was formed with a post office, town hall and churches. The new city colony was laid out in a grid pattern with a small central park; most of the buildings were warehouses for goods from the surrounding countryside or manufacturing workshops. Goods, both raw and processed, were quickly and efficiently exported to the rest of the world through Qingdao. In the late 20th century Jinan saw a massive urban expansion with the construction of a new administrative and business city to the east. Expansion of the city also took place in the west and south. Unfortunately, the southern expansion into the foothills of the Taishan ranges has led to both environmental degradation of the original limestone foothills and the compromising of the indigenous drainage networks.

Jinan City: environmental problems

With the rapid urbanisation of Jinan City, the underlying hydrological pattern of the cities drainage system has been forgotten. The rapid building programme has both covered pervious surfaces and piped and channelled existing stream networks. These measures have often been undertaken in a contingent and piecemeal fashion without understanding the consequences for the city. The significance of this work has had tragic consequences for the city with a number of serious floods.

Jinan City: environmental remediation: Sponge City

Urban flooding is not an isolated event but has become a growing phenomenon in many Chinese cities. With the construction of new cites, existing hydrological control systems like lakes and moats have been forgotten (Yu et al., 2008).

This has led to the Sponge City initiative (Xia et al., 2017), promoted by the Chinese government to improve water absorbency and to avoid flooding in urban areas. In 2015, guidelines for the building of a Sponge City were issued by the State Council. The goal is to construct the city in a way that allows rainwater to be naturally stored, purified and absorbed. The target is to collect and utilize 70 per cent of the rainwater with the aims that 20 percent of urban areas in China achieve the goal in 2020 and 80 percent in 2030. Jinan was one of the 16 pilot cities chosen in 2015 to explore and demonstrate this new model of urban flood control.

Xinglong catchment

Xinglong catchment site analysis

The Xinglong catchment is located to the south of the old city of Jinan (Figure 73). The site is in the foothills of the Taishan Mountains and discharges into the Xiaoqing River and the Huang He. The catchment is dominated by one large valley that runs in a north-south direction between the western edge of the foothills, the Qianfoshancun, and an isolated foothill, Yingxiongshan (Figure 74). They are classified as scenic areas and nature reserves. The dominant vegetation is remnant native vegetation, a result of heavy deforestation. In contrast, the flat valley floor is heavily urbanised from recent urban development. Two large green zones can be also found in the valley, Quancheng Park and the Hanjiao hotel and garden complex; both are located between the two foothills.

Hydrological pattern

The main overland flow path for the catchment is located in the centre of the valley (Figure 75). Two subsidiary flow paths are located on the west side of the Yingxiongshan, and the other is on the eastern side of the Qianfoshancun. The three flow paths meet on the southern side of the old city in Quancheng Square. There are two major sub-catchments. The hills within the catchment retain their natural hydrological pattern; however, the original river and streams of the valley catchment have been heavily modified by the construction of an urban stormwater infrastructure, a combination of piped infrastructure and channelisation. The two streams in the central part of the catchment have been canalised and flow adjacent to the Yuhan Road and the Shungeng Road before disappearing into the underground piped system as Wenhua West Road.

Figure 73 **Xinglong aerial**

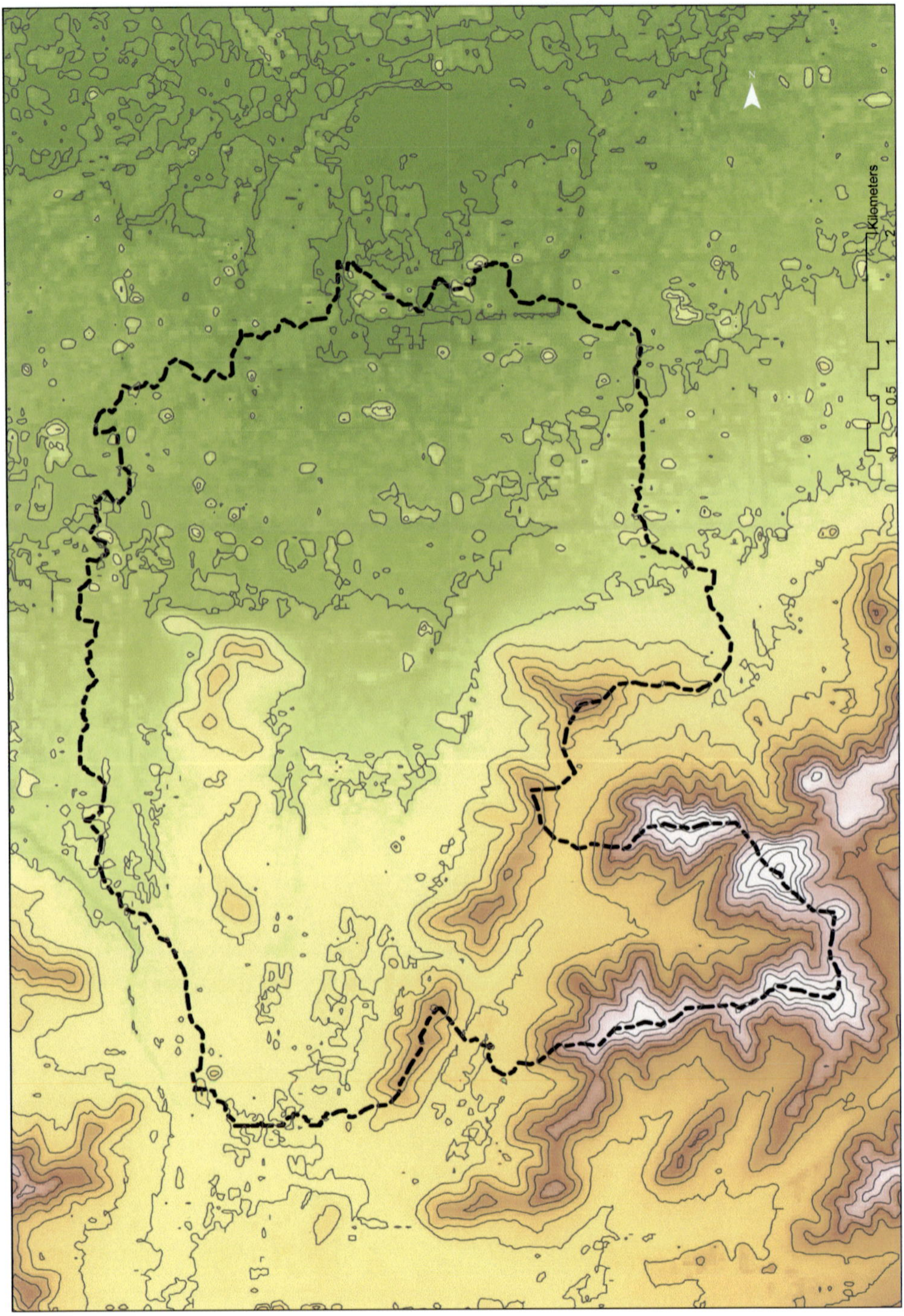

Figure 74 **Xinglong contours**

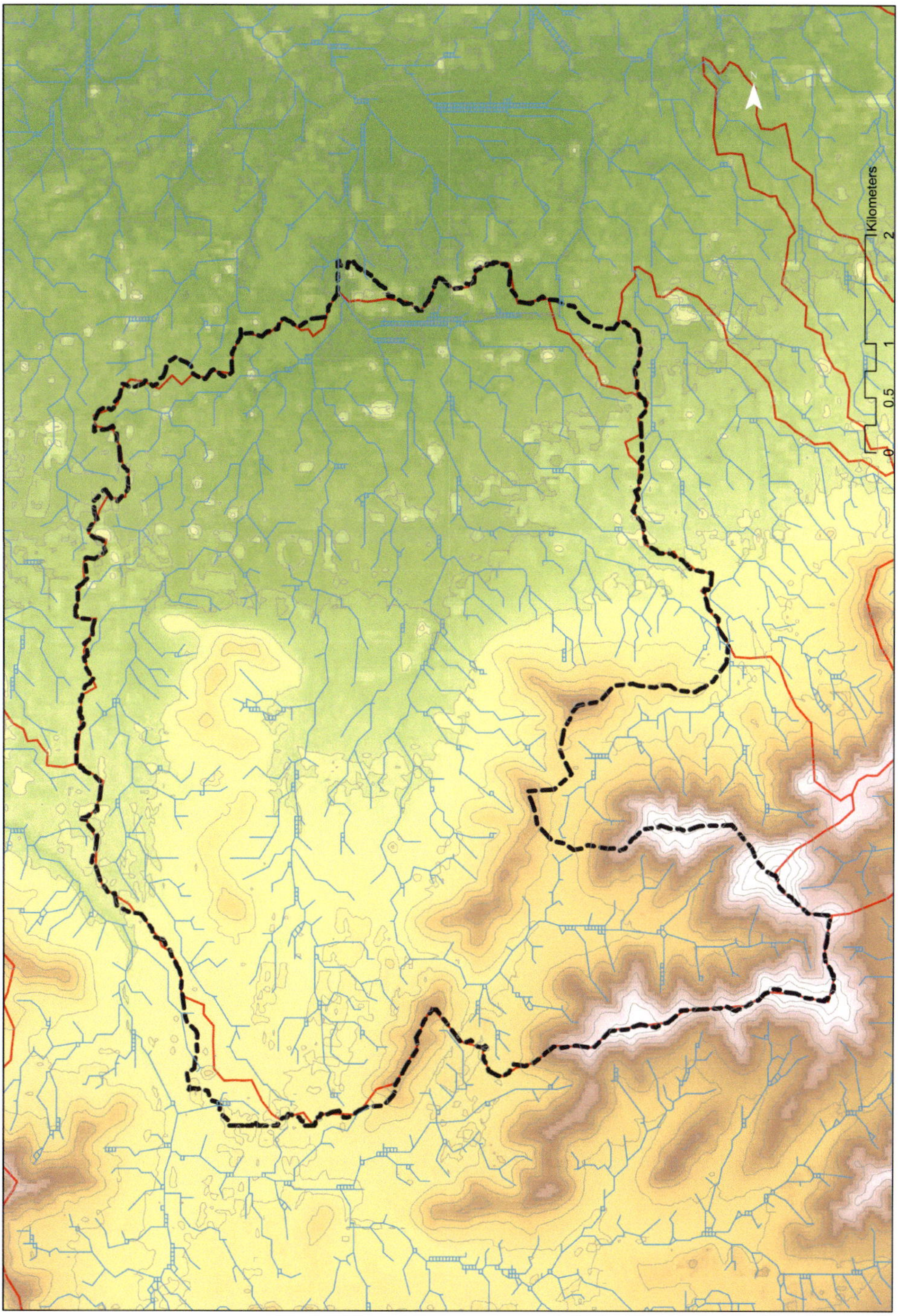

Figure 75 **Xinglong overland flow**

Aspect/slope

The aspect of the site is shown in Figure 76. The slope of the site is from 0 to 5 degrees (Figure 77).

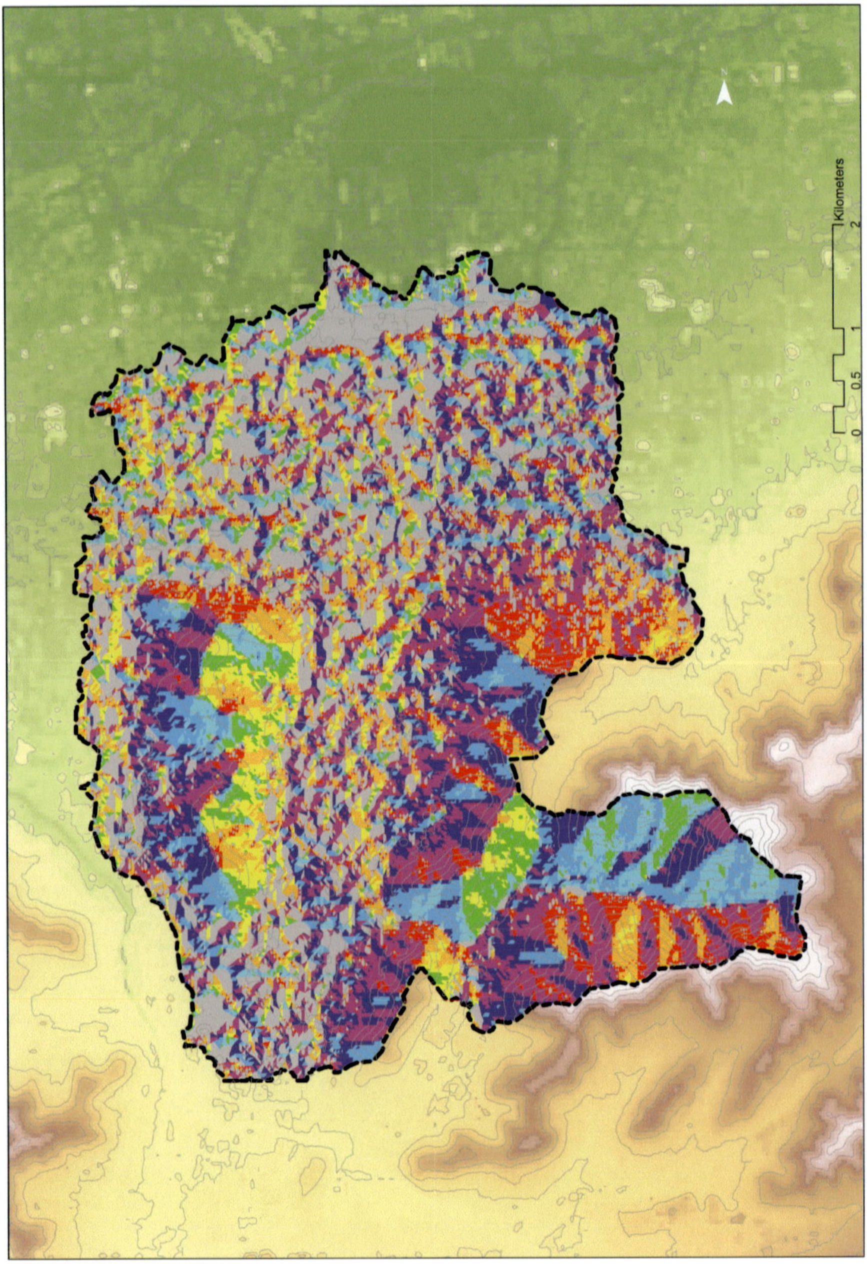

Figure 76 **Xinglong aspect**

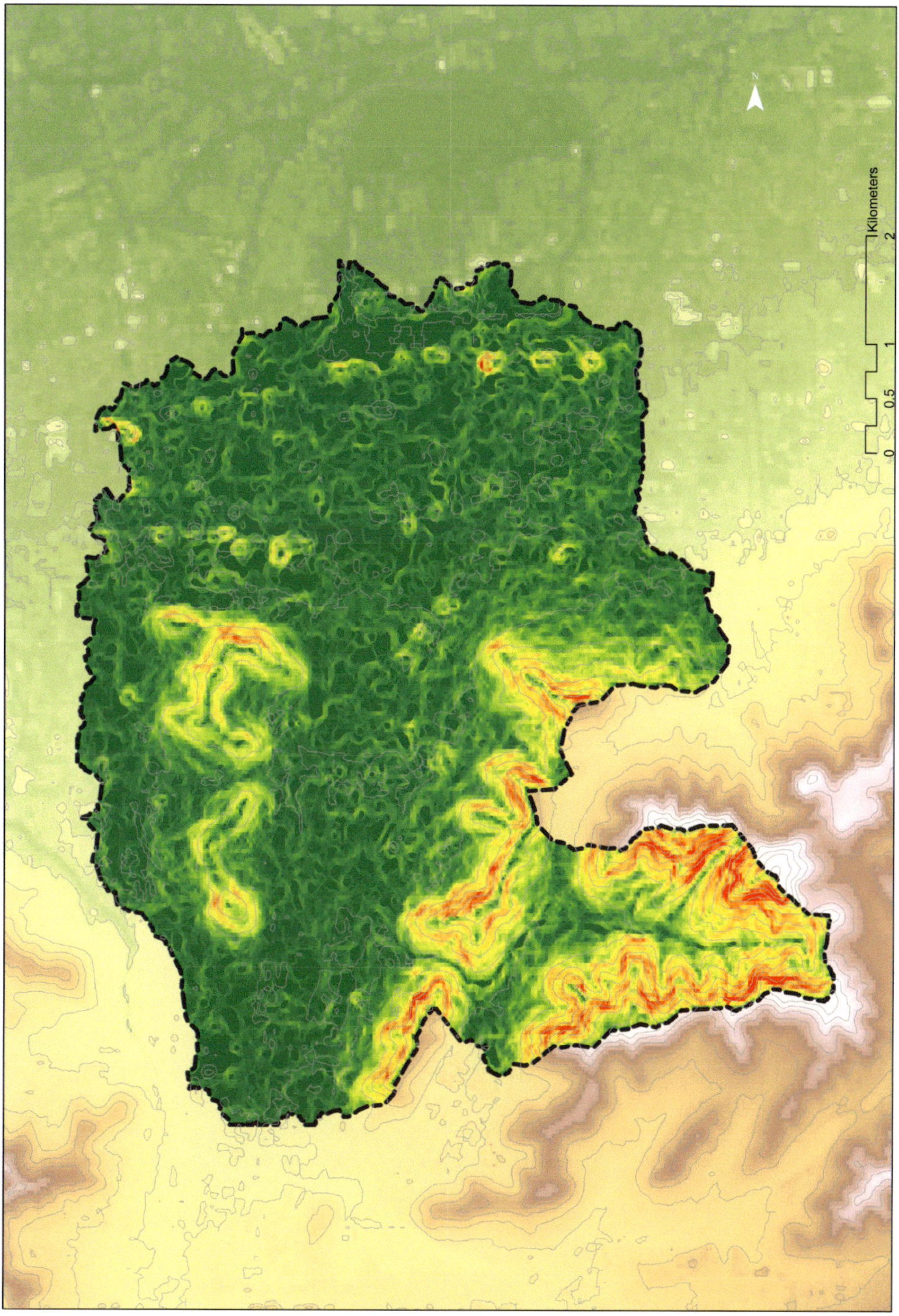

Figure 77 **Xinglong slope**

Land use

The total land area of the catchment is 3,663 ha. The dominant land use is for residential apartments. Business and commercial buildings are located mainly along Jingshi Road and Yuhan Road, two arterial roads across the catchment. Due to its mountainous character, the Xinglong catchment contains more green spaces than other parts of urban Jinan.

Pervious/impervious surface

The Jinan catchment covers an area of 3,663 ha. The existing city catchment has 69 percent impervious surface (2,517.80 ha) (Figure 78). Thirty-one percent of the existing city catchment is pervious surfaces (1,145.07 ha) (Figure 79). The higher than normal amount of pervious surface is a result of the surrounding hills being included in the catchment.

Using the Rational Method, the two-year runoff discharge flow rate (m^3/s) will be 974,427.1951 m^3/hr.

Xinglong catchment: environmental problems

On 18 July 2007, 180 mm of rain fell within three hours, causing a flash flood. The main economic damage was the flooding of Quancheng Square and the underground Yinzua Shopping Centre.

The reason for this damage was the location of Quancheng Square at the end of the Xinglong catchment. Due to the large number of impervious surfaces, buildings and roads, runoff within the 36 km^2 catchment accumulated in a very short time, causing a flood at the discharge point of the catchment.

The area south of Quancheng Square was chosen as one of the first pilot projects for the Sponge City initiative. The project plan divided the area into six sub-areas, and proposed a number of stormwater control goals and criteria. The stormwater control methods include the construction of water tanks to detain stormwater, permeable paving to absorb stormwater and rain gardens and water ponds to both detain and clean stormwater.

However, the proposed study area of the Jinan South Sponge City pilot project is based on administrative boundaries of the urban site. This has led to an engineering-driven solution that addresses the city hydrological condition defined by a collection of discrete urban blocks. An urban catchment analysis reveals that the chosen study area is actually split between two catchments; thus runoff will spread beyond the study area boundary. This leads to a difficulty in assessing and managing the movement and accumulation of stormwater runoff within the study area. Any study area for flooding remediation should be based on a catchment analysis. Through GIS modelling, the catchment boundaries and the hydrological pattern, including overland flow paths, water flow and intensity, can all be modelled. This data can contribute solutions to the critical problem of flooding in Jinan.

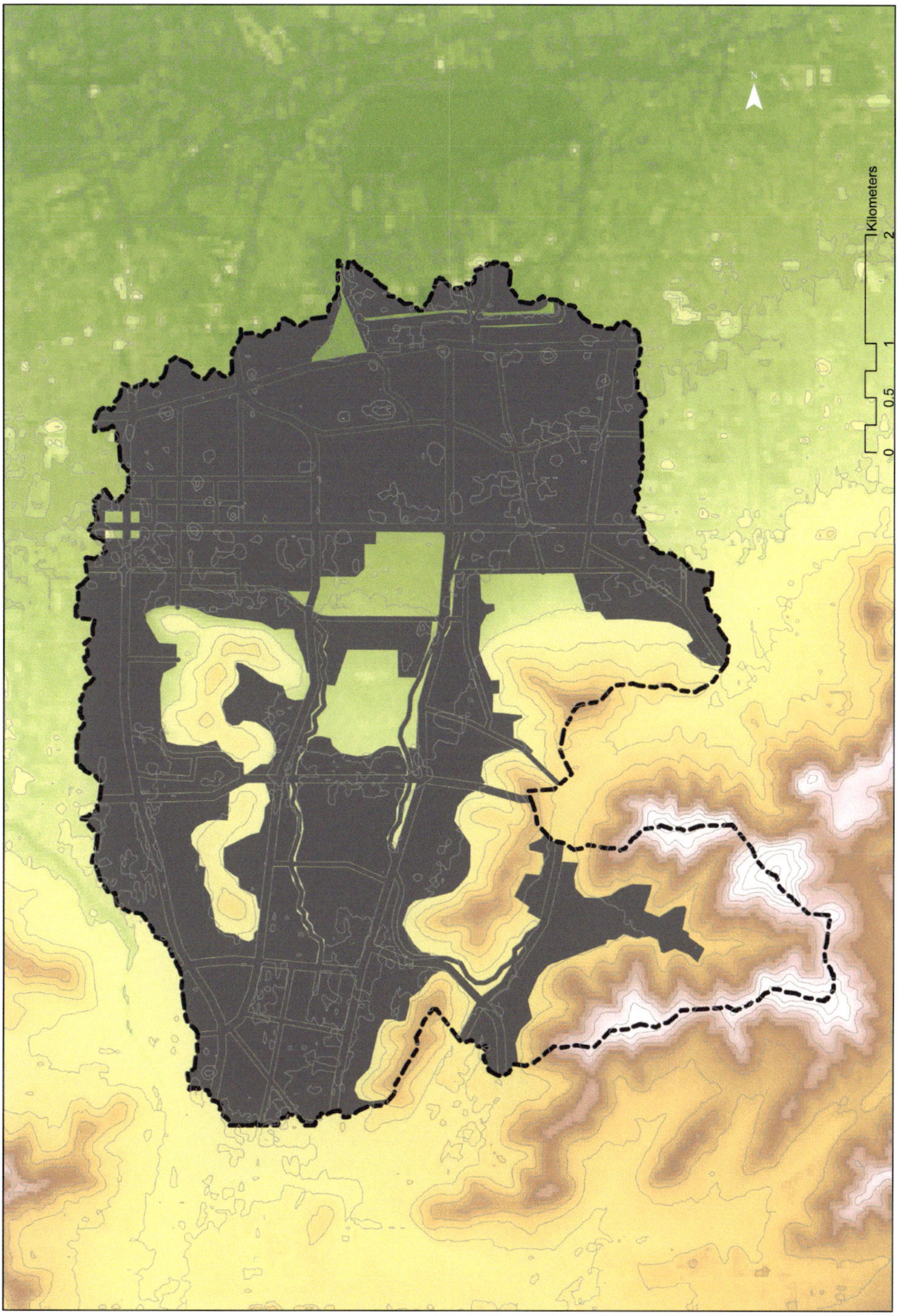

Figure 78 **Xinglong existing impermeable surface**

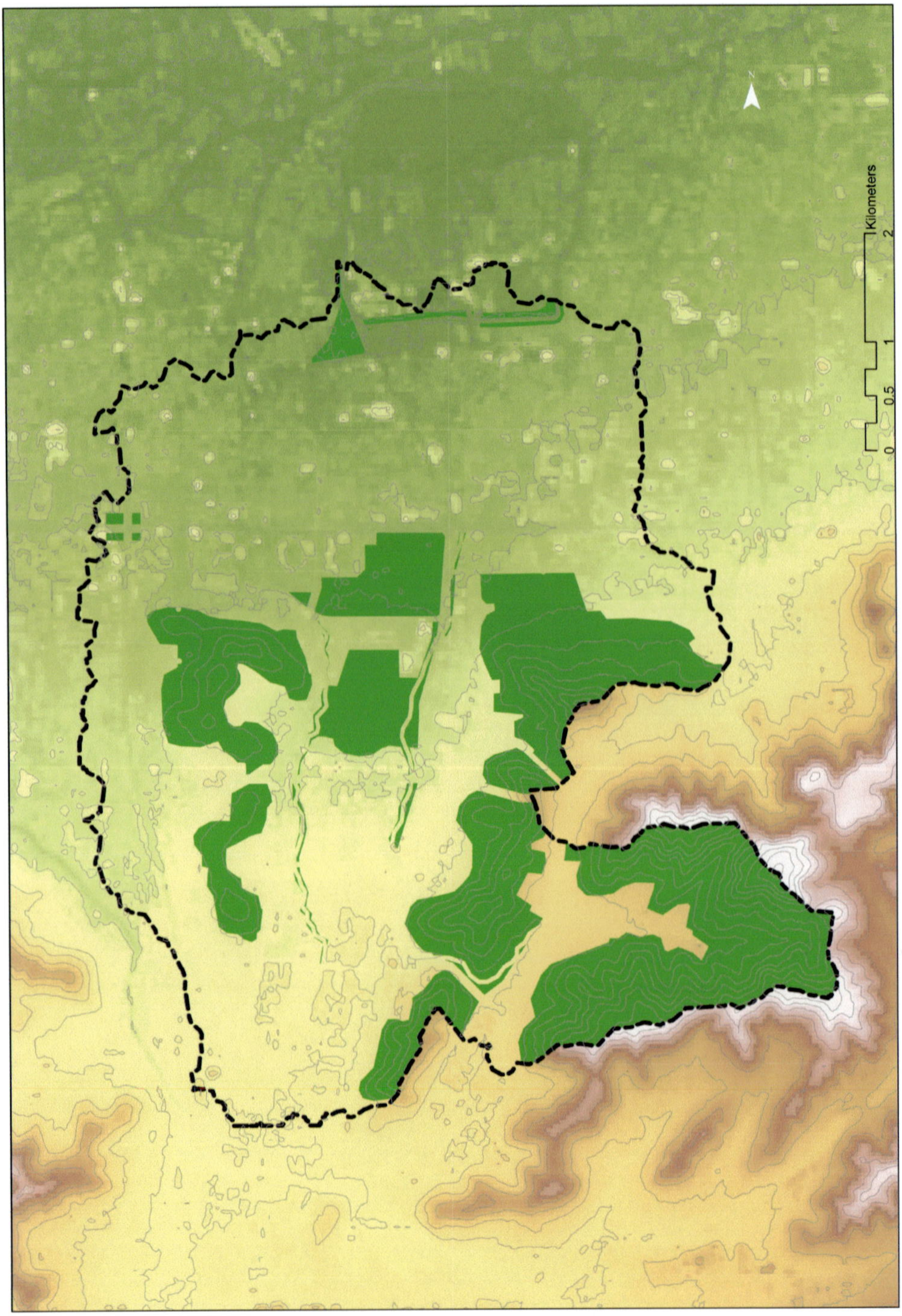

Figure 79 **Xinglong existing permeable surface**

Xinglong catchment: environmental remediation: design process

Hydrology

Increasing the amount of permeable surface within the existing urban catchment is an important way of reducing the build-up of urban runoff. Reducing the runoff at the head of the catchment would help in lessening the accumulation of flood water. However, increasing permeable surfaces within an existing city, with complex infrastructure systems and multiple ownership, is fraught with difficulties. However, by mapping the existing flow paths over the existing urban plan, city authorities and interested stakeholders can use these maps to guide and direct urban development in the future. This data could inform the future location of any new development that would be positioned away from an overland flow path.

Using GIS analysis, the contours, slope, aspect and underlying hydrological pattern of the two catchments can be analysed. The overland flow paths within the catchment can be mapped and classified to identify the main water courses within the site. A 30 to 100 m buffer zone alongside the stream edges should be protected as green spaces (Figure 80). To store stormwater, two large-scale retention ponds could be built along the stream buffer. Combining the existing green spaces and the buffered overland flow paths gives an indication of a new remediation network (Figure 81).

Pervious/impervious surface

The Xinglong catchment covers an area of 3,663 ha. The proposed city plan results in a decrease of impervious surface to 59 percent (2,167.68 ha) (Figure 82) and an increase of the permeable surfaces to 41 percent of the existing plan (1,495.19 ha) (Figure 83).

Using the Rational Method, the two-year runoff discharge flow rate (m^3/s) will be reduced to 911,611.1 m^3/hr.

Urban design

The stream and OLFP network could be used to form a new park system that could be revegetated with native plants. This park network would make a deep connection between the surrounding hills and city centre. The proposed new park system can also provide space for natural stormwater treatment devices, such as wetlands, rain gardens and swales. Construction of the new park system could run concurrent with the expected urban renewal of the area over the next 50 years (Figure 84).

Jinan City: environmental implications of the Xinglong catchment case study investigation

Retrofitting the existing urban catchment with a new park network will help to absorb rainwater and reduce the risk of urban flooding. Through the revegetation of existing stream systems and the construction of retention ponds, stormwater can be treated, stored and reused as a water resource. The land value around the new park system will increase, compensating for the lost building area and creating new investment opportunities to help in the construction of the park system.

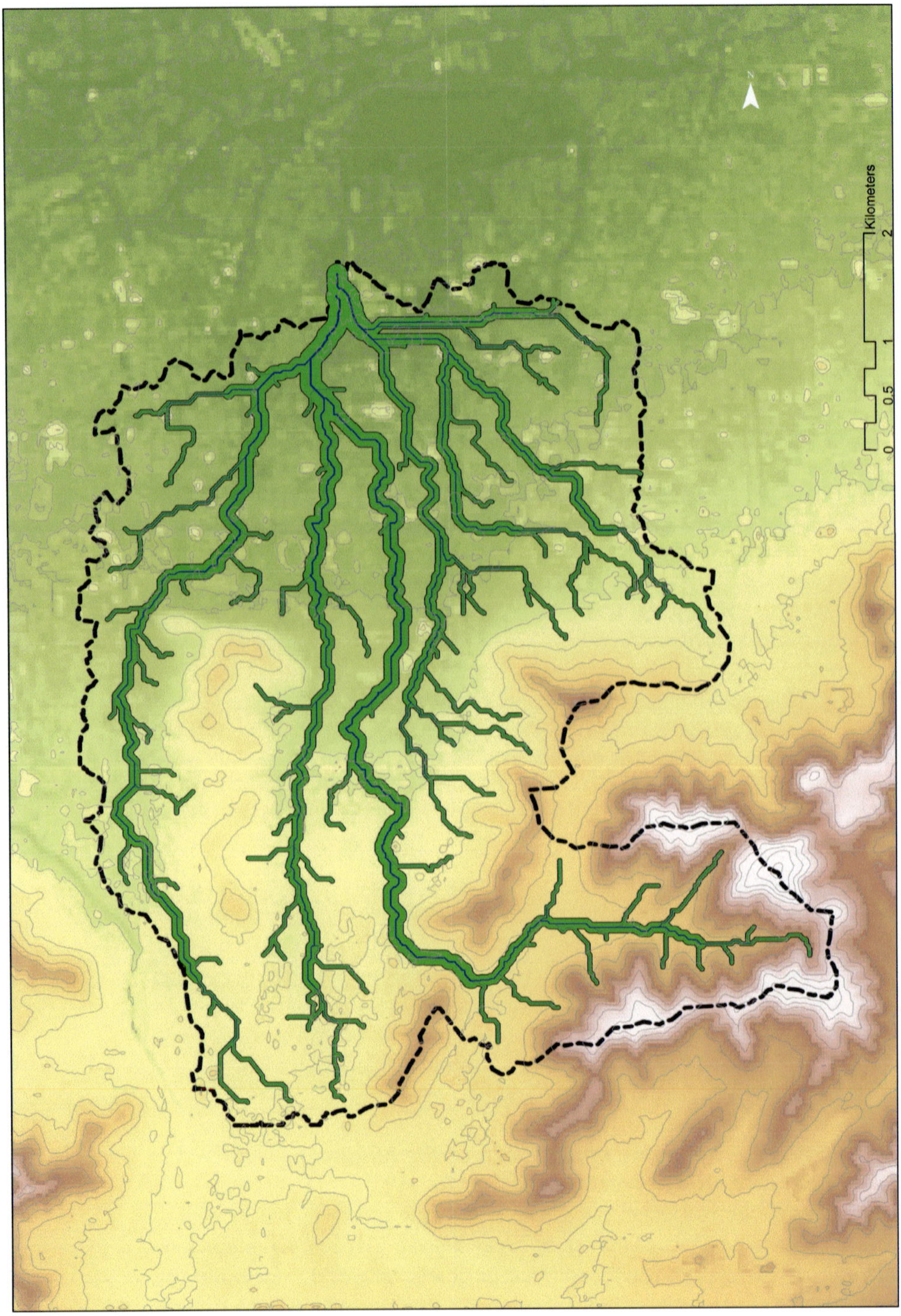

Figure 80 **Xinglong buffer OLFP**

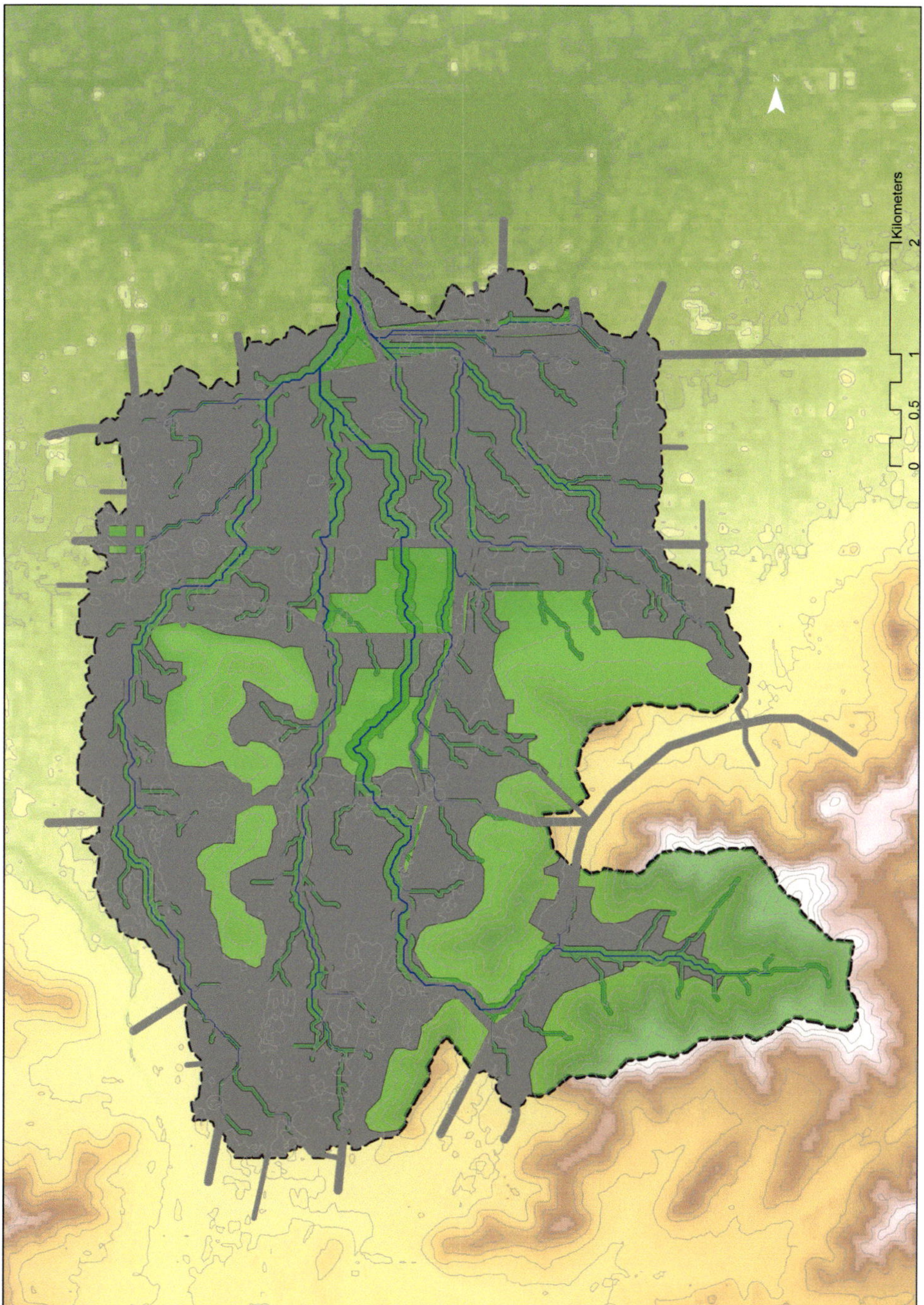

Figure 81 **Xinglong buffer existing green**

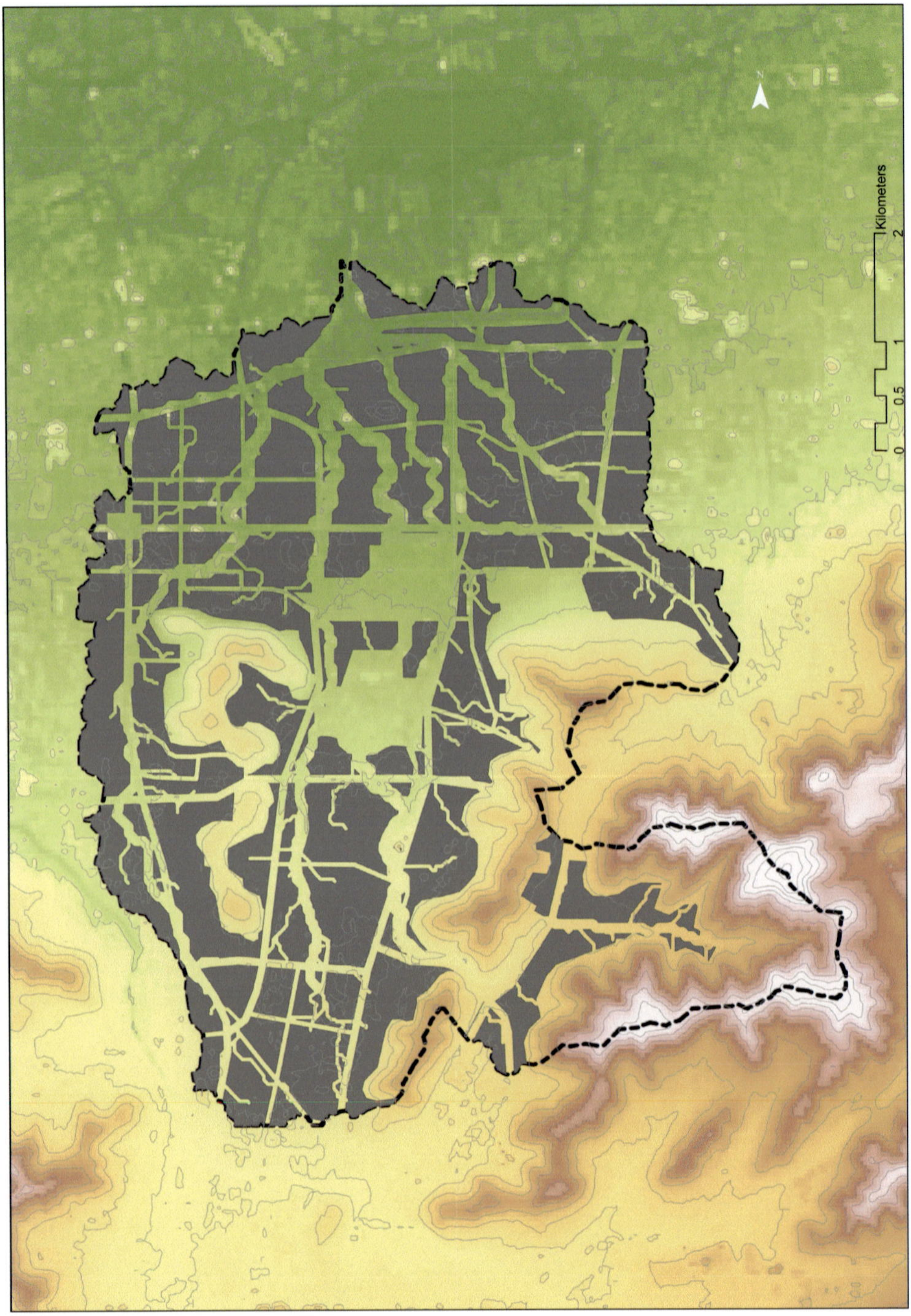

Figure 82 **Xinglong proposed impermeable surface**

Figure 83 **Xinglong proposed permeable surface**

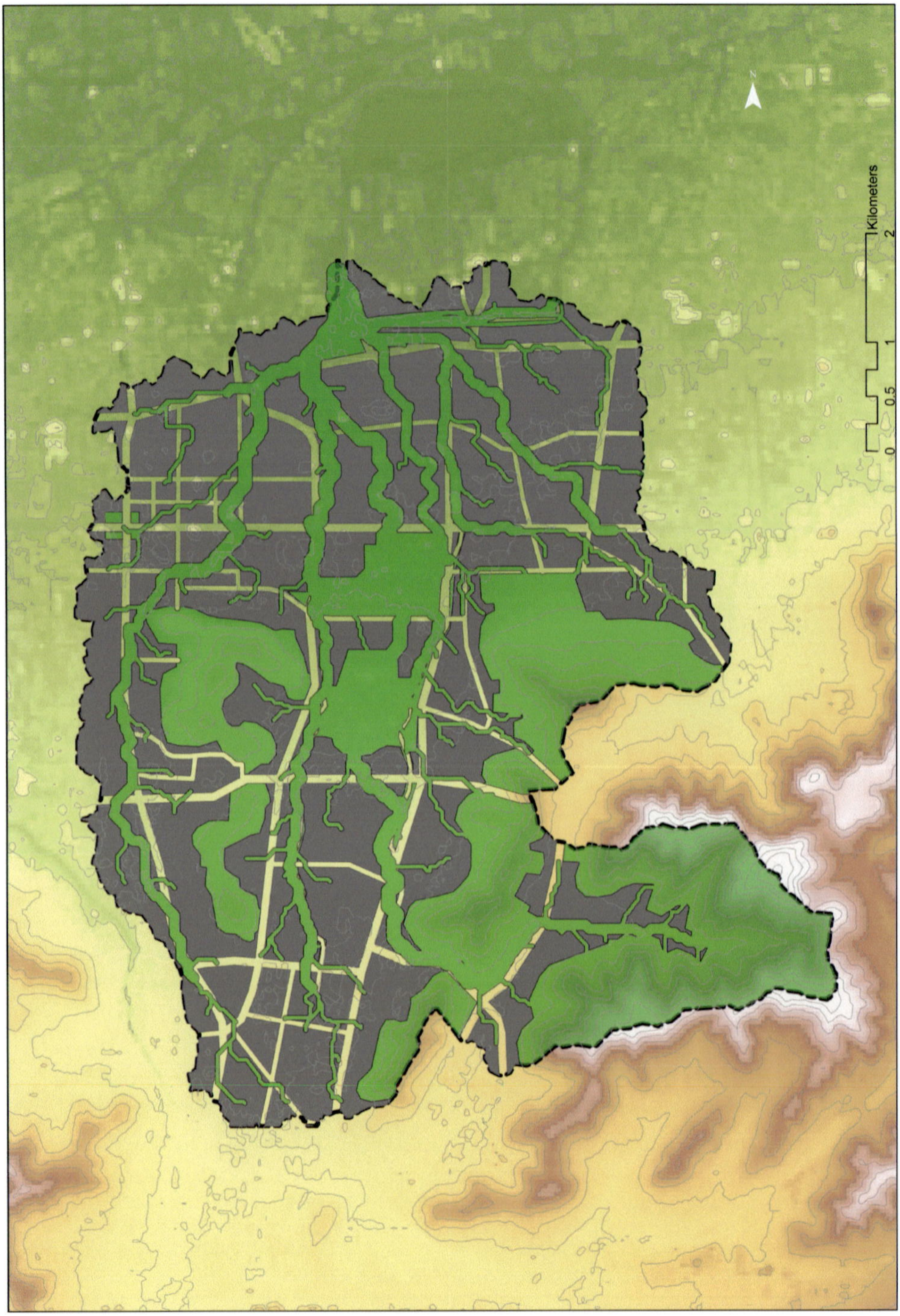

Figure 84 **Xinglong proposed plan**

Hazelwood Green

Introduction

Hazelwood Green is a new urban district planned for Pittsburgh, Pennsylvania, USA (ReMake Group, 2018), a typical riverfront brownfield redevelopment site.

Hazelwood Green catchment analysis

Hydrology

The site is at the discharge point of two catchments (Figure 85), the Greenwood catchment and the Hazelwood sub-catchment. The Hazelwood sub-catchment is approximately 146 ha. The Greenwood sub-catchment is considerably larger. The average annual rainfall in Pittsburgh is 936 mm. The average rainfall in October, the driest month, is 57 mm. The wettest month is June, with an average rainfall of 104.64 mm.

Aspect/slope

The aspect map (Figure 86) of the larger catchment shows clearly the topography of the hinterland of the site, as does the slope map (Figure 87).

Vegetation

The original vegetation of the site is classified as the Eastern Deciduous Forest Biome (Braun, 2010). Typical tree species include maple, sycamore, cottonwood, cherry, oak, ash, beech, chestnut, willow, elm and hickory, and the typical understory plants include rhododendron, buckthorn, sumac, witch hazel, honeysuckle, elderberry and dogwood. The present-day vegetation is grass with a number of weed species.

Hazelwood Green site analysis

The Hazelwood Green site is a long, narrow, 72 ha river terrace running roughly north-south. The site is bounded by the Monongahela River to the west and parallel railway track and roads, Irvine Street and Second Avenue, to the east. To the east of the road, the land rises to the suburb of Greenfield. To the southwest are the suburbs of Hazelwood and Glenwood, while directly to the south is the suburb of Scotch Bottom. To the north is the Pittsburgh Technology Center and the Hot Metal Bridge. The CSX spur railway runs along the riverfront before crossing the site roughly in the middle and then running parallel with the CSX mainline and Second Avenue. The site is a moderately flat river terrace, 6 to 12 m above the Monongahela River. The terrace has been heavily modified through site filling and reclamation.

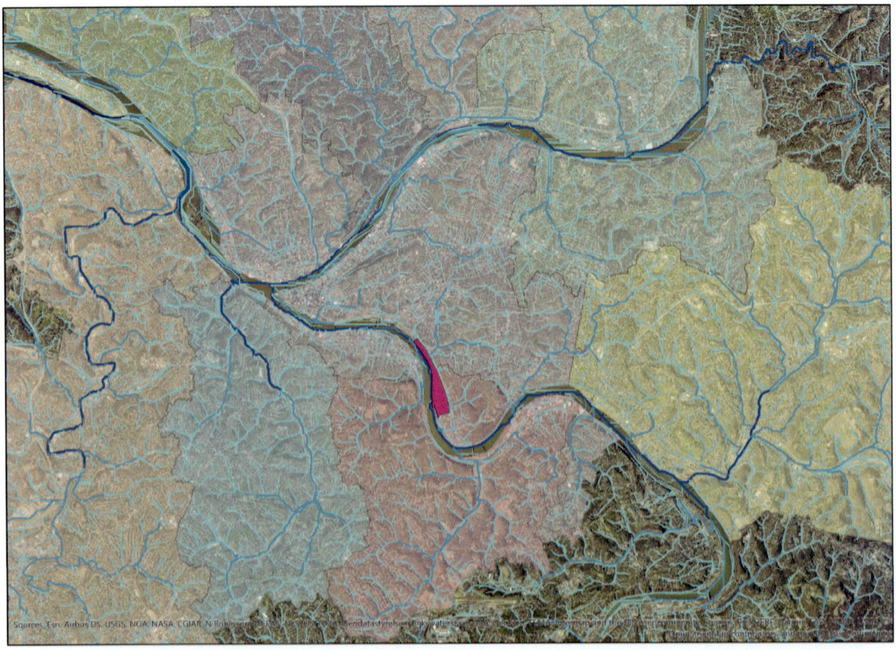

Figure 85 **Pittsburgh catchment**

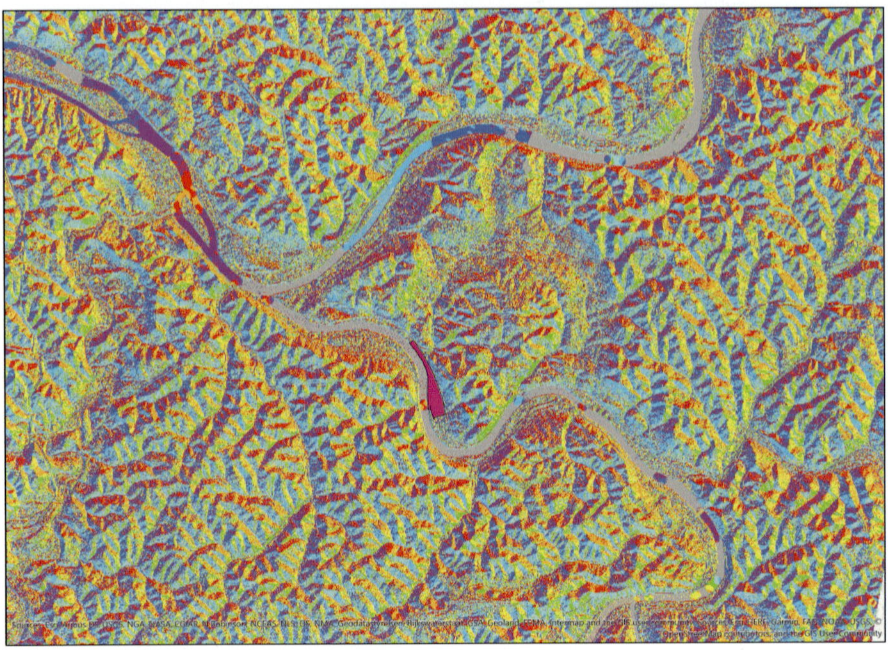

Figure 86 **Pittsburgh aspect**

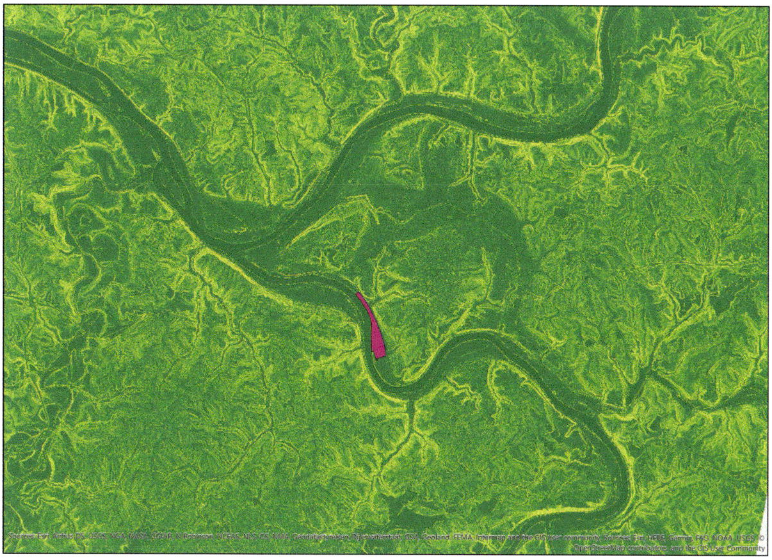

Figure 87 **Pittsburgh slope**

Figure 88 **Pittsburgh OLFP**

Hydrology

The two catchments drain into the Monongahela River. The OLFP for the Greenwood catchment crosses the site near the interchange of Irvine and Saline, while an OLFP for a sub-catchment of the Hazelwood catchment crosses the site near the intersection of Minden and Irving streets (Figure 88).

The site forms an internal sub-catchment with a bisecting OLFP leading to the Monongahela River in the centre of the site.

River flooding

The Monongahela River floods the site along the edge, with the worse effects at the northern end (Figure 89). The combined river flooding and overland flow path clearly demarcates the site (Figure 90).

Figure 89 **Hazelwood Green river flooding**

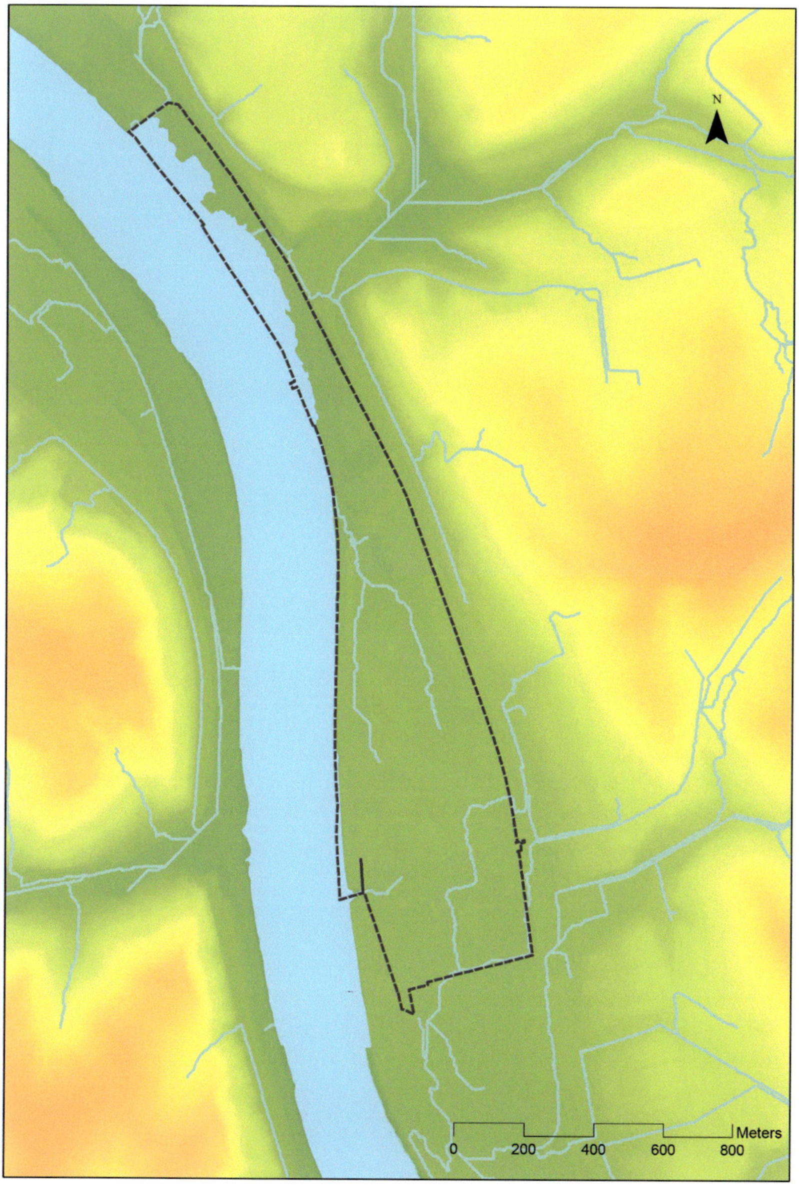

Figure 90 **Hazelwood Green OLFP**

Aspect and slope

The aspect of Hazelwood Green is mostly westerly. The slope of the majority of the site is flat (0 to 5 degrees); however, alongside the Monongahela River the slope increases from 5 to 16 degrees (Figures 91 and 92).

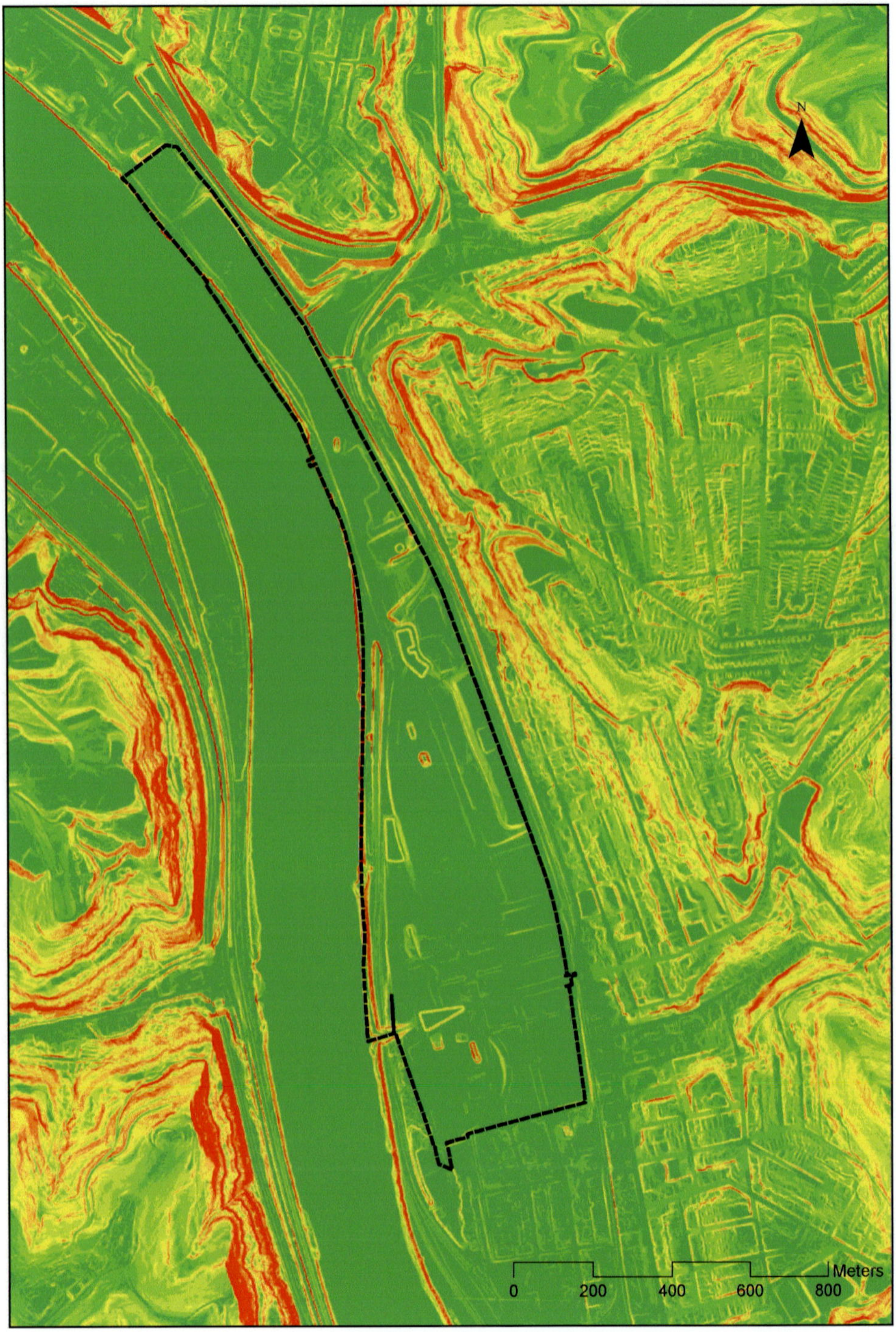

Figure 91 **Hazelwood Green aspect**

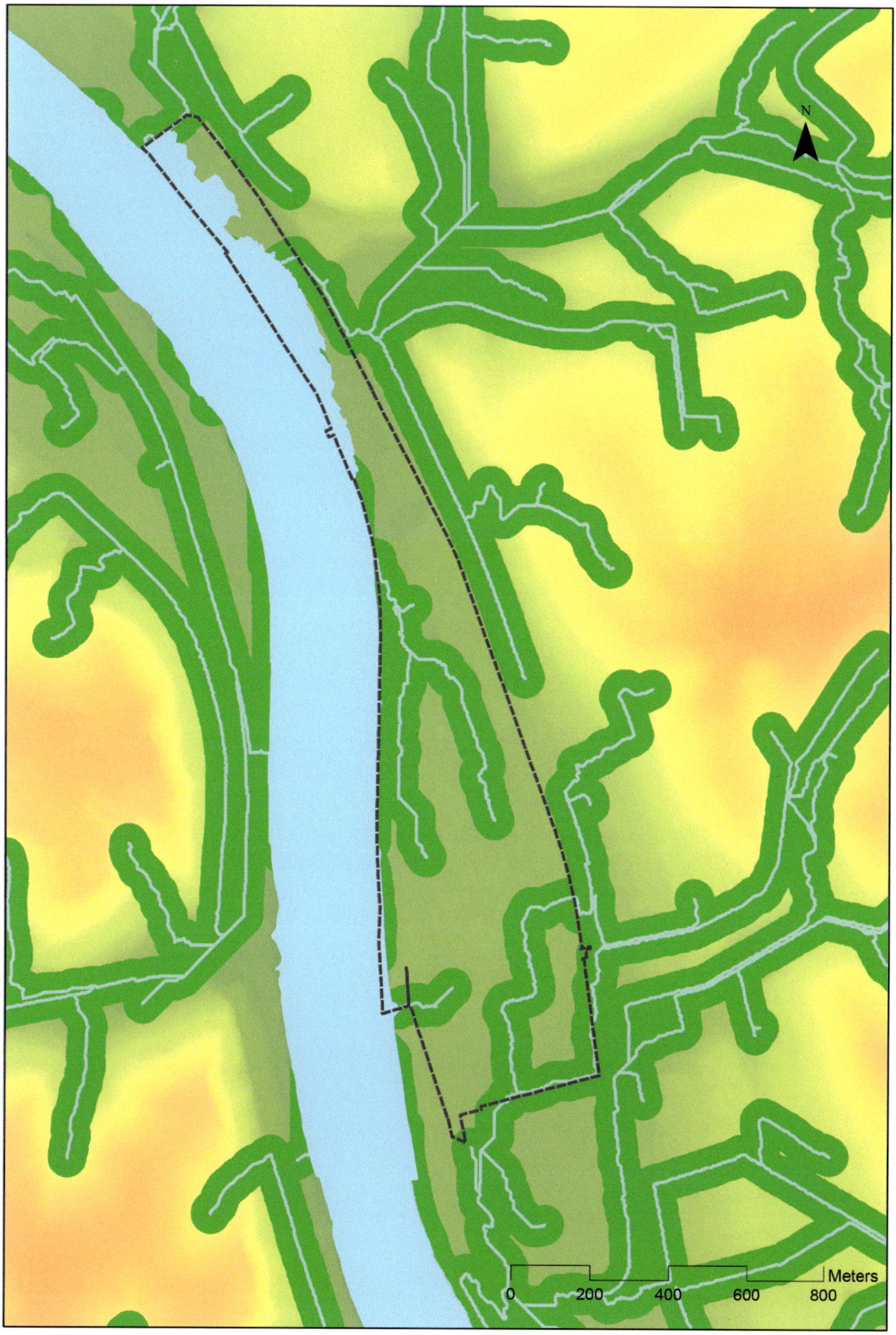

Figure 92 **Hazelwood Green slope**

Land use

The site was the location of an industrial steel plant. The industry was established in 1883 with the formation of the Jones and Laughlin Steel Company and closed in 1998. The site was connected with another steel-making facility across the Monongahela River and formed an important centre for steel making in the USA. The predominant land use of the site now is a deserted postindustrial site. At the southern end of the site is a 17.7 ha autonomous vehicle testing track (ReMake Group, 2018).

Pervious/impervious ratio

The existing site is largely made up of pervious surfaces. The impervious areas are the roading, the remnant industrial building and an autonomous car track.

- The existing site area is 72 ha.
- The impervious surface area is made up of roads and existing industrial buildings and an autonomous race track.
- The total impervious surface area is 18.7 ha.
- The total pervious surface area is 53.3 ha.
- Giving a ratio of pervious to impervious of 1:035.

Hazelwood Green master plan

In 2018 a development proposal was commissioned by the Almaono LP and the Regional Industrial Development Corporation (ReMake Group, 2018). The consultants, ReMake Group, Perkins + Will and Nelson \ Nygaard, have developed a comprehensive proposal that folds together site analysis as well as a comprehensive development proposal.

The site is 72 ha. The development plan allows for 12.4 ha of open space and 39.7 ha of development land; the total building area is 742,852.7m^2.

The development is divided into three zones along the eastern boundary: the River district, at the northern end of the site, the Mill district, in the middle of the site around the remnants of the steel mill, and the Flats district at the southern end of the site (Table 4.2).

Table 4.2 **Hazelwood Green development plan**

District	GLA	Open space	Development land	Total building area	Ratio	Building height
River	17 ha	4.3 ha	9.2 ha	253,439.5 m^2	1:2.75	73 m (24 floors) 46 m (15 floors)
Mill	31 ha	5.58 ha	18 ha	255,467.7 m^2	1:14	46 m (15 floors)
Flats	19.2 ha	2.5 ha	12.6 ha	233,929.8 m^2	1:18	46 m (15 floors)

Table 4.3 **Hazelwood Green development plan impervious/pervious ratio**

	Area	Pervious	Impervious	Ratio	Difference	Percent
Existing site	72 ha	53.3 ha	18.7 ha	1:035		26 percent
Proposed	72 ha	32 ha	40 ha	1:125	21.3 ha	55 percent

Hazelwood Green: environmental problems

With the construction of the proposed master plan, the hydrological pattern of the site will be changed. The increase in impervious surfaces will cause more stormwater and the possibility of more localised flooding. With climate change, increased rainfall will result in an increase in the runoff from the two catchments. This will result in an increase in pluvial flooding across the site. The existing flooding from the Mononga-hela River will also increase.

Pervious/impervious ratio

In the proposed master plan, the impervious surface of the Hazelwood Green site development would increase by 21.3 ha to 55 percent of the site, an increase of 30 percent (Table 4.3).

Hazelwood catchment: environmental remediation: design process

To ameliorate the effects of climate change on the site, an understanding of the hydrological behaviour of the site is necessary. The first step is to determine the structure, shape and size of the catchment, through mapping with ArcGIS. This data can be manifested as a series of maps showing catchment boundaries and a network of overland flow paths.

Hydrology

The environmental damage from an increase in pluvial and river flooding and an increase in stormwater discharge into the Monongahela River can be ameliorated using a number of practical strategies. An important technique is to establish a protective zone around these hydrological networks. Establishing a buffer zone of at least 50 m around the existing OLFP network (Figure 93) would result in a new public space of 21.58 ha. Protection of the Monongahela River edge is another important environmental measure; a buffer of 50 m would give a public river promenade of 20.19 ha (Figure 94). These interventions would have the effect of developing a new 41.58 ha park system for the site. The new park system would then connect the river's edge with the suburban hinterland.

Decreasing the amount of impervious surface through the removal of infrastructure such as roads and housing will lead to an increase in the amount of pervious surface, leading to an increase in the absorption of stormwater runoff (Table 4.4).

Table 4.4 **Hazelwood Green new development plan impervious/pervious ratio**

	Area (ha)	Pervious (ha)	Impervious (ha)	Ratio	Difference	Percent of imperious surface
Existing site	72 ha	53.3 ha	18.7 ha	1:035		26
Proposed	72 ha	32 ha	40 ha	1:125	21.3 ha	55
New development	72 ha	41 ha	31 ha	1:067	10 ha	40

Hazelwood catchment: urban design

To accomplish the increase climate change-proofing through a series of hydrologically remediatory measures means a change in the site development ratio.

In the River district the proposed ratio of development to site area is 1:275; with the installation of the proposed buffer zone, the ratio of development to site changes to 1:02.

In the Mill district the proposed ratio of development to site area is 1:14; with the installation of the proposed OLFP buffer zones, the ratio of development to site changes to 1:18.

In the Flats district the proposed ratio of development to site area is 1:18; with the installation of the proposed OLFP buffer zones, the ratio of development to site changes to 1:07 (Figure 96).

Hazelwood catchment: environmental implications of the design process

River zone

Establishing a riverine buffer zone enables the establishment of a soft-engineered flood prevention solution. Critical native riparian ecologies can be restored and protected. The result is a new kind of riverfront promenade for citizens (Figure 93).

OLFP network

By building a buffer zone around the OLFP network, a number of remediatory measures can be created, depending on what is judged to be the most critical environmental threat: pluvial flooding, stormwater contamination or the lack of biodiversity.

Addressing pluvial flooding, the buffered zones can be dedicated as part of a conveyance and detention system for flooding from the greater catchment. The new buffer system can also help contribute to the increase in pervious surfaces on the site. The OLFP zones can also contribute to the cleaning of urban stormwater by allowing for the location and positioning of structural stormwater devices such as wetlands and swales adjacent to urban zones. The OLFP zones can also allow for an increase in the site's biodiversity through revegetation with native species. The competed OLFP network would create a new public space for the residents and workers, linking the site from the river bank to the forested escarpment behind the site, creating ecological corridors (Figure 95).

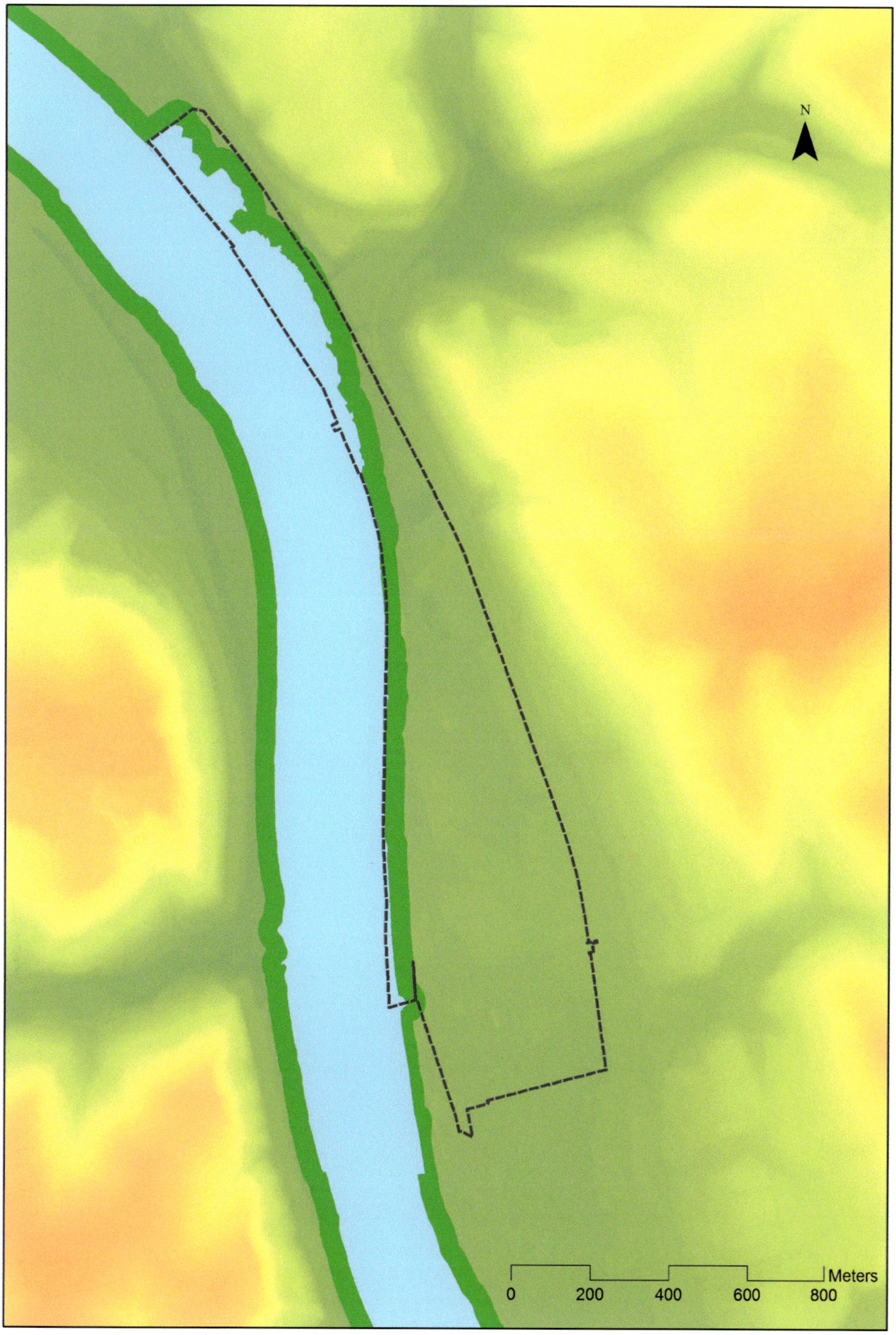

Figure 93 **Hazelwood Green OLFP 50 m buffer**

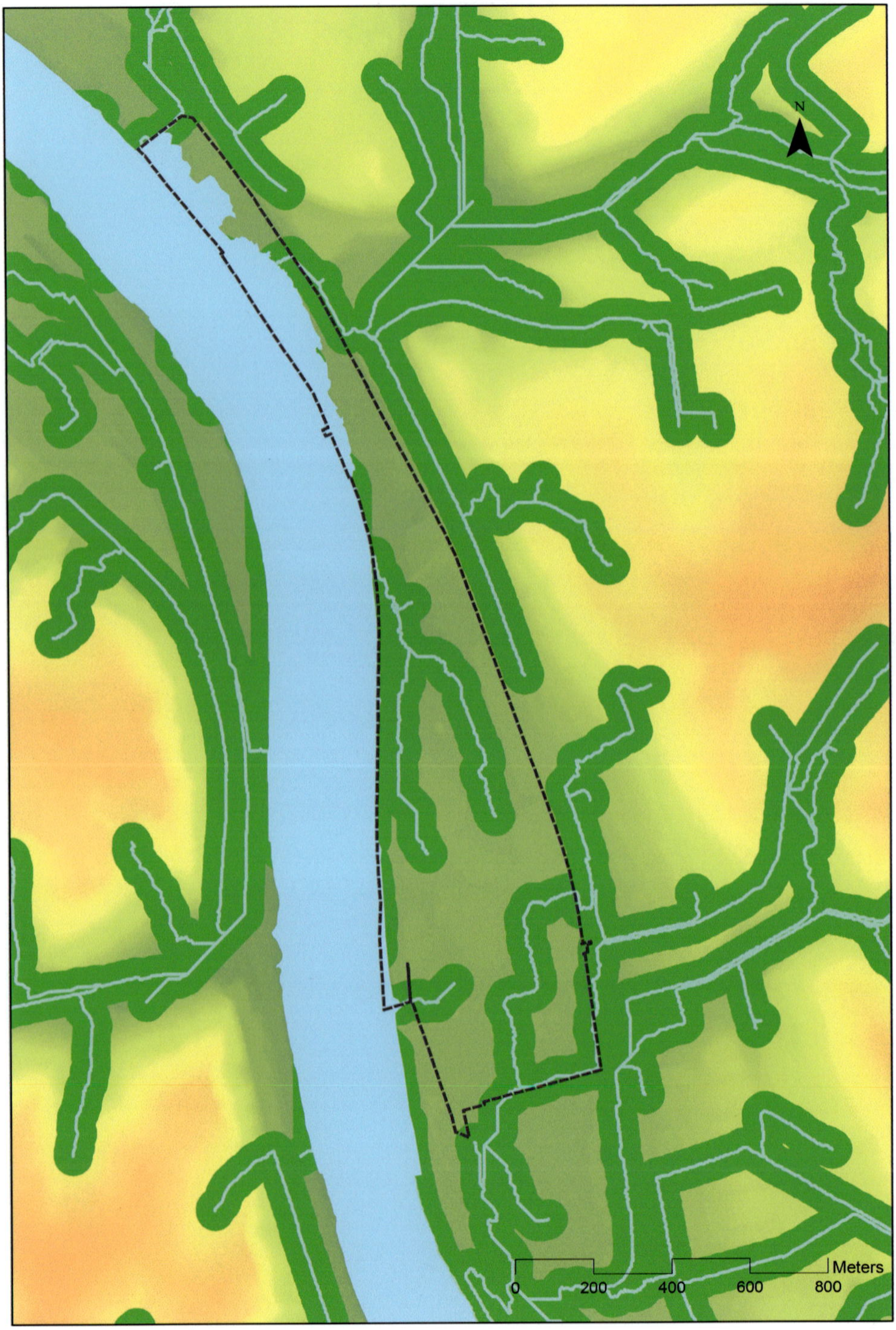

Figure 94 **Hazelwood Green river 50 m buffer**

Figure 95 **Hazelwood Green park**

Figure 96 **Hazelwood Green building zone**

Hazelwood catchment: environmental implications of the investigation

The mapping demonstrates a design process where a development project can be safeguarded against the problems of climate change through the simple device of identifying and protecting the river's edge and OLFPs through buffering and replanting. In this way the revegetated buffer zones protect the existing hydrological network from an influx of contaminated stormwater that will be exacerbated by both the building programme and the increased in rainfall from climate change. The ratio of impervious to pervious surfaces is then modified from the proposed master plan to one in which the hydrological network is given precedence. This ensures that a greater percentage of rainfall is able to be absorbed by unbuilt surfaces. A social consequence of this new green network is the establishment of a new path/park system that links the development and the surrounding landscape. The clustering of the building GFA into a new, denser urban form (Figure 96) makes the demarcation between landscape/public space/remediation territory and building more peremptory, yet perhaps more tangible.

Osney Mead

Introduction

Osney Mead is a new urban development planned for Oxford, UK.

Osney Mead site analysis

Osney Mead is located on the western side of Oxford city, UK (Figure 97). The site is a 15 ha light industrial estate that was developed from 1961 (Shepheard Epstein Hunter, 2016). A number of businesses are located on the estate, including the publishers Holywell Press and Alden Mowbrey, as well as the publisher of the Oxford Mail and Oxford Press. Two organisations from the University of Oxford, the Department of Engineering Science and the Bodleian Library, also have buildings on the site.

The site is on the periphery of the city. To the north of the site is the Oatlands Road recreation reserve. The west and south of the site are bounded by a tributary of the Bulstake stream and beyond the stream are agricultural fields. To the north-east, the site is adjacent to the 19th-century suburb of Osney, separated by the Osney Ditch and the River Thames. At the intersection of these two waterways is the Osney Lock.

Figure 97 **Oxford aerial**

The site is in the Thames (Evenlode to Thame) sub-catchment. The area of the sub-catchment is 149,59.089 ha (EAUK, 2020).

Hydrology

The Evenlode to Thame catchment is made up of rivers and streams in semi-natural landscapes. The landscape of this sub-catchment is characterised as a river meadowland (OWLS, 2020).

Typically, these landscapes are a flat riverine floodplain (Figure 98). They are mostly agrarian with different types of pasture according to whether they are flood-prone or not. The topography is flat and the hydrological character is a number of river channels that flood seasonally. The landscape is agrarian in pattern with small fields and meadows and trees; both white willow and crack willow are lined along streams and ditches.

The average annual rainfall in Oxford is 631 mm. The average rainfall in February, the driest month, is 39 mm. The wettest month is December, with an average rainfall of 62 mm. The contours of the site vary very little (Figure 99).

The site is within the River Thames, Oxford Flood plain. The site is defined as Flood Level 3, Zone 3a: High Probability of land having a 1 in 100 or greater annual probability of river flooding (DCLG, 2012) (Figures 101, 103).

Figure 98 **Oxford flood catchment**

Figure 99 **Oxford contours**

Vegetation

Tree species are ash, poplar, hawthorn and alder. The pasture flora is made upon a number of native grasses and herbs that include fescue and crested dog's tail. Herbs include oxeye daisy, bird's-foot trefoil and knapweed. Rare species include fritillaria. Species that like wetter conditions include pepper saxifrage, meadow sweet and great burnet (Rothero, Lake, & Gowing, 2016).

Aspect/slope

The aspect of Osney Mead is flat. The slope of the site is flat (0 to 5 degrees). The OLFP network shows the site draining equally to the Bulstake stream and the Thames (Figure 100).

Pervious/impervious ratio

- The existing site is 15 ha.
- The impervious surface area is made up of roads, 44 percent (7.5 ha), and buildings, 38 percent (5.7 ha).
- The total impervious surface area is 13.2 ha.
- The total pervious surface area is 1.8 ha.
- Giving a ratio of pervious to impervious of 1:7.

Figure 100 **Oxford OLFP**

Osney Mead development plan

A development plan was prepared for this site in 2016 for the owners, the University of Oxford by Shepheard Epstein Hunter (2016).

The university is responding to a worldwide trend in academia to establish collaborative relationships with business to develop joint research and design projects. The opportunity for business to collaborate with university researchers is done in four ways: sites for business to relocate to Oxford and be part of the new development; the provision of research space, both offices and laboratories; and dedicated space for engineering research and the provision for researcher housing (Shepheard Epstein Hunter, 2016).

The total footprint of the development is 47,000 m^2, the company building zone is 23,000 m^2, the innovation research and business incubators are 12,000 m^2, the engineering innovation centre is 8,000 m^2 and the researchers' housing is 4,000 m^2. The maximum height of any development is 18.2 m (approximately 6 storeys at 3 m). The total GFA would then be 282,000m^2.

Pervious/impervious ratio

- The existing site is 15 ha.
- The impervious surface area is made up of asphalt 6 percent (1 ha) and buildings 27 percent (4 ha).
- The total impervious surface area is 5 ha.
- The total pervious surface area is made of water, vegetation, soft landscape and permeable paving, 67 percent (10 ha).
- Giving a ratio of pervious to impervious of 2:1.

Figure 101 **Oxford flooding**

Osney Mead: environmental problems

There are two environmental issues that the proposed development faces: the effect of increasing impervious surface and the effect of the existing flooding. The effect of increased impervious surfaces on the proposed new urban development does not seem to be onerous. The impervious/pervious ratio of the proposed development is in fact better than the impervious/pervious ratio of the existing development. However, the existing flooding of the site must call into question the viability of any development without extensive remediation. The existing flooding will certainly increase with the effects of climate change.

Environmental remediation: design process

Hydrology

To ameliorate the effects of flooding on the development, an understanding of the hydrological behaviour of the sub-catchment is necessary. The first step is to determine the hydrology of the site through studying the OLFP. By buffering this network, a hydrological pattern starts to emerge (Figure 102).

The second step is to map the site flooding. From this mapping, roughly 6 'islands' or dry areas are revealed that are out of the flooding zone. The total size of the islands is approximately 7 ha (Figure 104). Through a process of cut and fill, the dry zones can be raised above the flood zone and the damage that would be occasioned by an increase in flooding from climate change.

Figure 102 **Osney Mead OLFP buffer**

Figure 103 **Osney Mead flooding**

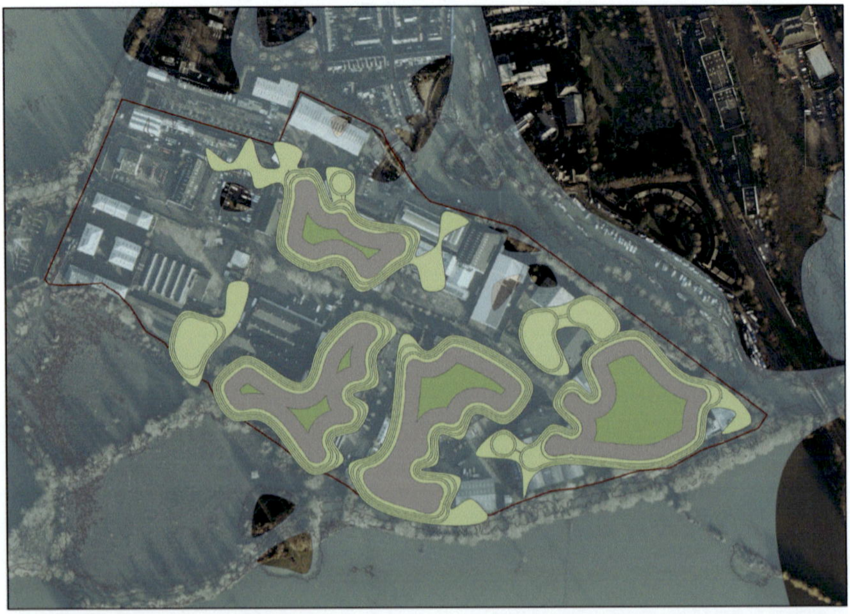

Figure 104 **Osney Mead building zones**

Biodiversity

By using the buffering function in ArcGIS, a serried zone around each of the islands at different levels can be created to allow for the creation of an indigenous ecotone. A native transect of planting from flood plan to marginal to dry ground can be established around each island. This planting helps to restoring the native biodiversity of the area.

Osney Mead: urban design

To accommodate the flooding and to preserve the necessary GFA of the development plan, the shape of the building zone will be determined by the location, size and shape of the 'islands' revealed in the flood mapping. Thus, the islands form the development plan of four new building zones (Figure 105). The buffering function in ArcGIS can be used to determine a possible building footprint. Giving the building form an internal depth of 20 m allows for the provision of an internal courtyard. Extruding the building by six storeys gives an indicative shape of the new developments within the landscape.

Pervious/impervious ratio

- The existing site is 15 ha.
- Islands are 46.8 percent (7.02 ha).
- The impervious surface area is made up of buildings: 36 percent (5.4 ha).
- The total impervious surface area is 5.4 ha.
- The total pervious surface area is made of restored landscape: 64 percent (9.6 ha).
- Giving a ratio of pervious to impervious of 1.7:1.

Figure 105 **Osney Mead building zones 1**

Figure 106 **Osney Mead building zones 2**

Osney Mead: environmental implications of the design process

The new development plan (Figure 106) demonstrates how the environmental consequences of flooding can be remediated through two operations, firstly acknowledging the spatial pattern that flooding creates and using that as the basis for a new development strategy. Through topographic manipulation, a series of islands can be created that form a series of building zones over which an urban programme can be shaped (Figure 107). The building zones form a closed loop that maximises the space to be occupied on the island, while the provision of an inner garden ensures that the building users don't suffer from a deep floor plan. The building typology is perhaps closer to the Smithson concept of a Land Castle (Smithson & Smithson, 1967). Allowing the site to be party to the seasonable ebb and flow of the flood waters also gives a chance to restore the native flora of the site, in this way reestablishing the natural biodiversity of Oxford and enabling the site to connect to other ecological restorations within parts of the catchment.

Figure 107 **Osney Mead building zones 3**

Conclusion

Greenfield

The two greenfield projects demonstrate how a catchment based approach to two greenfield urban developments, one in New Zealand, the other in the PRC, can result in reducing the amount of contaminated stormwater entering the receiving environment.

Placing the proposed urban development within the larger context is carried out by mapping the hydrological catchment. The existing rainfall runoff can then be measured via the Rational Method. By then placing the urban development within the catchment, the implications of the increase in the volume of stormwater through an increase in impervious surfaces can be measured.

A number of techniques can be then be deployed to help alleviate these problems, especially identifying and protecting the existing hydrological network.

The first part of the design process is to map the existing hydrological system using GIS. The second part is to protect the networks by establishing a planted buffer zone along the streams/river corridors. This stage also has the effect of increasing the pervious surfaces. A recalculation of the amount of stormwater runoff using the Rational Method shows a decrease in the volume of stormwater.

However, the increase in pervious surfaces is accomplished at the expense of the building programme. This is rebalanced through the clustering of building. In the Rarawara case study, the housing that is removed to allow for the buffered stream system is simply clustered as apartments that are positioned at the intersection of the stream corridor and Waitamata Harbour.

In the Furong case study, the waterfront site is transformed into a hydrological remediation zone. The four prescribed development zones are clustered as 'islands' while the rest of the site is transformed into a remediation wetland to clean the water from the urbanised catchment and to detain pluvial flooding.

Brownfield

The four brownfield projects demonstrate a number of techniques drawn from conventional remediation regimes and from an adaptation of catchment based techniques. All four projects share a common theme: the mapping and analysis of the existing hydrology of the site. GIS mapping and analysis was used to identify the existing hydrological network, the streams and overland flow paths and flooding, and then using the buffering function in ArcGIS, to make protection zones around each OLFP and stream. The effect of this operation was to also increase the amount of pervious surface on the sites.

Clustering the urban form was the other important design technique. By buffering the existing hydrological system, the loss of the development GFA was inevitable. Clustering the development GFA into a new urban form was a way of ensuring that the projected real estate programme could still be accomplished

There are a number of urban implications of the remediatory work. The suggested solution for the Wynyard Point case study was to assemble the building programme into four towers, the location driven by the exergies of the landscape remediation programme. In Jinan, the mapping of the OLFP gives a future map to the city authorities. This can be a guide in any future construction programme in the catchment to allow for conveyance and detention. In Pittsburgh, the building programmes are clustered around the high ground, above both the river flooding and the pluvial flooding from the hinterland. In Oxford, the building programmes are gathered into islands that are raised above the floodplain. The next chapter of the book draws together the key themes and the implications of the proposed design method for building urban resilience to the effects of climate change.

References

ARC. (2003). *Stormwater Treatment Devices: Ddesign Guideline Manual*, Auckland. Retrieved from www.aucklandcity.govt.nz/council/documents/technicalpublications/TP10%20Stormwater%20management%20devices%20design%20guideline%20manual%202003.pdf

Architectus. (2007). *Wynyard Quarter Urban Design Framework*. Retrieved from www.waterfrontauckland.co.nz/Waterfront-Auckland/What-s-Next/Planning.aspx

Aronson, M. F. J., Lepczyk, C. A., Evans, K. L., Goddard, M. A., Lerman, S. B., MacIvor, J. S., . . . Vargo, T. (2017). Biodiversity in the city: Key challenges for urban green space management. *Frontiers in Ecology and the Environment, 15*, 189–196.

Auckland Council. (2003). *Stormwater Management Devices Design Guideline Manual*, Auckland, New Zealand. Retrieved from www.aucklandcity.govt.nz/council/documents/technicalpublications/TP10%20Stormwater%20management%20devices%20design%20guideline%20manual%202003.pdf

Auckland Council. (2016). *Whenuapai Structure Plan*. Retrieved from www.aucklandcouncil.govt.nz/plans-projects-policies-reports-bylaws/our-plans-strategies/place-based-plans/Documents/whenuapai-structure-plan-september-2016.pdf

Braun, E. L. (2010). *Deciduous Forests of Eastern North America*. Caldwell, New Jersey, USA: The Blackburn Press.

DCLG. (2012). *Technical Guidance to the National Planning Policy Framework*. Retrieved from https://assets.publishing.service.gov.uk/government/uploads/system/uploads/attachment_data/file/6000/2115548.pdf

EAUK. (2020). *Thames (Evenlode to Thame)*. Retrieved from https://environment.data.gov.uk/catchment-planning/ReasonsForNotAchievingGood/510915

Falconer, R. (2009). *Pluvial Flooding and Surface Water Management*. Paper presented at the 5th EWA Conference, Brussels. Retrieved from www.dwa.de/portale/ewa/ewa.nsf/C125723B0047EC38/CC41A2CC77C52058C125768E0030232E/$FILE/Pluvial%20Flooding%20and%20Surface%20Management.pdf

Fletcher, T. D., Shuster, W., Hunt, W. F., Ashley, R., Butler, D., Arthur, S., . . . Viklander, M. (2015). SUDS, LID, BMPs, WSUD and more – The evolution and application of terminology surrounding urban drainage. *Urban Water Journal, 12*(7), 525–542. doi:10.1080/1573062X.2014.916314

Gibson, A. (2018, May 25). Hobsonville point proposed 15-level apartment block exceeds maximum height by 40.8m. *NZ Herald*. Retrieved from www.nzherald.co.nz/business/news/article.cfm?c_id=3&objectid=12077330

Gunawardena, K. R., Wells, M. J., & Kershawa, T. (2017). Utilising green and bluespace to mitigate urban heat island intensity. *Science of the Total Environment, 584–585*, 1040–1055.

Intergovernmental Panel on Climate Change. (2014). *Climate Change 2014 Synthesis Report, Summary for Policymakers Chapter*. Retrieved from www.ipcc.ch/pdf/assessment-report/ar5/syr/AR5_SYR_FINAL_SPM.pdf

Lucas, D., & Head, J. (1997). *Native to the West: A Guide for Planting and Restoring the Nature of Waitakere City*, Waitakere. Retrieved from www.waitakere.govt.nz/cnlser/pw/greennetwk/pdf/NativeToTheWest.pdf

Maksimović, Č., Prodanović, D., Boonya-Aroonnet, S., Leitão, J. P., Djordjević. S., & Allitt, R. (2009). Overland flow and pathway analysis for modelling of urban pluvial flooding. Journal of Hydraulic Research, 47(4), 512–523.

Malaviya, P., & Singh, A. (2012). Constructed wetlands for management of urban stormwater runoff. *Critical Reviews in Environmental Science & Technology, 42*(20), 2153–2214. doi:10.1080/10643389.2011.574107

Meurk, C. D., & Hall, G. M. (2006). Options for enhancing forest biodiversity across New Zealand's managed landscapes based on ecosystem modelling and spatial design. *New Zealand Journal of Ecology, 30*(1), 131–146.

Morton, J. (2004). *Seashore Ecology of New Zealand and the Pacific*. Auckland: David Bateman.

Myers, S. (2014). *Opportunities for Promoting Ecological and Biodiversity Values in the Wynyard Quarter and throughout the Waterfront*, Auckland. Retrieved from www.wynyard-quarter.co.nz/wqsmart/www/pdfs/environmental/smyers-biodiversity-opportunities-for-wynyard-quarter-11-feb-2014.pdf

New York State Department of Environmental Conservation. (2014). *Shoreline Stabilization*. Retrieved from www.dec.ny.gov/docs/permits_ej_operations_pdf/shorelinestable.pdf

OWLS. (2020). *River Meadows*. Retrieved from http://owls.oxfordshire.gov.uk/wps/wcm/connect/occ/OWLS/Home/Oxfordshire+Landscape+Types/River+Meadowlands/River+Meadowlands+Information/

ReMake Group, P. W., & Nelson\Nygaard. (2018). *Hazelwood Green: Preliminary Land Development Plan: Special Planned District 10 (SP-10) Pittsburgh, PA*. Retrieved from www. hazelwoodgreen.com

Rothero, E., Lake, S., & Gowing, D. (Eds.). (2016). *Floodplain Meadows: Beauty and Utility: A Technical Handbook*. Milton Keynes: Floodplain Meadows Partnership.

Shepheard Epstein Hunter. (2016). *Osney Mead Master Plan*. Retrieved from www.ox.ac.uk/sites/files/oxford/media_wysiwyg/16_07_06_Osney_Mead_boards_FINAL.pdf

Smedley, R. (2011). *Freemans Bay Stormwater Options Assessment*. Auckland: Auckland Council.

Smithson, P., & Smithson, A. (1967). *Urban Structuring*. Studio Vista.

Stone, R. C. J. 2001. *From Tamaki-makau-rau to Auckland*. Auckland: Auckland University Press

Thompson, D. B. (2007). *The Rational Method*. Retrieved from https://pdfs.semanticscholar.org/a4e9/37c1b58958f3add38f934df85810d41b63b3.pdf

van Roon, M., & van Roon, H. (2009). *Low Impact Urban Design and Development: The Big Picture: An Introduction to LIUDD Principles and Methods Framework* (Vol. 37). Lincoln, NZ: Manaaki Whenua Press.

West 8. (2015). *Toronto Central Waterfront*. Retrieved from www.west8.nl/projects/all/toronto_central_waterfront/

Xia, J., Zhang, Y., Xiong, L. Xiong, L. H., He, S., Wang, L. F., & Yu, Z. B. (2017). Opportunities and challenges of the Sponge City construction related to urban water issues in China. *Science China Earth Science*, *60*, 652–658.

Yu, Kongjian, Lei, Z., & Dihua, Li. (2008). Live with water: Flood adaptive landscapes in the Yellow River Basin of China. *Journal of Landscape Architecture*, 6–17.

Chapter five

Climate change has rapidly moved from being a fringe conversation to a central global concern. Yet this welcome attention has often led to an apocalyptic sense of doom and gloom where people feel that they can only wait for the end of the world. This book offers a way in which all stakeholders in the urban realm, planners, engineers, designers, civic authorities, citizens and developers, can both understand the spatial consequences of climate change and the scope and shape of the necessary environmental remediation measures.

The consequence of these remediation measures on the future shapes of our cities will be profound; however, the consequences of not changing our present urban model will be overwhelming.

This book argues that conventional urban development follows an urban design model based on new urbanist thinking, ideas and techniques. The result has been the production of a knowable urban design formula, block planning, active street edges and the insertion of public buildings. The result is a generic urban prescription accompanied by a knowable real estate formula that provides property professionals with a broad understanding, within the vagaries of the property cycle, of what the expected return will be on individual buildings within the overall master plan. The continuing repetition of this urban model is evidence of its success.

However, a critical issue in any urban development, which hasn't been properly acknowledged, is the environmental effects of climate change. The book argues that the success of the current urban development model is predicated on an intensive building and infrastructure development, buildings, roads, streets, footpaths and urban squares that are highly impervious. The consequences of this urban development model for the environment are the production of contaminated stormwater and pluvial and maritime flooding. The traditional conventional response to these problems has been engineering-based. Environmental problems such as pluvial flooding were traditionally dealt with by a conventional piped system, and the occasional flood was accepted as something beyond the design of the system. Likewise, the protection of the sea edge from storm surges was traditionally met through the construction of a hard-armoured sea wall. The production of contaminated stormwater by a new urban development was seen as an inevitable byproduct of a development, and the subsequent discharge of contaminated stormwater into the existing natural stream/river/harbour network was traditionally accepted.

The growing consequences of climate change – increased rainfall, rising sea levels and an increase in global air temperature – will exacerbate these environmental problems. There will be an increase in the production of contaminated stormwater, an increase in pluvial flooding from the urban catchment, a rise in sea level causing marine flooding and, with increased temperatures, an increase in the urban heat island effect.

The book acknowledges that these environmental problems and the associated remediation techniques are well-known but they remain either elided or adopted in a half-hearted manner.

The book offers three insights. The first is that by bringing together the existing known environmental problems within a catchment framework, remedial solutions can be identified, assessed, analysed and tested. The urban catchment offers a measurable and geographically defined system into which a series of criteria can be introduced that privilege good environmental outcomes. For example, the problem of the production of contaminated stormwater and the consequences for the receiving environments can be remediated through several measures, such as rain gardens and wetlands.

By placing an urban development, no matter what scale, within the larger context of the hydrological catchment, the extent of any environmental problem can be understood.

This has two consequences when applied to a brownfield site. Firstly, the environmental consequences of decisions in the large catchments can be apprehended in the smaller urban development site. The most obvious example is the production of stormwater within an urban catchment and the discharge/outfall. Secondly, the same understanding can be made around pluvial flooding, a condition produced within the hinterland of the catchment.

The second insight that the book offers is that any new urban development should strive towards a more equitable hydrological future through the provision of more open spaces/pervious surfaces. These spaces can simply be used to absorb rainwater that would have become runoff if falling on an impervious surface. The spaces can also be used to plant trees to help increase water absorption through transpiration, and the open spaces can be used for environmental remediation such as wetland treatment ponds, flood conveyance and detention zones.

The third insight is that if the amount of pervious space available must be increased, then the current urban model/building programme must change. A densely populated, gridded master plan is a positive impediment to the adoption of measures that will help to address the serious environmental problems that affect the viability of urban development. Consequently, by clustering the building programme, the impervious footprint of a building could be reduced by increasing height, thus freeing up the ground plane for the necessary remediation measures.

This book poses a different urban design model that contradicts almost all traditional urban design mores; however, as the effects of climate change on cities are gradually being realised, then the exigencies of the environmental issues facing urban developments must force a radical rethinking of a conventional urban design model that either does little to help build urban resilience to these effects or, worse, actively contributes to harming citizens.

The IPCC Special Report (Intergovernmental Panel on Climate Change, 2018) clearly lays out the latest evidence of climate change and the consequences: increasing precipitation, increases in the mean temperature and increasing sea-level rise are all now inevitable consequences of 1.5°C of global warming. The consequences for the continuing viability of urban development are clear and unambiguously articulated. If governments, agencies and stakeholders wish to continue with urban developments, then the current design model simply will not be resilient against these effects.

This book demonstrates that for the urban realm to be resilient to climate change, a new urban design process is required. This design process puts the remediation of environmental issues first. A reconfigured urban plan is the result, one in which the landscape is prioritised over the traditional urban plan. The book provides a strategy for urban designers, developers and stakeholders to rethink the ways in which an urban development can be planned. The book offers the promise of an agreeable landscape for citizens of the new city, whilst at the same time ameliorating the worst effects of climate change.

In Aotearoa/New Zealand, all citizens, Māori and Tauiwi, have specific obligations under the Treaty of Waitangi. Māori are partners in any decision making in the public realm. Future research into the ways that Matauranga Māori can shape the environmental processes that lead to the building a more resilient and equitable city are critical for the success of the future Aotearoa/New Zealand city.

Epilogue

While finishing this book, the COVID-19 pandemic struck. The spectacle of the world's cities shutting down has given rise to an avalanche of writing about the implications of this pandemic for the shape of the future city. Opinion is divided, from Blake's Glad Day (Blake, 1794–1796) to a Darwinian advocacy of letting the poor and old die so that business can survive. However, some implications for the way our cities may develop can be discerned.

Increasing urban density is a critical part of the ideology of New Urbanism's child, the Compact City (Orum, 2020). The argument advanced is that by increasing residential density in the centre of cities, a number of benefits for urban life will transpire, public transport will become sustainable, restaurants, cafés and bars will have enough locals to survive, business will be established and a virtuous circle begins. The key is increasing proximity and connection between people, culturally and socially.

With the hindsight of the pandemic, all these desirable qualities are now problematic. Opponents of the Compact City are now gleefully piling in. Prominent are the new suburbanists like Joel Kotkin (2017) are extolling the virtues of low-density suburbia as a panacea for effects of the pandemic. The supposed evils of suburbia (low density, single houses and gardens and reliance on the car) are, in the light of the pandemic, being revealed as shining safety measures.

How does this book fit into this new world? Of course, the reality of climate change has not disappeared, but the pandemic has opened up new possibilities for urban design that seemed so fixed just a few months ago. I see the book as a kind of halfway house between these two positions. I argue that making a city resilient to climate change will involve questioning the way we design and build new cities and the way in which we retrofit existing cities. I argue that to help cities build resilience to the some of the effects of climate change, like flooding and stormwater pollution, the form of the city will have to change: to become more open, to allow for the installation of the necessary remediation measures that will build resilience to the effect of climate change: wetlands, detention ponds and engineered soft flood barriers. These measures, these landscapes, are multi-functional; while they have an immediate purpose, the remediation of certain problems, they can also function as public spaces.

Here the book's argument is connected to a point agreed on by all the protagonists in the arguments around the shape of our cities post-pandemic. The provision of green public space has become a critical part in the fight against the pandemic. The urban park has offered an open green space away from the conditions that lead to the pandemic spread. In the park, citizens can enjoy space, sunshine and exercise while safely distancing from their fellow citizens. As such, the city park is seen by Compact City advocates as a legitimisation of the traditional city form. For the suburbanist, the park is equally an integral part of suburbia. This is the space where citizens and families go to walk, enjoy nature and exercise. The suburban park is seen as a legitimatisation of suburbia in the fight against the spread of COVID.

Predicting the effect of the pandemic on the future city form is impossible, but there seems to be a common idea that the provision of public green space is something that will help build urban resilience to the spread of the pandemic. If the effect of the pandemic starts a great park building campaign, as happened in European and American cities in the middle of the 19th century, then we will have prepared for the effects of the next pandemic. We will be, at the same time, starting the process to use the new parks to build resilient green systems to ameliorate the worst effects of climate change.

The new parks will help to keep us healthy while at the same time making a serious start in our forthcoming struggle to survive climate change.

References

Blake, W. (1794–1796). *Albion Rose*. London: William Blake.

Intergovernmental Panel on Climate Change. (2018). *IPCC Special Report*. Retrieved from http://report.ipcc.ch/sr15/pdf/sr15_spm_final.pdf

Kotkin, Joel. (2017). *The Human City: Urbanism for the Rest of Us* Evanston, IL: Agate B2.

Orum, A. M. a. J., M. (2020). Compact city. In A. M. Orum (Ed.), *The Wiley Blackwell Encyclopedia of Urban and Regional Studies*. Hoboken, NJ: Wiley Blackwell.

Index